THE SEARCH FOR MEANING

Paavo Pylkkänen obtained an M.Sc. in Logic and Scientific Method at the University of Sussex and is now studying towards a Ph.D. in Theoretical Philosophy at the University of Helsinki, where he has lectured on David Bohm's philosophy of nature. He has worked as an Expert Secretary for the Division of Cognitive Science of the Academy of Finland. His interests include the philosophical foundations of cognitive science, the implications of quantum theory to our world view, and cultural criticism.

Dear Dad   Dec '94

Hoping that you have a wonderful x-mas and a very happy new Year! all the best

love
Rona & Tahera
Kamelot.

Cover illustrations: The quantum potential for two Gaussian slits viewed from a position on the axis beyond the screen. The quantum potential was introduced by Bohm in 1952 and plays an important role in giving an intelligible explanation of quantum phenomena. What is striking about the quantum potential is that it depends on the *form* of the environment. Thus, Bohm has proposed that the way in which the quantum potential *informs* the motion of quantum particles is *analogous* to how information and meaning organize human physiological activities and actions. (From J.P. Vigier et. al., 'Causal particle trajectories and the interpretation of quantum mechanics', pp. 169-204, in *Quantum Implications: Essays in Honour of David Bohm*, ed. B.J. Hiley & F.D. Peat, London: Routledge 1987.)

THE
SEARCH
FOR
MEANING

THE NEW SPIRIT IN SCIENCE
AND PHILOSOPHY

EDITED BY

PAAVO PYLKKÄNEN

First published 1989

© PAAVO PYLKKÄNEN 1989

British Library Cataloguing in Publication Data

The search for meaning.
1. Meaning — philosophical perspectives
I. Pylkkänen, Paavo
121'.68

ISBN 1-85274-061-2

*Crucible is an imprint of The Aquarian Press,
part of the Thorsons Publishing Group,
Wellingborough, Northamptonshire, NN8 2RQ, England*

Printed in Great Britain by Mackays of Chatham, Kent
Typeset by MJL Limited, Hitchin, Hertfordshire

1 3 5 7 9 10 8 6 4 2

Acknowledgements

The editor would like to thank especially Dr Juan Luis Hancke, formerly of the Max Planck Institute in Göttingen, and now working as a scientific adviser to the Swedish Herbal Institute Ltd in Gothenburg. Dr Hancke, whose interests range from the foundations of medicine to more general questions such as the quality of communication in science and society, has been instrumental in bringing together many of the contributors and thus initiated this common search. He has just that spirit of warmth, friendship and inquiry that makes projects like this happen.

Of the contributors, Francis Steen and Srinivas Aravamudan have helped me in many ways, as well as David Bohm, John Briggs, Matti Bergström and David Peat. At the final stages of the work, discussions with Tiina Seppälä and Matti Vaittinen have been particularly useful.

Many of the contributors were initially brought together by meetings held at Brockwood Park Educational Centre in Bramdean, Hampshire, England. Later symposiums have taken place in the country conference centre of the University of Sussex (1986) and more recently in Härsjögården, Hyssna in Sweden (1988). On behalf of the contributors I would like to thank all those who have participated and contributed to these meetings.

The later symposiums were made financially possible by kind donations from Richard Evans and John Kesselstatt, and especially from Georg Wikman and Kari Holmberg, the directors of the Swedish Herbal Institute Ltd. Their company has very generously supported these symposiums and the editing of this book. My own research has been supported by the Emil Aaltonen Foundation, Tampere, Finland.

Finally, I should like to thank Eileen Campbell, editorial director at Thorsons, and her staff for a very pleasant co-operation in which this book became a reality.

Contents

Foreword

About 20 years ago there was throughout the industrialized world a sudden rise in consciousness which was associated with the extraordinary events of 1968 in Paris, Berkeley, Prague and many other centres. This new consciousness was concerned with the nature of our industrial society; the nature of the relationship of human beings with each other and with their environment in the widest sense. A crisis in modern culture was recognized; suddenly people became conscious that the world could not continue with relationships based on force, domination and exploitation. Scientific study of pollution, destruction of natural resources and ecological balance showed that the future of humanity depended not only on recognizing the common interests of all races and nations, but one needed to go further and recognize that human beings and all other types of life, and even the physical features of the earth, were interdependent and shared a common future. The whole earth was seen as one and, in a sense, as alive. Instead of man using science to control nature, man needed to establish with nature a relationship based on the new vision of unity: a creative relationship like that between two human beings who, as a result of mutual understanding, feel no need to try to control each other.

The environmental studies, supported by broader interests in medicine and new ideas physics, stimulated holistic thinking; people realized that our tradition of fragmented thinking (to use David Bohm's term) did not correspond to the nature of reality. Our fragmented culture was not only uncreative, but the lack of relation between our search for scientific knowledge and our moral concern put at risk the future of humanity and of the biosphere as a whole.

But how is a new type of thinking to be developed? There has been a long holistic tradition going back to Pythagoras who linked the search for knowledge of the material world with the spiritual salvation of the one who searched. But, in contrast, the extraordinary development of science has been largely based on analytical and abstract thinking which focuses attention on certain sets of relations in nature while ignoring all others. Science has searched for the general by studying the particular, but its view of the general is limited; it does not attempt to deal with the universal as, for example, religion does.

The main tradition of science has been reductionist; higher levels of complexity have been interpreted in terms of simpler, and supposedly more basic, levels. Reductionism is probably an essential aspect of science; but can we develop a deeper and broader science which includes a complementary aspect which would be non-reductionist and spiritual? If we could do that we might transform science so that it is no longer a limited materialistic enquiry but acquires the wider dimensions of a spiritual quest. The thoughts of A.N. Whitehead moved in that direction. More recently there has been new interest in trying to develop further such holistic thinking; for example, David Bohm has throughout his life struggled to find ways of grasping the whole. The importance of the present book in my opinion lies in its contribution to very far-reaching developments of this kind which should restore moral quality to human knowledge and help to give our lives higher meaning.

MAURICE WILKINS

If we do not care enough now, future generations may not exist to thank us for their existence and for our caring.
—Douglas Hofstaedter

Introduction

PAAVO PYLKKÄNEN

It is part of our nature to find coherent meaning because we *are* meaning. An incoherent meaning means that we are in some ways unhealthy. Our being will not be right. Just simply the aim to be whole inspires the search for a coherent meaning...there isn't much of a coherent meaning in society. People have...come to take it for granted that there isn't one. They can hardly imagine what it would be like to have one. That's a temporary state of affairs, I hope. If there were a generally coherent meaning which was true and not self-deceptive, you would appreciate its value without question in the same way you appreciate being healthy. You don't ask 'Why should I be healthy?' — David Bohm 1986.[1]

The aim of this book is to inquire what a coherent meaning, suitable for our own time, would be like. That is, how are we to coherently think about our relationship to each other individually and globally, to nature and even to the whole of the cosmos? What is it that makes a meaning, or more generally, a world-view, coherent?

Clearly, a coherent world-view helps us to grasp a deeper unity beyond apparently fragmented phenomena. In a scientific culture, perhaps the most radical fragmentation persists between the objective, scientific experience and the subjective, mental experience. For science treats everything, including the human mind, as a mechanistic object, a complex machine, whereas our more inward perception of ourselves gives a strong impression that we are mental subjects. Clearly these two views are incoherent in a very radical way. Western science has left the subject out of the universe, and insofar as the religions are gradually losing their importance, many of us may feel that we have no place in the larger scheme of things. We are often isolated from other people, and may feel that our lives have no meaning, except in a very limited, egoistic sense.

Of course, the world is full of signs telling us that such crisis is not only in our personal lives. Apart from the threat of nuclear annihilation and global ecological catastrophy, there are numerous other problems: famine, violence, oppression, and economic, racial and sexual inequality, to name a few. Of course, there has recently been some reason for optimism as the Superpowers have been able to at least begin to reduce nuclear weapons, and as some governments have at least promised to give priority to environmental issues.

But it is clear that a much more radical change is required for humanity to survive. Is it possible to even conceive of such a change? One of the suggestions of this book is that only a radical change in what the world *means* to us would constitute a change in what the world *is*. This proposal is put forward by the physicist and philosopher David Bohm, who says that we have a reason for a much greater optimism than we commonly assume, provided we are willing to consider the nature of meaning more carefully:

> . . .we have open to us a tremendous possibility. . . .it's the present meanings . . . that are leading us to all these troubles. . . .the fact is that the world means a place where everybody must scramble for himself, and where each nation must defend itself . . . A change of meaning is necessary to change this world politically, economically and socially. But that change must begin with the individual; it must change for him. . . .if meaning itself is a key part of reality, then, once society, the individual and relationships are seen to mean something different a fundamental change has *already* taken place.[2]

How can a change in what things mean to me or to you be a fundamental change in, say, social reality? Bohm answers:

> Suppose . . . we apply meaning to society. Karl Marx says society means to me a place where there are classes and where people are exploiting each other and where they should stop that. By creating that meaning Marx has already effected a change in society which he has spread to other people. In other words, the meaning is part of the very thing he is talking about either coherently or incoherently. Hitler was hoping his would be coherent. Other people say it wasn't.[3]

Usually we may think that what society is and what it means

to us are two different things. And we may then look for a meaning that corresponds to society in a correct way. But, as Bohm points out, meaning helps to create the very thing that is meant. After Marx had communicated to others what society meant to him, and many people had accepted it, society was no longer the same — Marx's view changed society, it did not merely describe it.

So when, as an example, we try to evaluate Marx's view, we must also ask whether, on the whole, it had a positive effect on society. It is clear that Marx's view had a great value in that it drew attention to serious problems in nineteenth century society but at the same time it has not been able to bring about a classless society. In the twentieth century the need to transcend global fragmentation is stronger than ever.

It is still very possible that we are going to have a nuclear war because of the various divisions within humanity. It is thus clear that prevailing political and economic views have failed to bring about a unity and equality between all people on the earth. At the same time nationalism and religion bring unity for a limited group but are a hindrance to true global unity.

When we are talking about society and telling others what it means to us, it is clear that what we say can change society in a significant way. The question is, does it change it into a good direction? Does it help the whole of society work without conflict, without breaking up? If it does, then it is a coherent meaning. A meaning is coherent when its overall effect, the reality it helps to create, is harmonious. But insofar as the world is still fragmented into nations, religions and ideologies which are opposed to each other, it is clear that humanity has no over-all, coherent meaning. And yet such a coherent meaning is absolutely necessary if we are to communicate about important matters and survive as a species.

This does not imply that there is only one correct way of looking at the world, one absolute meaning to everything. In fact, it is just this tendency for our meanings to become absolute that leads to conflict with others. With five billion people on the earth it is very unlikely that everybody will agree about everything. But on the other hand, the whole world is now so interconnected, that we need some overall world-view which is common to all humanity. What is required of such a view?

It is clear that such a world-view must recognize that the

world will always mean something different to different people. It accepts that there will always be a plurality of meanings, and yet it seeks unity in this plurality so that a *global dialogue* is possible. In such a dialogue, based upon a coherent common meaning, the differences between the various views could manifest themselves as creative tension, instead of meaningless conflict.

We have thus suggested that meaning plays a key role in determining what human society is. It seems clear that what society means to us and what it *is* are really not separate. The great revolutions have shown that the moment people took autocracy to mean something bad that must be stopped, this was the beginning of its decline. So it is quite easy to see how changes of meaning *are* changes of being at the human level. But what is the relation between nature and its meaning to us? At first, we might readily say that what nature is and what it means to us are two entirely different things.

But obviously this is not the case. For we have taken nature to mean an objective resource to be ruthlessly exploited, and as a consequence, our actions have polluted the earth in just one century. Clearly, if nature had meant something different, such as an integral part of ourselves, we would not have begun to destroy it. It is clear that already the 'being' of the earth has changed as a consequence of what it has meant to us. Its ozone skin is torn apart and its temperature is rising as a consequence of human action.

The fact that science and technology took nature to mean a grand mechanistic machine with no inherent value and meaning has actually facilitated the exploitative attitude. But why is it that our scientific culture still sees nature as a mechanistic machine in spite of the fact that this attitude facilitates the destruction of the ecosphere and reduces the universe, including ourselves into an object with no inherent meaning? Does modern science support this attitude?

Here we come to a very important point which is also central to this book: the mechanistic view, although it has a great value in limited areas, is an incoherent characterization of nature in the light of modern physics and possibly also biology. The quantum theory, the most fundamental theory of matter, especially calls for a radical revision in our concept of reality. David Bohm writes:

The quantum theory ... presents us with a great challenge, ... for in this theory there is no consistent notion ... of the reality that underlies ... matter. Thus, if we try to use the prevailing world-view based on the notion of particles, we discover that the 'particles' (such as electrons) can also manifest as waves [and] that they can move discontinuously. ... If on the other hand we apply the [equally possible] world-view in which the universe is regarded as a continuous field, we find that this field must also be discontinuous, as well as particle-like... It seems clear ... that we are faced with deep and radical fragmentation [and] confusion, if we try to think of ... the reality that is treated by our physical laws.[4]

There have been many attempts to respond to this situation but, all in all, these attempts have failed to give us a coherent view of reality. According to Bohm,

at present physicists tend to avoid this issue by adopting the attitude that our overall views concerning the nature of reality are of little or no importance. All that counts in physical theory is supposed to be the development of mathematical equations that permit us to predict and control the behaviour of large statistical aggregates of particles. Such a goal is not regarded merely for its pragmatic and technical utility: rather, it has become a presupposition of most work in modern physics that prediction and control of this kind is all that human knowledge is about.[4]

Bohm notes that the above presupposition reflects the general spirit of our age, but he insists that we cannot dispense with an overall world-view. If we try to do this, we are left with those, generally inadequate, world-views that happen to be at hand:

Indeed, one finds that physicists are not actually able just to engage in calculations aimed at prediction and control: they do find it necessary to use images based on *some* kind of general notions concerning the nature of reality, such as 'the particles that are the building blocks of the universe': but these images are now highly confused (e.g. these particles move discontinuously and are also waves). ...we are here confronted with an example of how deep and strong is the need for some kind of notion of reality in our thinking, even if it be fragmentary and muddled.[5]

In this book we search for less confused images, for it is clear that our concept of reality has a tremendous effect on how we behave in relation to nature and to other people, and also on the meaning life has for us as individuals. But images that are less confused are not necessarily the most familiar ones. For the quantum theory suggests that the universe is more like a living organism than a dead machine.[6]

As Bohm (1987) points out, according to the mechanistic view, everything that exists is thought to be a system consisting of separate elements. In general, these are *particles*, such as atoms, protons and quarks, but can also include continuously extending *fields*, such as the electromagnetic and the gravitational field. These elements are thought to be basically *external* to each other, not only in that they are separated in space but especially in that the fundamental nature of each element is independent of that of the others. Such elements interact externally and mechanistically by pushing and pulling each other either directly or through forces which diminish as the distance between the elements increases. What is essential is that these forces are external and do not affect the inner natures of the elements.

In an organism the elements grow organically as parts of the whole. This means that the very nature of any part can be profoundly affected by changes of activity in other parts, and by the general state of the whole. So in contrast to the mechanistic view, the parts are *internally* related to each other as well as to the whole.

In what sense does the quantum theory then challenge the mechanistic view? First of all, according to the theory all action takes place in the form of indivisible and small amounts of energy or quanta. This means that all interactions between the elements of the universe constitute an indivisible whole, which weaves the whole universe into one. Secondly, light and matter act either as waves or as particles, depending on the experimental context. This is in contradiction to mechanism, according to which the inner nature of a thing is not affected by the context which it is in. Thirdly, and perhaps most radically, quantum theory predicts, and experiments show, that two separate particles can be non-locally correlated. In certain situations, what happens to particle A influences a distant particle B even if no force known to physics mediates between them. This points to a new holistic feature of nature which is incompatible with the mechanistic idea that forces between particles diminish as their distance increases.

Thus, all the above points are in contradiction with the mechanistic view, and suggest instead that the universe is more like a holistic organism. In the light of the above, how would we then characterize, say, an electron? This is how Bohm sees it:

> The electron must behave in all sorts of strange ways, like being a wave and a particle at the same time and jumping from one state to another without passing in between — and doing all sorts of things that cannot be understood but only calculated. If you don't want to say it's alive ... you should say that the electron is a total mystery and all you can do is compute statistically how it will reveal itself phenomenally in certain kinds of measurements.[7]

We can thus, in general terms, characterize nature, including inanimate matter, as being 'alive'. But in what sense is it alive? Thinking in the holistic framework, is it possible to give a sharper image of reality at the quantum level?

David Bohm thinks that presently the most intelligible way of making sense of the paradoxes of quantum theory is to say that quantum particles are actively guided by a wave or a field containing something analogous to *information*. An electron, for example, moves with its own energy, but the information in the *form* of the quantum field directs this energy. The essential point is that when the information meets the energy of the particle, it becomes active.

Bohm generalizes this idea to what he calls *active information*. The basic idea of this is that a form which has very little energy enters into and directs a much greater energy. This is what happens in many areas beyond the quantum theory. As examples of such active information Bohm sees the radio wave, information in a computer, the DNA molecule, and also human experience of meaning. Indeed, he thinks that meaning in general can be seen as the activity of information, in a similar way as William James thought that meaning is the activity which a sign gives rise to.

In quantum theory, the field that guides the particle reflects essentially the *form* of the particle's environment. It is from this role of form as a guiding factor that Bohm draws the link to the concept of in*form*ation. To inform means literally 'to put form into' something. We need to postulate this field of information in order to explain and understand why the form of the environment is reflected in the behaviour of the particles.

In Bohm's paper in this book you will see how this new way of thinking leads to a fascinating concept of matter at the quantum level.

Those familiar with the roots of Western science know that such an emphasis on the causative role of form echoes Ancient Greek philosophy and especially Aristotle's notion of formal (and final) cause.[8] But nowadays science undergraduates all over the world are taught that it is not appropriate to attribute formal and final causes to nature; partly to avoid anthropomorphism, and partly because in classical physics it was possible to explain the behaviour of material bodies in mechanistic terms.

Consequently, there is a widespread conviction that physics, at least, can do without formal cause. This, indeed, was the case in classical physics, but in quantum mechanics the situation is totally different. One must emphasize here that Bohm's way of illustrating quantum phenomena in terms of the field of active information is not '. . . arbitrarily imposed from the outside, (e.g. by assumption) but it has been demonstrated to follow from the overall theory itself'.[9]

So, striking as it may seem, the most fundamental theory of modern physics is totally compatible with the notion of formal cause. But the truly radical point is that the quantum theory is *not* compatible with the mechanistic view. Thus, according to Bohm, the causative role of form (and thus something *analogous* to information and its meaning) enters physics in a fundamental way.

Another common argument against seeing meaning and purpose as objective features of nature is to say that this is anthropomorphic. But is the mechanistic view any less anthropomorphic than any other view? According to the biologist Rupert Sheldrake

> (i)ronically, the mechanistic approach itself seems to be more anthropomorphic than the animistic. It projects one particular kind of human activity, the construction and use of machines, onto the whole of nature. The mechanistic theory derives its plausibility precisely from the fact that machines *do* have purposive designs whose source is in living minds. . . . The fact of the matter is that the machine analogy is entirely anthropomorphic.[10]

In a similar vein, David Bohm suggests that the mechanistic view in classical physics is based upon the idea of the mechanical system and forces, which is a model of how people push things around. According to him, mechanism began with people pushing things around: it is based on projecting into matter the sort of things that we do with our body. Further, Bohm notes that even space and time are anthropomorphic concepts.[11]

Thus, anthropomorphism is not an inferior intellectual strategy. It may even be inevitable to some extent, for every scientific model comes from the creative action of the human mind. Modern physics requires that we introduce new concepts in order to explain and understand nature. And if the best explaining concepts happen to be anthropomorphic, we should not *a priori* discard them just because of this — unless we are also going to discard other anthropomorphic concepts such as force, or even space and time. Clearly, we must ask the deeper questions about what is a good explanation, and what kind of concepts provide the most fruitful context for further discoveries.

And yet the new way of talking about matter is truly striking to our common sense, as the following extract from a discussion between David Bohm and the American philosopher Renée Weber shows. They are discussing the participatory universe, in which everything is the observer and everything is the observed:

> **Bohm:** The electron, in so far as it responds to a meaning in its environment, is observing the environment. It is doing exactly what human beings are doing. The word 'observe' means to gather, to pay attention.
> **Weber:** So the electron is observing us?
> **Bohm:** It is gathering information about us, about the whole universe. It is gathering-*in* the universe and responding accordingly. Therefore it is observing, if you take that in its literal sense.[12]

So if you ever wondered what it is like to be an electron, Bohm gives you at least some idea!

According to Bohm, the field of information is essential to what an electron *is*. And this information is not a usual notion of physics, such as energy or electric charge. Instead, he sees it as '. . . a condensed form of meaning, which has to be unfolded.'[13] Thus, insofar as meaning has some inherent subjectivity, so do quantum processes, at least in a very elementary

way. But do we then have to say that stones think? Bohm
answers:

> ...I am not attributing consciousness as we know it to nature
> ...matter may not have the same sort of consciousness that
> we have, but there is still a mental pole at every level of mat-
> ter... And eventually, if you go to infinite depths of matter,
> we may reach something very close to what you reach in the
> depths of mind. So we no longer have this division between
> mind and matter.[14]

The proposal that meaning plays an objective role even at the
quantum level opens up a new way of conceiving the unity
of mind and matter. And it is just this kind of unity that a
coherent world-view should provide. This kind of view makes
it possible to understand how we can be at the same time conscious subjects and material objects. It also articulates the holistic implications of quantum theory: we are internally related
to other people, to nature, to the whole of the cosmos.

The distinction between what is meaning and what is not
is yet another way how our mechanistic world-view splits up
existence. Although this is a reasonable division in many situations, it need not be made absolute. Meaning does not necessarily fade out altogether as we glide down the Great Chain
of Being from man towards inanimate matter. Renée Weber
notes:

> That is one of the beautiful aspects of this world-view. It envi-
> sions a universal coherence and points to an all-encompassing
> principle that runs throughout the system; it doesn't just start
> at the human or organic level.[15]

The fact that there is no mechanistic bottom level to reality suggests that meaning and subjectivity are in some sense irreducible features of reality, at all levels. Meaning would thus be
the essence of being, and changes of meaning would give rise
to changes of being. I think this has to do with the tremendous possibility that David Bohm sees opening up in this exploration into meaning:

> **Weber:** What does all this imply to the human world? Look-
> ing at the universe in this way changes our lives in what
> way? ...
> **Bohm:** The mechanistic view has created a rather crude and
> gross meaning which has created a crude and gross and con-
> fused society. [But I'm saying that] the being of matter is mean-

ing; the being of ourselves is meaning; the being of society is its meaning. [This new view] encourages us . . . toward a creative attitude, and fundamentally it opens the way to the transformation of the human being because a change of meaning is a change of being. At present, . . . because of the confused fragmentary meanings we have a confused fragmentary being, both individually and socially. Therefore this opens the way to a whole being, in society and in the individual.
. . .

Weber: This view . . . would make human beings feel rooted and have their dynamic place in the whole scheme of things.
Bohm: At least they would have a chance to find it there. It's a view within which it makes sense to observe, to find out where your place is.[16]

Let us now move on to look at how this book relates to the above questions. *The Search for Meaning* is above all an exploration in which people from various fields come together to discuss our concept of meaning and to extend it into new directions. On the other hand, as many of the contributors have used David Bohm's approach as a framework for their own inquiry, the book can partly be seen as a further development and application of this approach in different contexts.

In the first article, Bohm presents his new theory in more detail. Afterwards, his views will be discussed by a group of people which includes many of the contributors. This discussion touches on some very important topics, and it clarifies and further unfolds the basic ideas of the book. So should Bohm's approach awaken questions in your mind, you may find many of them explored in the discussion.

In the next paper Rupert Sheldrake examines how the status and role of meaning in science, and especially biology, has changed through history since Aristotle. Against this historical background he gives reasons why modern biology favours a return of meaning, purpose and life to nature, who lost these as mechanistic science developed. Sheldrake also sketches how his well-known concept of morphic fields relates to meaning and purpose.

The hypothesis of formative causation Sheldrake put forward in 1981 in his *New Science of Life* proved to be one of the most thought-provoking scientific ideas of the Eighties. The basic idea was that the forms and behaviour of past organisms of a species influence the forms and behaviour of similar organisms in the present. He proposed that this influence takes place across both space *and* time via what he called morphogenetic fields. Sheldrake's hypothesis is not only meant as an alternative interpretation of the existing biology, but it also makes experimental predictions that differ from those of the orthodox theory.

For example, if several rats in Australia have learned to perform a certain task, Sheldrake's hypothesis says that other rats of the same species ought to learn the same task more easily anywhere in the world, even when they have had no physical contact with the Australian rats. No wonder these proposals, made on the basis of some already existing experimental results, created a storm of controversy: *Nature* magazine wanted Sheldrake's book burnt, whereas *New Scientist* hailed it as an exciting and reasonable hypothesis in the best tradition of science, and set up a competition for the best experiments to test it.

In his new book *The Presence of the Past* (1988), Sheldrake extends his earlier ideas and proposes that what we usually think of as the laws of nature are more like habits. This was also the idea of the American philosopher Charles Peirce, who held that 'Matter is merely mind deadened by the development of habit to the point where the breaking up of these habits is very difficult', or '...matter is effete mind, inveterate habits becoming physical laws.'[18] Sheldrake sees a dynamic aspect in this view, for it is peculiar to habits that they can change: '...the invisible organizing principles of nature, rather than being eternally fixed, evolve along with the systems they organize.'[19]

From a purely philosophical point of view it is interesting and important that Sheldrake is keeping alive the idea that laws of nature are habits. Formative causation suggests in a poetic way how both 'persistence of memory' and true creativity could be inherent in nature. And it is clear, that if the predictions of his hypothesis proved to be true, it would change our view of reality very radically — it would be for biology and psychology what relativity and quantum theory were for physics.

The following extract from a discussion with Renée Weber illustrates how Sheldrake looks at meaning:

Sheldrake: You will always have people who say that any meaning we attribute to the universe is simply a projection of our own minds and the only thing we can know is our way of seeing things. . . .

Weber: Kant!

Sheldrake: Then there will be people who say our world is full of meanings, that it is a kind of messy and provisional reflection of a much more ideal world of mathematical formulae.

Weber: Plato!

Sheldrake: . . . The third view is . . . [Aristotle's] doctrine of hylomorphism: with form and matter as two sides of the same thing. Since his interpretation of the meaning is teleological in terms of things having purposes or goals, the meaning of both sides gives coherence to a thing and also defines a unity of its different aspects related to its goal. My own view is in the Aristotelian tradition. In any case, there is a coherent tradition of looking at the world which is similar to what we are talking about.[17]

Thus, morphic fields are teleological, they are fields of information which guide the development of the form of an organism, its behaviour and even its mental functioning. Fields that guide mental functioning could be called 'meaning fields'. For if it is reasonable to talk about fields of information, even at the level of the electrons, is it not much more plausible that our consciousness can be thought of as a 'field of meaning' which is associated with the brain and the body, in an analogous way as the field of information is associated with the electron?

We pointed out earlier that quantum systems are more like holistic organisms than mechanistic machines. Of course, it does not follow from this that human beings and other biological organisms would not be like machines. Bohm (1987) writes:

> . . . there's no way to exclude the possibility that organisms have a mechanistic base in their supposed constituent particles. But if we say that the particles themselves haven't got a mechanistic base, then why should the organisms have it? It would be peculiar to say that the particles of physics are not mechanistic, but as soon as they make organisms they are mechanistic.[20]

Modern physics thus gives intuitive support to the conceptual structure of Sheldrake's hypothesis.

The second part of the book shifts the focus of attention from nature in general to human beings in particular and uses the viewpoints of medicine, neuroscience and psychology. We move smoothly from Sheldrake's biological paper to look at the human body and its health. Larry Dossey, the author of *Space, Time and Medicine*, explores here the relevance of Bohm's concept of *soma-significance* to medicine. You may have already wondered about this 'cryptogram' which figures in the title of three papers. Dossey's paper discusses soma-significance at great length, but let me give you a little bit of its background here.

After writing a paper on language, Bohm began to think about the commonly used term *psycho-somatic* which implies that there are two separate things, mind and body. 'Psyche' comes from a Greek word and means mind or soul and 'soma' means the body. Generally we use the word psycho-somatic to refer to physical illness which is supposed to be caused by psychological factors. Bohm then thought that if we use the word psycho-somatic to denote that mind affects body, we also ought to have a word for the reverse effect, the effect of body on mind; for the word psycho-somatic does not get across the fact that the soma affects the psyche as much as the psyche affects the soma. Logically, one could then use the word soma-psychic to refer to this reverse process.

But Bohm was not merely looking for a new word. He was also dissatisfied with the implication of 'psycho-somatic' that mind and body are two separate entities. His own intuition was more like that of Spinoza, namely that mind and body are *aspects* of one reality. In this connection Bohm then thought that the *soma is significant*. That is, there is no mental entity separate from a somatic entity, as the word psycho-somatic implies. Instead, he saw soma and significance to be the two aspects of one reality, corresponding to the physical and the mental. His point (which will be explored in much greater detail later) was that the soma is significant to the mental side but the mental side is *at the same time* the activity in the soma.

Thus he felt that the term soma-significance would help us to view the relationship of mind to matter in a proper way. It emphasizes that the soma is significant and also emphasizes that it is meaning, significance in the mental side that affects the soma, rather than a 'psyche' or soul which tends to imply some separate entity. 'Soma-significance ' suggests that there is no mental entity separate from a somatic entity. Rather, there is one process which is simultaneously both soma-significant and *signa-somatic*. Note that it follows from soma-significance that we can consistently replace 'psycho-somatic' by the new word signa-somatic.

The wider implications of soma-significance have also been described by Renée Weber:

> If the physical universe is the *soma*, as in Spinoza — nature's or God's body — then the non-soma or meaning is the cosmic mind or nature's thought. Meaning is therefore part of *all* the levels of being. . . . Since all meaning is purposive and active, that adds up to a claim that everything is a partner in the evolution of the universe — at all levels from the subatomic, biological, historical, and social domains, to something beyond that we can dimly conjecture about.[21]

The idea of soma-significance, introduced by Bohm in his *Unfolding Meaning*,[2] which was certainly one of the concepts that prompted the present book. Larry Dossey has found that the concept is not only philosophically interesting, but has potential to transform our thinking about health and disease and thus our whole medical approach. Dossey brings out striking examples about how meaning of life events — such as the death of one's spouse — can affect the immune system profoundly. He thinks that Bohm's theory of soma-significance can be developed to give an intelligible account of how the uniqueness of the meaning of life events crystallizes into actual medical problems. Traditional medicine, with its mechanistic view, has generally de-emphasized the role of meaning and consciousness in health and disease. And yet some of the most serious illnesses of our time, such as heart disease or cancer, are nowadays thought to be related partly to mentally induced stress. Dossey's search for a more comprehensive view of illness and health on the basis of Bohm's theory is thus clearly of utmost importance. He develops the idea that meaning is the determinant of health in a much more fundamental sense than we commonly assume.

The next paper focuses on a specific part of the human body — the brain and the nervous system. Its author Matti Bergström has much research experience as a neurophysiologist. He is very well-known in Finland and also in Sweden as a creative and imaginative scientist whose interests extend far beyond the laboratory and concern the state of our culture and the future of humanity as a whole.

His model presents the brain as a dynamic system which has two interacting parts or poles: the *core part* of the brain stem and the *outer shell* of the cerebral cortex. The role of the brain stem is to regulate consciousness with its chaotic signal flow, whereas the cerebral cortex carries sensory data in its more ordered signal flow. As these two processes interact there is a meeting of chaos and order, out of which our behaviour is born. This paper is highly interesting as it is related to the current dicussion of 'neural Darwinism' in the brain sciences. Bergström is one of the pioneers of this revolutionary concept, and in this paper he also extends this notion beyond Darwinism in exciting ways.

On the basis of his many years of research, Bergström has — like Sperry — come to believe that we need to refer to the concept of value when talking about the brain. Bergström works from the bold assumption that certain overall processes of the living brain, known to us presently, correspond in a relatively accurate way to some basic features of the human mind.

His approach to understanding consciousness is, in some ways, quite different from that of Bohm, for example. But what is common between them is the recognition of the causative role of values and meaning in the human world, mentally and physically. So working within quite a different framework, Bergström has come to emphasize that if we want to understand the brain and meet the problems facing humanity today, it is to meaning and values that we should give our attention.

From the brain the book shifts its focus to the mind. David Shainberg practised psychiatry for many years before he dedicated himself to painting. In his paper, Shainberg points out how already infants seek order and meaning in their experience, and describes the spontaneous creativity in this process of making meaning. Unfortunately such spontaneity tends to get lost as we grow older. Shainberg inquires into this fundamentally important question and contrasts two alternatives as a psychological way of life: either we search for security in the established and fixed old structures of meaning, or we see life and relationship as a process of *making new meanings*, thus allowing creativity and uncertainty to play a part in life. He points out that, especially in a dialogue, the possibilities for this experience open themselves up.

There is a clear parallel between Bergström and Shainberg,

for both see the essential dynamics of human life to lie in the dynamic interaction and balance between creativity and fixed structures of knowledge. Bergström discusses the neurophysiological basis of this dynamics, whereas Shainberg views it more from the inside.

The next part consists of philosophical explorations that expand on the issues introduced before, and make new openings. In his paper 'Beyond Cezanne's Mountain' David Peat, a physicist and the author of *Synchronicity*, reminds us that meaning is an aesthetic topic which cannot be understood with intellectual and scientific means alone. Peat discusses the creative dynamics of meaning; and with a vision of a renaissance man he sketches how there might be a deeper unity between the arts and the sciences, philosophy and religion through the common, generative role that meaning plays within them.

Arleta Griffor takes us to the deep waters of philosophy. She begins by discussing Descartes' formulation of the mind-body problem. Descartes thought that mind and matter are two distinct substances, and that they were primarily differentiated by matter having extension, which the mind did not have. But modern physics has challenged the traditional concept of matter as extended, and thus it is possible to reconsider the relation between mind and matter. Can we, in the light of modern physics, see new common features that mind and matter share? Can these features be considered as a basis for conceiving their relationship in a new way? Griffor, who is working on a PhD thesis on Bohm's philosophy, discusses these questions in the context of Bohm's concept of the *implicate order*.

Again, as this concept will be referred to in a number of articles, let me introduce it here. Bohm's initial response to the mind-body problem was his notion of enfolded or implicate order which he originally developed in order to understand relativity and quantum theory on a deeper basis common to both. The essential feature of the implicate order was that

> . . . the whole universe is in some way enfolded in everything and that each thing is enfolded in the whole. . . . The basic proposal is that this enfoldment relationship is not merely passive or superficial. Rather, it is active and essential to what each *is*. It follows that each thing is internally related to the whole and therefore to everything else. The external relationships are then displayed in the unfolded or *explicate* order in

which each thing is seen as separate and extended and related only externally to other things.[22]

Bohm suggests that the implicate order provides an intuitive way of understanding the properties of matter as implied by quantum theory. He also says that the implicate order can even more obviously be used to describe mind

> ...with its constant flow of evanescent thoughts, feelings, desires, and impulses, which flow into and out of each other, and which in a certain sense enfold each other (as, for example, we may say that one thought is *implicit* in another, and this word means literally 'enfolded').[23]

Bohm suggested that the implicate order is common to both mind and matter, and their relation could be expressed by means of it. But he also recognized that the implicate order does not provide a clear understanding of just how mental and material sides are to be related. Concepts like soma-significance and active information can be seen as a step towards such understanding, and Griffor will also discuss them.

In my own paper I will look in more detail at the implications of quantum physics, and especially the question of what is the nature of the reality that underlies our everyday experience of matter. It seems that one of the founders of the quantum theory, Niels Bohr, did give a *consistent* interpretation of the theory. But at the same time, he almost categorically refused to discuss the nature of quantum reality, thus leaving room for a lot of confusion. It is against this confusion that the value of David Bohm's new interpretation of quantum theory featured in this book can be appreciated more fully. My paper places Bohm's notion of active information in its context in physics, and also discusses its implications for our concept of the relation between matter and consciousness.

It is exciting to relate the above considerations to cognitive science, the rapidly growing interdisciplinary study of consciousness. For most cognitive scientists and philosophers of mind still assume that the mind can be reduced to matter in the human brain, or more generally, that mind is a property of any suitably organized material system, be it a brain or a computer.

Such a view *presupposes* that consciousness has its base in some unambiguous bottom level of material reality. This can be contrasted with Bohm's approach, which starts from questioning our concept of matter instead of assuming it. His analysis makes it clear that it is not consistent to think that consciousness is ultimately grounded in a mechanistic material process. At the end of my paper, I will make some tentative suggestions about what could be a more consistent way to characterize consciousness.

In the next paper Karl Georg Wikman discusses the human creation which is mysterious above all others: mathematics. He first illustrates with many examples how creativity plays an extraordinary part in the development of mathematics: he will then proceed to ask why is it that surprisingly frequently, physical phenomena are organized in ways which can be accurately described by mathematics. It is as if the mind, for no apparent reason, discovers the keys that open the locked doors of nature's secrets. Wikman goes through the main attempts to explain this mystery, and ends with a radical suggestion: if we consider mathematics and nature as aspects of a larger system, then mathematics can be seen as a way in which the universe refers to itself. From time to time Wikman will note how Bohm's notion of soma-significance allows us to discuss phenomena which would otherwise be left in total mysteries.

It may seem like a quantum jump from mathematics to deconstruction — and it certainly is! But Srinivas Aravamudan will start his juxtaposition of Bohm with the French literary philosopher Jacques Derrida by discussing the fact that humanities, too, have a temptation to build their theories upon formulas or structures. Aravamudan discusses the strengths and limitations of structuralism in modern linguistics and proceeds to consider the radically anti-formalist thought of Jacques Derrida, and its concept of deconstruction in particular.

Deconstruction is an interesting philosophical approach which looks at a system of thought from within. Its principal aim has been to examine the presuppositions of Western philosophy. It is a radical critical approach with still unclear political, social and intellectual implications. Deconstruction is not exactly what Bohm is suggesting, but both approaches can be seen as a radical examination of what culture and human thinking is. Bohm is more accessible to the general reader than deconstruction, which is more directly concerned with literary and philosophical *texts* than our sensory experience in the usual sense.

Both Bohm and Derrida are reminiscent of Spinoza, who presented a monist alternative to Descartes' dualism. Derrida has addressed the problems with Cartesian dualism, and Bohm, too, developed his soma-significance as a response to it.

Deconstruction views text as a field which is not categorically different from reality, which strikes a chord with Bohm's view about fields of information as essential to reality. One can also see an analogy between quantum interconnectedness and so called intertextuality.

Deconstructive criticism shies away from absolute categories because it feels that Western philosophy has always sought these and failed to see their limits. Thus, it aims to show the problems of absolute systems and ways of *displacing* them. A deconstructive critic does not think that texts can be understood exhaustively, for a text is always thought to have a field which is beyond the grasp of thought. This undercuts the Hegelian tendency to grasp totality. Here, too, one can see a similarity to Bohm for whom meaning is inexhaustible, and regarding the tendency to grasp totality, Bohm points out that

> ...to have an approach of wholeness doesn't mean that we are going to ... capture the whole of existence within our concepts and knowledge. Rather it means ... that we understand this totality as an unbroken and seamless whole in which relatively autonomous objects and forms emerge. And ... it means that, in so far as wholeness is comprehended with the aid of the implicate order, the relationships between the various parts or sub-wholes are ultimately internal.[24]

There is at least an apparent difference between the 'Bohmian' and the deconstructive approach in that the latter does not ask directly what is transformation; perhaps because transformation often has to do with absolute categories. But the deconstructive attempts to displace systems of thought contain implicitly the idea of transformation.

Aravamudan's paper illustrates how radical parallels can be drawn between the sciences and the humanities, by showing how Bohm's ideas about meaning and dialogue stand dynamically together with those of Derrida. Also, the ideas of Bakhtin and Marx will be brought into the picture.

The last paper in this part asks what would a soma-significant cosmology be like. Francis Frode Steen explores this question by embarking on a multi-level literary journey. There is a historical aspect to this journey as Bohm's concepts are reformulated in Meister Eckhart's (1260-1327) terminology. The protagonist has a dialogue with himself on the nature of the finite and the infinite, structure and freedom. And as he begins his journey, he reminds us that his ideas are put forward in the spirit that no description can be ultimately correct. This is Zen along the Tiber.

It then remains to relate the theory to the practice. We have suggested that, if we give our attention to meaning in an appropriate way, this would result in a radical change of our world-view, and our behaviour individually, socially and even globally. The last part of the book consists of papers which attempt to illustrate how this very important and subtle question of change can be approached.

David Schrum opens the discussion by giving a very clear presentation of the aspects of meaning relevant here. He suggests that meaning to life as a whole depends on a context and builds up gradually over the years. He also raises the problem of meaninglessness, pointing out that what is involved is not a total absence of meaning but rather that our relationships are disharmonious and have an *inadequate* meaning. Schrum suggests that those very fixed patterns of human life we may wish to alter contain the energy required for the change. This paper starts from elementary concepts and then develops a clear and sophisticated insight into the nature of meaning and human transformation.

John Briggs and Frank McCluskey continue to ask how theoretical insights about meaning can be awakened and then realized in practice. Following Bohm's suggestion, they see the major cause of conflict in human relationships to be the tendency of human thought to believe in absolute meanings which result in absolute positions. But the nature of meaning, as seen in this book, suggests that there are no absolute meanings because each meaning can be taken into a larger context. There is thus a fundamental *ambivalence* to meaning.

Briggs and McCluskey suggest that this ambivalence can be a source of creativity and evoke what they call a state of *omnivalent meaning* in the human mind, similar to one's experience of a Shakespeare play or a Picasso painting. In omnivalence many meanings converge in so many ways that one may feel the immensity of meaning without being able to say what it means.

They also report an informal experiment in which a person

approached her difficult life situation through a dialogue based on ultimate questions — in her case, 'What is happiness?'. This intimate report illustrates the way in which the present approach to meaning can have a great practical value. Briggs and McCluskey close their article with a history of ultimate questioners, suggesting that philosophical inquiry has in its highest peaks not been a search for rigid truths, but rather, it has aimed to produce an omnivalent state of mind.

The final paper by Arleta Griffor brings together many of the topics discussed earlier. She starts her inquiry by asking why there is such a lack of harmony in the world. If a perception of new, creative meanings does not take place in humanity, what is preventing it? Her analysis will take us through historical attempts to resolve this issue by Descartes, Kant, Hegel and Marx to Bohm's 'meaning view'.

She also gives a glimpse of the radical approach of the philosopher J. Krishnamurti (1895-1986), who has been influential to many of the contributors in this book. Bohm's dialogues with Krishnamurti mark one of the most interesting meetings of the scientific and the contemplative mind in this century, and Krishnamurti's insights into the nature of human conditioning have certainly encouraged Bohm's own optimism about the possibility of a transformation in human consciousness.[25]

A very important part of Bohm's view on human transformation is dialogue, which he sees as a way for the fragmented subcultures of society to come together and form common intentions. In this respect Bohm has been influenced by the English psychiatrist Patrick De Mare, who has proposed that just as individuals and families may need therapy, so the whole of society could engage in a creative dialogue which could be called 'sociotherapy'.[26]

Such dialogue is one of the recurring themes in this book and Arleta Griffor concludes by asking whether it could be the context in which the movement of the human mind could find a new creative mode individually, socially and cosmically.

We hope that *The Search for Meaning* will be a step to a new direction. It is possible to be realistic and scientific, and yet to convey a sense of optimism: something *can* be done, or rather, something can be *seen*. By inquiring into our human problems openly and rationally, in the spirit of friendship, an *insight* may begin to develop. It isn't that *The Search for Meaning* offers itself as a means to an end, or as a 'solution' to all our problems; but in joining the inquiry and looking at our whole mode of individual and collective action critically and from new angles, the kind of insight that is able to change things can be awakened.

In fact, in this inquiry we may begin to see that the very rationality which uses everything only as a means to achieve its ends may be one of the key factors of the present crisis of humanity. We may begin to develop a new kind of rationality which sees other people and possibly even nature as also having a subjective aspect: an intrinsic meaning.

Such a view about nature and other people would encourage us to explore the potential of human consciousness in a new way and to ask whether it has the capacity for deeper love and affection, friendship and compassion. If we felt this way about all humanity and nature, we would never kill each other for our nations, nor destroy the earth because of our greed.

But our inward reality is too often filled with hatred. And we think that we have a good reason to hate, we do not just hate arbitrarily. There is thus a close link between meaning, reason and emotion. Bohm suggests that our emotions depend upon verbally articulated meanings which are backed up by reason. For example, when we are angry we say something like 'I have a *good reason* to be angry, *because* he treated me like dirt'. And the anger and hate that is thus generated builds up between individuals, groups and nations.

So if we want to have world peace, one of the key points to look at may be the power of reason and meaning to generate destructive emotions. We usually view our thought as an abstract instrument, a mere describer of what happens. We may think that our thoughts have no significant effect upon our experience, or to the reality of our emotions. But this view may be wrong: perhaps thought is a much more powerful factor in creating mental reality than we commonly assume. Bohm tells how he was particularly struck in the early Sixties by Krishnamurti's suggestion that

something has gone wrong with human thought as a whole and that the confusion in thought is behind all the trouble. Thought, which we regarded as our highest achievement, was actually what was destroying us. Not that thought itself is wrong, but something had gone wrong with it.[27]

Another point by Krishnamurti which had an impact on Bohm

was the question '...whether there was not some reality beyond thought, from which we had to move — even our thinking must move from there.'[27]

Thought in its movement of attributing reasons and meanings may act as a guide to mind and body — whatever emotion my thought says I have a good reason to feel will actually manifest as a real emotion with physiological effects. Clearly here is a strong contrast between two ways of seeing thought. Either thought merely *describes* the processes between the person and other people, or else, thought may be the *determinant* of the person's emotions, and thus also determines his or her behaviour towards others. The independent power of thought may be far greater than we assume.

If we could choose not to hate, would we still want to hate? But what is there to be done — if my thought says I have a good reason to hate, what can I do? Bohm suggests that

> We need a kind of self-perception whereby the concept or thought would be aware of its own activity. The deeper mind would see that this is only a thought, and then it could say 'it's not very significant' and then it wouldn't have an effect.[28]

Note how Bohm is emphasizing that whether or not a thought will make us hate depends on what we take it to *mean*: '...when we see that an idea is false it goes away; when we see that something is unreal, it goes away; when we see that something is not necessary, we don't do it'.[28] Thus, if I take a thought like 'I have a good reason to be angry because he insulted me' to mean 'true, real and necessary', I will certainly get angry. But at the same time we may think that it is even more true and necessary that we should not get angry and hate other people. How can we reconcile this conflict? Bohm suggests that

> one way is to observe what is going on inside you. What this means is not to suppress it and not to carry it out. If you carry out an impulse you must accept the assumptions behind it. If you suppress it, you can see nothing. There is a state in between where it is being suspended. Suppose you are angry. You don't hit somebody verbally or physically, but you see what the anger is doing to you. So if you can stay with anger, observe it, then you begin to get an insight into how it is working. That is the beginning of how you can start to change.[28]

By giving attention to the meaninglessness of our aggressive thoughts we can learn not to hate, not to create destructive realities within us. The emotions in themselves, such as hatred, do not help us to act properly. The alternative of not hating need not be indifference or submission to 'hateworthy' actions. But instead of our energy being wasted in hatred, we could act intelligently and creatively. Hate is destructive and what we need in problematic situations is creative intelligence.

The above also underlines the importance of forgiving, as Bohm has pointed out. The actual forgiving to somebody may not be the most important thing. But what is important to realize is that all the hurts and mistakes that we take to be *unforgivable* darken our own lives. We do not realize the price we pay for not forgiving — our life-energy which could be free and full of joy is bound by hatred and the memories of all the 'unforgivable' things that have happened to us. And ultimately, our intelligence will be blocked by the rigidity of our hatred. Can we thus realize that we are spoiling our own lives, and ultimately the life of those close to us, because of our hatred? Can we see how these emotions build up socially and globally, and thus sense how urgent it is to change?

In summary, this book can be seen as a tentative sketch of what science, and more generally, human inquiry could be like. Scientific creativity depends crucially upon the psychological character of a person, and not only upon her or his knowledge and rational abilities. It is a function of aesthetic sensitivity, of the ability to communicate and listen to others, and even of one's overall sense of the cosmos and of one's role in it.

But because our modern scientific culture is primarily concerned with knowledge and experimentation, we do not know how radical a change in creativity would take place if we gave importance to these other factors. Our culture takes too much for granted. We hope that this book breaks some ground in showing how a wider basis for human inquiry and creativity can be established.

Much of our culture is thus based on the tacit assumption that the mode of being and communication of the scientists is either unimportant, or that we, in the Western culture, have found the right mode. But this may be our fatal mistake — for it is clear that overall we, as a species, must learn to communicate better with each other about the most important matters. This requires a change at the individual level, for often what is preventing communication are our personal blocks and fears.

In this sense science and philosophy, as well as all human relationships are facing a tremendous challenge: can we develop a new individual and a social consciousness, a new meaning and a new mode of being, which is able to respond to the urgent problems facing humanity at all levels today? In search of this new meaning and being, we must also turn to other cultures than the Western one. And yet we probably need something entirely new, something that can emerge out of a true dialogue — a dialogue between the East, the West and the South; between the man and the woman; between art, religion, philosophy and science.

We need to change our approach to the whole of life, if we want to survive. And the point is not just to survive, but to have a *meaningful* survival, not only for the developed countries but for the whole world.

Notes and References

1. In Bohm, D., Sheldrake, R. and Weber, R. (1986), 'Matter as a Meaning Field', in Weber's *Dialogues with Scientists and Sages*, p.123 London, Routledge.
2. Bohm, D. (1987), *Unfolding Meaning*, ed. by Factor, D., p.107; pp.95-6 London, Routledge & Kegan Paul.
3. *Dialogues with Scientists and Sages*, p.121.
4. Bohm, D. (1980), *Wholeness and the Implicate Order*, p.xiii. London, Routledge & Kegan Paul.
5. Ibid, p.xiii-xiv.
6. *Unfolding Meaning*, pp. 1–25.
7. *Dialogues with Scientists and Sages*, p.114.
8. These will be discussed in more detail in Sheldrake's and Griffor's papers, this volume. But here, let it suffice to say that a formal cause is that which makes an object what it is. The formal cause of a sculpture is the form of the thing it represents. The final cause is the end or purpose of the thing, e.g. for a sculpture the final cause could be its being sold in a market place.
9. Bohm, D. (1987), 'An Ontological Foundation for the Quantum Theory', in Lahti, P. and Mittelstaedt, P. (ed.), *Symposium on the Foundations of Modern Physics 1987*. Singapore, World Scientific.

10. Sheldrake, R. (1988), *The Presence of the Past*, p.314. London, Collins.

11. *Dialogues with Scientists and Sages*, p.116.

12. Ibid. p.120.

13. Weber, R. (1987), 'Meaning as being in the implicate order philosophy of David Bohm: a conversation', in *Quantum Implications: Essays in honour of David Bohm*, ed. by Hiley, B.J. and Peat, F.D., p.442. London, Routledge & Kegan Paul.

14. *Unfolding Meaning*, p.87, pp.89-90.

15. *Quantum Implications*, p.444.

16. *Quantum Implications*, p.450.

17. *Dialogues with Scientists and Sages*, p.122.

18. *The Presence of the Past*, p.14.

19. Ibid., p.114.

20. *Unfolding Meaning*, p.21.

21. *Dialogues with Scientists and Sages*, p.119.

22. Bohm, D., (1985) 'A new theory of the relationship between mind and matter', p.2. Preprint.

23. Ibid, p.3.

24. *Unfolding Meaning*, p.21.

25. Krishnamurti, J. and Bohm, D. (1985), *The Ending of Time*. London, Gollancz. See also Krishnamurti, J. (1971), *The Urgency of Change*. London, Gollancz. See also Krishnamurti, J. (1971), *The Urgency of Change*, London, Gollancz.

26. De Mare, P. (1985), *Group Analysis*, vol. XVII, no. 78, Sage, London.

27. Bohm, D. in *Resurgence* No. 121 March/April 1987, p.17.

28. Ibid., p.19.

PART ONE

The Meaning Revolution
in Science and Culture

Meaning and Information
DAVID BOHM

In this book our specific aim is to explore the notion that meaning is a key factor of being, not only for human beings individually and socially, but perhaps also for nature and for the whole universe.

When we use the term 'meaning', this includes *significance, purpose, intention* and *value*. However, these are only points of departure into the exploration of the meaning of meaning. Evidently, we cannot hope to do this in a few sentences. Rather, it has to be unfolded as we go along. In any case, there can be no exhaustive treatment of the subject, because there is no limit to meaning. Here, we can usefully bring in Korzybski's statement that whatever we say anything is, it isn't. It may be similar to what we say, but it is also something more and something different. Reality is therefore inexhaustible, and so evidently is meaning. What is needed is thus a creative attitude to the whole, allowing for the constantly fresh perception of reality, which requires the unending creation of new meanings. This is especially significant, in the exploration of the meaning of meaning.

Meaning is inseparably connected with information. The operative notion here is that information has to do with *form*. Literally 'to inform' means 'to put form into' something. First of all, information has to be held in some form, which is carried either in a material system (e.g. a printed page) or in some energy (e.g. a radio wave). We find that in general a pure form cannot exist by itself, but has to have its subsistence in some kind of material or energetic basis; and this is why information has to be carried on such a basis. Thus, even the information in our sense impressions and in our thought processes has been found to be carried by physical and chemical processes taking place in the nervous system and the brain.

What is essential for a form to constitute information is that it shall have a *meaning*. For example, words in a language that we cannot read have no meaning, and therefore convey no information to us. Gregory Bateson has said, 'information is a difference that makes a difference'. But to be more precise, we should put it this way: Information is a difference of *form* that makes a difference of *content*, i.e., meaning. (For example, a difference in the forms of letters on a printed page generally makes a difference in what they mean.)

Meaning is the activity of information

Just how is information related to meaning? To go into this question, it is useful to consider the notion of *active information*. As an example, let us take a radio wave, whose form carries information representing either sound or pictures. The radio wave itself has very little energy. The receiver, however, has a much greater energy (e.g. from the power source). The structure of the radio is such that the form carried by the radio wave is imposed on the much greater energy of the receiver. The form in the radio wave thus literally 'informs' the energy in the receiver, i.e. puts its form into this energy, and this form is eventually *transformed* (which means 'form carried across') into related forms of sound and light. In the radio wave, the form is initially inactive, but as the form enters into the electrical energy of the receiver, we may say, that the information becomes active. In general, this information is only potentially active in the radio wave, but it becomes actually active only when and where there is a receiver which can respond to it with its own energy.

A similar notion holds in a computer. The form is held in the silicon chips, which have very little energy, but this form enters into the much greater energy of the overall activities of the computer, and may even act outside the computer (e.g. in a ship or an aeroplane controlled by an automatic pilot guided by the information in radar waves).

In all these cases, we have been considering devices made by human beings, that respond actively to information. However, in modern molecular biology, it is assumed that the DNA molecule constitutes a code (i.e. a language), and that the RNA molecules 'read' this code, and are thus in effect 'informed' as to what kind of proteins they are to make. The form of the

DNA molecule thus enters into the general energy and activity of the cell. At any given moment, most of the form is inactive, as only certain parts of it are being 'read' by the RNA, according to the stage of growth and the circumstances of the cell. Here, we have a case in which the notion of active information does not depend on anything constructed by human beings. This shows that the idea of active information is not restricted to a human context, and suggests that such information may apply quite generally.

It is clear, of course, that the notion of active information also applies directly to human experience. For example, when the form of a road sign is apprehended in the brain and nervous system, the form is immediately active as *meaning* (e.g. if the traffic sign says 'stop', the human being brings the car to a halt).

A still more striking example is that of a person who encounters a shadow on a dark night. If this person's previous experience is such as to suggest that there may be assailants in the neighbourhood, the meaning of an assailant may be immediately attributed to this form. The result will be an extensive and powerful activity of mind and body, including the production of adrenalin, the tensing of the muscles, and an increase in the rate of the heart. But if, on closer inspection, this person sees further evidence indicating that it is only a shadow, all this activity stops, and the body and mind become quiet again. It is clear then that *any* form to which meaning can be attributed may constitute information. This is generally potentially active, and may become actually active in the mind and body of a human being under suitable conditions.

Such relationships of activity in mind and body have been called psychosomatic, where 'psyche' means 'mind' or 'soul' and 'soma' means 'the body'. This suggests two separate systems that interact. But the examples that we have been discussing indicate a relationship much closer than mere interaction of separate entities. Rather, what is suggested is that they are merely two sides or aspects of an overall process, separated in thought for convenience of analysis, but inseparably united in reality.

I would like to suggest then that the activity, virtual or actual, in the energy and in the soma *is* the meaning of the information, rather than to say that the information affects an entity called the mind which in turn operates somehow on the matter of the body. So the relationship between active information and its meaning is basically similar to that between form and content, which we know is a distinction without a real difference or separation between the elements distinguished.

To help focus attention on this kind of distinction, I shall suggest the term *soma-significant*, instead of psychosomatic. In doing this, I am generalizing the notion of soma to include all matter. Each manifestation of matter has form, and this form has meaning (at least potentially, if not actually). So we see quite generally that soma is significant. But in turn, this significance may give rise to further somatic activity (e.g. as with the shadow on a dark night). We shall call this activity *signa-somatic*. So we have the two inseparable movements of soma becoming significant and the significance becoming a somatic activity. This holds not only for human beings, but also for computers (e.g. computers can now 'recognize' forms and act in a way that differs according to differences of form). Similarly the RNA in the cell can respond to the form of the DNA, so that the 'soma' of the DNA becomes significant, and this acts signa-somatically to produce proteins that differ according to differences in the form of the DNA. So the actions of soma-significant and signa-somatic can thus be extended beyond the domain of human experience, and even beyond the domain of devices constructed by human beings.

It is important to consider the fact that the activity of meaning may be only virtual, rather than actual. Virtual activity is more than a mere potentiality. Rather, it is a kind of suspended action. For example, the meaning of a word or of any other form may act as imagination. Although there is no visible outward action, there is nevertheless still an action, which evidently involves the somatic activity of brain and nervous system, and may also involve the hormones and muscular tension, if the meaning has a strong emotional charge. However, at some stage, this action may cease to be suspended, so that an outward action results. For example, in reading a map the forms on the paper constitute information, and its meaning is apprehended as a whole set of virtual activities (e.g. in the imagination), representing the actions that we might take in the territory represented by the map. But among these, only one will be actualized externally, according to where we find ourselves to be at the moment. The information on the map is thus potentially and virtually active in many ways, but actually and externally active at most in one way.

If, however, we can find no place, at least for the moment, to which the map is actually relevant, all such external activity may be suspended. As has indeed already been indicated, this sort of suspension of outward activity is nevertheless still a kind of inward activity that flows out of the total meaning of the available information, (which now includes the realization that there is no place to which the map is actually relevant). More generally then, all action (including what is called inaction) takes place at a given moment directly and immediately according to what the total situation means to us at the moment. That is to say, we do not first apprehend the meaning of the information and *then* choose to act or not act accordingly. Rather, the apprehension of meaning *is*, at the very same time, the totality of the action in question (even if this should include the action of suspending outward activity).

This inseparable relationship of meaning and action can be understood in more detail by considering that meaning indicates not only the *significance* of something, but also our *intention* toward it. Thus 'I mean to do something' signifies 'I intend to do it'. This double meaning of the word 'meaning' is not just an accident of our language, but rather, it contains an important insight into the overall structure of meaning.

To bring this out, we first note that an intention generally arises out of a previous perception of meaning or significance of a certain total situation. This gives all the relevant possibilities and implies reasons for choosing which of these is better. As a simple example, one may consider the various foods that one may eat. The actual choice may be made according to the significance of the food as something that one likes or dislikes, but it may depend further on the meaning of the knowledge that one has about the nutrient qualities of the food. More generally, such a choice, whether to act or not to act, will depend on the totality of significance at that moment. The source of all this activity includes not only perception and abstract or explicit knowledge, but also what Polanyi called *tacit knowledge*; i.e., knowledge containing concrete skills and reactions that are not specifiable in language (as for example is demonstrated in riding a bicycle). Ultimately, it is this whole significance, including all sorts of potential and virtual actions, that gives rise to the overall intention, which we sense as a feeling of being ready to respond in a certain way.

It must be kept in mind, however, that most of the meaning in this process is *implicit*. Indeed, whatever we say or do, we cannot possibly describe in detail more than a very small part of the total significance that we may sense at any given moment. Moreover, when such significance gives rise to an intention, it too will be almost entirely implicit, at least in the beginning. For example, implicit in one's present intention to write or speak is a whole succession of words that one does not know in detail until one has actually spoken or written them. Moreover, in speaking or writing, these words are not chosen one by one. Rather, many words seem to be enfolded in any given momentary intention, and these emerge in a natural order, which is also enfolded.

Meaning and intention are thus seen to be inseparably related, as two sides or aspects of one activity. In actuality, they have no distinct existence, but for the sake of description we distinguish them (as we have done also with information and meaning). Meaning unfolds into intention, and intention into action, which, in turn, has further significance, so that there is, in general, a circular flow, or a cycle.

Closely related to meaning and intention is *value*. Thus, to say 'This means a great deal to me' signifies 'This has a very high value to me'. The word 'value' has the same root as *valor*; and it therefore suggests a kind of strength or virtue. Generally speaking, that which has for us a broad and deep significance will give rise to a sense of value, which arouses us to some kind of response, and infuses us with a corresponding strength or intensity of tne kind of energy that is needed to carry out our intention. Without such a sense of value, we will have little interest and energy, and our action will tend to be weak and ineffective. It is thus clear that meanings implying some kind of high value will bring about strong and firm intentions. When such intentions are focused on a determinate end or aim (once again dependent on the overall meaning) they are called *will*. Thus, intention, value and will may be seen as key aspects of the soma-significant and signa-somatic cycle. It follows then that all three of these, together with meaning, flow and merge into each other in an unbroken movement. The distinctions between them are only in thought. These distinctions are useful in trying to understand and talk about this process, but should not be taken to correspond to any real separation between them.

Thus far, we have been discussing how already-known meanings take part in the cycle described above. Generally speaking, such meanings implicitly contain a *disposition* to act in a corresponding way. Thus, if our view of a road suggests that it is level, our bodies will immediately be disposed to walk accordingly. Moreover, if there are unexpected pot-holes in the road, these may 'trip us up' until we see the meaning of the new situation, and thus immediately alter the disposition of our bodies. All meanings indeed imply (or enfold) various kinds of such *disposition to act* (or not to act), and these are an essential part of the signa-somatic activity of meaning.

As long as the action flowing out of a given set of such already-known meanings is coherent and appropriate, this sort of disposition will constantly be re-enforced, until it becomes a habit, or a *fixed disposition*.

But sooner or later, a situation will be encountered in which this disposition is no longer appropriate. It is then necessary to suspend the older dispositions, and to observe, to learn, and to perceive a new meaning, implying a new disposition.

As an example, consider a very young child, to whom bright objects have always signified goodness, happiness, pleasant excitement, etc., in which are implied a disposition to reach out and take hold of such objects. Suppose now that for the first time the child encounters a fire, and acts according to its habitual disposition. It will burn itself and withdraw its hand. The next time the child sees a fire, the initial disposition to reach out for it will be inhibited by the memory of the pain. When action is thus suspended, the mental energy in the intention to act will tend to go into the calling up of images of previous experiences with such objects. These will include not only images of many pleasing bright objects, but also the memory of the fire, which was pleasing when experienced far enough away but painful in the experience of contact. In a way, these images now constitute a new level of somatic form, resembling that of the original objects, but of a more subtle nature. This form is, as it were, 'scanned' or surveyed from a yet deeper and more subtle level of inward activity.

We emphasize again that in such a process, that which was previously the meaning (i.e. the images and their significance) is now being treated as a somatic form. The child can operate on this form, much as it can operate on the forms of ordinary objects. Thus, the child is able to follow the image of the fire, as it gets closer and at a certain point it evokes a memory-based image of pain. Out of this emerges a new meaning, enabling the child to solve the problem of determining an appropriate relationship to the fire, without having to be in danger of burning itself again. In this new meaning, the fire is pleasant when the hand is far enough away and painful when it is too close. And a new disposition arises, which is to approach the fire more carefully and gradually, to find the 'best' distance from it. As the child engages in many similar learning experiences, there arises a still more subtle and more general disposition to learn in this way in approaching all sorts of objects. This makes for facility and skill in using the imagination in many different contexts to solve a wide range of problems of this general nature.

It is clear that this process can be carried to yet more subtle and more abstract levels of thought. In each stage, what was previously a relatively subtle meaning, can, as in the case of the fire, now be regarded as a relatively somatic form. The latter, in turn, can give rise to an intention to act on it. The energy of this intention is able then to give rise to an ever-changing sequence of images with yet more subtle meanings. This takes place in ways that are similar to those that took place with the image of the fire. Evidently, this process can go on indefinitely, to levels of ever greater subtlety. (The word 'subtle' is based on a root signifying 'finely woven', and its meaning is 'rarefied, highly refined, delicate, elusive, indefinable and intangible'.)

Each of these levels may then be seen from the mental or from the material side. From the mental side it is an information content with a certain sense of meaning as a subtle virtual activity. But from the material side it is an actual activity that operates to organize the less subtle levels, and the latter thus serve as the 'material' on which such an operation takes place. Thus, at each stage, the meaning is the link or bridge between the two sides.

It is being proposed then that a similar relationship holds even at indefinitely greater levels of subtlety. The suggestion is that this possibility of going beyond any specifiable level of subtlety is the essential feature on which *intelligence* is based. That is to say, the whole process is not intrinsically limited by any definable pattern of thought, but is in principle constantly open to fresh, creative and original perceptions of new meanings.

This way of looking at the subject contrasts strongly with the commonly-held notion, to which I have referred earlier, that matter and mind are considered to be separate substances. In the view that I have been proposing, the mental and the material are two sides of one overall process that are (like form and content) separated only in thought and not in actuality. So there is only one energy which is the basis of all reality. The form, as apprehended on the mental side, gives shape to the activity of this energy, which later acts on less subtle forms of process that constitute, for this activity, the material side. Each part thus plays both roles, i.e., the mental and the material, but in different contexts and connections. There is never any real division between mental and material sides, at any stage of the overall process.

This implies, in contrast to the usual view, that meaning is an inherent and essential part of our overall reality, and is not merely a purely abstract and ethereal quality having its existence only in the mind. Or to put it differently, in human life, quite generally, meaning *is* being. Thus, if one were to ask what sort of person a given individual *is*, one would have to include all his or her characteristic tendencies and dispositions to act, which, as we have seen, come out of what everything means to that person. Thus our meanings flow into our being, and because the somatic forms in this being are significant, such being flows back into meaning. Each thus comes to reflect the other. But ultimately, each *is* the other. For the activity to which information gives rise is our being, and this being is actuality and action that are thus 'informed'. So meaning and being are separated only in thought, but not in actuality. They are but two aspects of one overall reality.

It is clear that because there is no limit to the levels of subtlety of meaning that are possible, the being flowing out of meaning is in principle infinite and inexhaustible. One can see that this also follows in another way by noting that all meaning is to some degree ambiguous, because each *content* depends on some *context*. But this latter in turn can become a content, which depends on a yet broader context (which may include many levels of subtlety), and so on indefinitely. So meanings are inherently incomplete, and subject to change, as they are incorporated in broader, deeper, and more subtle meanings, arising in new contexts.

It is possible to look at this whole process in terms of the implicate or enfolded order (which I have discussed elsewhere). That is to say, all these levels and contexts of meaning enfold each other, and may have a significant bearing on each other. Meaning is thus a constantly expanding structure, in which the potential significance of any part is always being actualized by inclusion in greater contexts. It can therefore never be complete or final. At the limits of what has, at any moment, been comprehended are always unclarities, unsatisfactory features, and failures of actions flowing out of intention to fit what happens. The yet deeper intention is to be aware of these discrepancies and to allow the whole structure to change if necessary. This will lead to a movement in which there is the constant unfoldment of still more comprehensive meanings.

But, of course, each new meaning thus perceived has some limited domain in which the actions flowing out of it may be expected to fit what actually happens (e.g. as in the case of the child to whom 'bright' meant 'goodness' and 'happiness'). Such limits may in principle be extended indefinitely through further perceptions of new meanings. However, no matter how far this process may go, there will still be limits of some kind, which will be indicated by the disharmonies between our intentions, as based on these meanings, and the actual consequences that flow out of these intentions. At any stage, the perception of new meanings may resolve these discrepancies and disharmonies, but there will continue to be limits, so that the resulting knowledge is still incomplete.

What is implied then is what we have indeed already indicated; meaning is capable of an indefinite extension to ever greater levels of subtlety as well as of comprehensiveness. This can actually take place, however, only when new meanings are being perceived freshly from moment to moment. Of course, such fresh perceptions may flow freely into the short term memory, which does not hold a fixed content. It therefore seems natural to include the short term memory as a natural extension of fresh perception. However, the long term memory is a kind of relatively fixed recording, tending to have a certain stable quality. Of course, even long term memories may fade, or otherwise alter, as their meanings are seen to change in actual experience. Nevertheless, when the long term memory operates as the major factor in consciousness, it is not able to transform its own structure in a fundamental way.

It has indeed only a limited capacity to adapt to new situations (e.g. by forming combinations of known images, ideas, principles, etc.).

To go beyond these limits, a fresh perception of new meanings is needed. To create new meanings in this way requires at least a potentially infinite degree of inwardness and subtlety in our mental processes. Such mental processes of indefinitely deep inwardness and subtlety can, however, incorporate the content of memory along with the rest of perception into wholes, in which, for example, old long term memories may take on new meanings. Thus, though memory is essentially mechanical when it is the major factor operating, it is nevertheless able, in a secondary role, to participate significantly in creativity.

Physics and active information

Thus far, we have been focusing mainly on meaning insofar as this operates in a human being. We have seen, however, that the notion of active information can be extended beyond this, to apply to radio receivers, to computers, and to the activity of DNA in a cell. I would like now to go further and show that a similar notion may apply to all inanimate matter at the level of the most fundamental laws of physics that are known; those of the quantum theory.

I shall begin by considering a single particle of matter; e.g. an electron. According to the quantum theory, such a particle shows wave-like properties, as well as particle-like properties. I propose to explain this by assuming that while the electron is a particle, it is always accompanied by a new kind of wave field, determined by Schrödinger's equation (rather as the Maxwell's equations determine the propagation of the electromagnetic field). The electron as we actually encounter it must then be understood in terms of both the particle *and* the field, which always accompanies the particle.

When one looks at the meaning of Schrödinger's equation expressed in terms of this model, one sees that it implies the need to add to the classical forces acting on the particle an additional new kind of force, derivable from what I called the quantum potential.

The basically new features of the quantum theory come mainly from the new properties of the quantum potential. Of these, one of the most important is that this potential is related to the Schrödinger wave function in such a way that it does not depend on the intensity of the wave, but only on the form. This implies that the Schrödinger wave does not act like, for example, a water wave on a floating object to push the particle mechanically with a force proportional to its intensity. Rather, a better analogy would be one that we have already considered in connection with our discussion of information — that of a ship or aeroplane on automatic pilot — guided by radar waves. The ship or aeroplane (with its automatic pilot) is a *self-active* system, i.e. it has its own energy. But the *form* of its activity is determined by the *information content* concerning its environment that is carried by the radar waves. This is independent of the intensity of the waves. We can similarly regard the quantum potential as containing *active information*. It is potentially active everywhere, but actually active only where and when there is a particle.

We may illustrate what this means by considering what happens to a statistical distribution of electrons that pass through a system of two slits and are detected on a screen, as illustrated below

Each of these electrons follows a well-defined track that can be shown mathematically to be perpendicular to the wave front at the point where the particle is. Suppose then that we consider a specified particle which is so located that it goes through

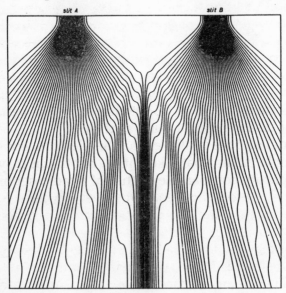

Particle trajectories through two slits

one of the slits. Afterwards, it will follow a complicated path, so that the particle is significantly affected by a quantum potential determined by the interference of waves from both slits. It is clear that even though the electron goes through only one slit, its movement will depend on information coming from both slits. Indeed, even at distances so great that the wave intensity is small, there may be a significant effect of this kind, because, as has been pointed out, the electron responds with its own energy to the form of the wave, however weak the latter may be, and not to its intensity. As has already been pointed out, this response can strongly reflect distant features of the environment, and this implies a certain new quality of wholeness of the electron with the environment that is not present in classical physics. In this way, we understand that the path of each particle depends very much on whether one slit is open or both are open (which is contrary to what one would expect in classical physics). This is the proposed explanation of how the electron can behave in some ways like a particle and in other ways like a wave.

Thus, as we have seen, each individual particle follows a complicated path, depending strongly on the information in the form of the wave that reflects the whole environment. Nevertheless, it ultimately arrives at a particular point on the screen, thus demonstrating the particle nature of the electron. Yet, in a random statistical distribution of electrons with the same Schrödinger wave, we can see, as shown in Fig. 1, that all these particles 'bunch' to produce a fringe-like distribution on the screen. The field of information in the Schrödinger wave is thus reflected in the statistical distribution, and in this way we understand how the dependence of each particle in this field of information brings about the wave-like behaviour of a statistical distribution of such particles.

This model implies however that an electron (for example) is not a simple billiard-ball-like entity, but that it may have an inner complexity comparable to that of a radio set or a vessel guided by an automatic pilot. However, to consider such a notion goes against the general approach in physics over the past few centuries, in which it is assumed that as we analyze matter into smaller and smaller units, its behaviour will become simpler and simpler. Here, we are implying that in the quantum domain such an approach is no longer adequate. Rather, the situation is more like that which is encountered in a large population of human beings. Whereas in a large mass of people we can often make some relatively simple statistical analyses, nevertheless when we come down to the individual, we discover a complexity and subtlety that defies our powers of analysis.

Current theoretical notions suggest that an electron cannot be larger than something of the order of 10^{-16} cm. Is it possible to have so much structure in such a small space? The application of the quantum theory to the gravitational theory suggests that our ordinary notions of space and time will hold down to a distance of the order of what is called the Planck length, which is about 10^{-33} cm (beyond which all our present concepts of physics would probably break down). Between the electronic size of 10^{-16} cm and the Planck length of 10^{-33} cm, there is a range of scales that is as great as that between every-day dimensions and the presumed size of the electron. Thus, there is ample room for the possibility of the requisite structural complexity.

Thus far, we have been discussing only the one-particle system. When we consider the many-particle system, the significance of active information for the quantum theory becomes yet more evident.

Firstly, it must be said that in the many-particle system, the Schrödinger wave is no longer capable of being represented in the ordinary three-dimensional space. Rather, it has now to be thought of in a multi-dimensional space, called *configuration space*, in which there are three dimensions for each particle. A single point in this multi-dimensional space corresponds to a certain configuration of the entire system of particles — hence the name, configuration space.

It is not possible directly to imagine such a configuration space. However, if we recall that the essential significance of the wave in the one-particle system was that it determines a kind of information, then the interpretation can readily be extended to the many-particle system. For it is well known that information, being a highly abstract sort of thing, can be organized and understood in any number of dimensions. This is a natural development of the idea that the Schrödinger wave is not to be regarded as a field of *force*, but rather as a field of information.

A more careful analysis of the mathematics for this case shows that the whole set of particles is now subject to a gener-

alized sort of quantum potential. This depends on the Schrödinger field of the entire many-body system. So we have an
extension of this interpretation to the many-body system, in
which each particle is self-active. However, the form of its
action may now depend on a common pool of information
belonging to the whole system.

The activity of such a common pool of information in the
quantum mechanical context can be most clearly seen in the
superconducting state of electrons in a metal. This is a state
that may arise at very low temperatures, in which an electric
current flows indefinitely without friction, because electrons
are not scattered by irregularities or obstacles in the metal in
which they are flowing. In terms of this model, one sees that
in the superconducting state, the common part of information
induces an organized and co-ordinated movement of electrons
resembling a ballet dance, in which the particles go around
irregularities and obstacles without being scattered.

As the temperature is raised, however, the state of the system
changes in such a way that the property of superconductivity
disappears. The explanation for this is that the Schrödinger
wave field begins to break up into independent factors, representing separate pools of information that apply to similar sub-
systems, and eventually, at high enough temperatures, to the
individual particles themselves. It is as if, in the ballet, the
dancers begin to break up into separate groups that are guided
by different 'scores', until eventually each individual is doing
his or her own dance, unrelated to those of others. The co-
ordinated state of movement therefore disappears, and the
electrons behave more like a disorganized crowd of people than
like an orderly group of ballet dancers.

More generally, one can show by an examination of the
mathematics that the behavior of large-scale objects, especially
at appreciable temperatures, will be determined by separate
pools of information. This explains why, in ordinary large-scale
experience, one finds no evidence of this new organized and
co-ordinated quantum mechanical behavior. Rather, as can be
shown, this latter will tend to become significant mainly in
the small scale (i.e. with atoms and molecules). It can appear
in the large scale, but only in special situations, which include
low temperatures, or with other unusual experimental conditions that may be set up in the laboratory.

The possibility that many particles may move in the way

described above according to a common pool of information, implies that there can be what is called a *non-local connection*. As in the one-particle case, this is because the quantum potential does not necessarily fall off to a negligible value when the particles are separated even by macroscopic orders of distance.

At first sight it seems that such a non-local connection, that can produce a kind of instantaneous contact of distant particles, would violate the theory of relativity, which requires that no signal can be transmitted faster than light. It is possible to show, however, that the quantum potential cannot be used to carry a signal, i.e. that it could not constitute a well-ordered series of impulses that could transmit a well-defined *meaning*. But I shall not, however, go into more detail at this point as it is not directly relevant to the main theme of this paper.

The notion of such a non-local connection evidently goes quite far outside the framework of concepts that have been generally accepted in classical physics. But, of course, it is a perfectly rational idea. And indeed, I would say that much of the resistance that it has encountered is of the nature of the kind of prejudice that tends to arise against any unfamiliar notion.

We have seen then that in the quantum theory, the quantum potential may quite generally be regarded as representing active information, which may be organized in pools of sizes that vary according to the conditions. In accordance with the suggestion that meaning is the activity, virtual or actual, that flows out of such information, we are led to regard the movements of the self-active particles as the meaning of this information. This implies, however, that the notion of active information and meaning that has been proposed in more limited contexts (that include human beings, computers and DNA) can now be extended to the basic physical laws that apply to all matter.

The notion that meaning *is* being has in this way been extended to inanimate matter at the level of the most fundamental laws of physics that are known to us so far. Thus, if we were to ask what an electron is, we would have to include in the answer to this a description of how it behaves under various circumstances. According to classical physics, an electron is an entity that moves mechanically and is deflected only by external forces and pressures, that do not in general significantly reflect distant features of its environment. But according to the quantum theory, an electron is something that can significantly respond to information from distant features of its environment, and this mode of response, which is the meaning of the information, is essential to what the electron is.

In analogy to what has been said about human experiences, the particles constituting matter in general may be considered to represent a more gross (explicate) somatic level of activity, while the Schrödinger wave field corresponds to a finer, subtler, more implicate and 'mind-like' level. In human experience however, it has been proposed that each 'mind-like' level can be regarded as a somatic bearer of form when seen from a yet finer and more subtle level. This would imply firstly that the information represented by the Schrödinger wave field is being 'carried' by a finer and subtler level of matter that has not yet been revealed more directly. But even more important, it also implies that there may be a finer and more subtle level of information that guides the Schrödinger field, as the information on the Schrödinger field guides the particles. But this in turn is a yet more subtle 'somatic' form, which is acted on by a still more subtle kind of information, and so on. Such a hierarchy could in principle go on indefinitely. This means, of course, that the current quantum mechanical laws are only simplifications and abstractions from a vast totality, of which we are only 'scratching the surface'. That is to say, in physical experiments and observations carried out this far, deeper levels of this totality have not yet revealed themselves.

In this way, we arrive at a notion of matter in general which is closely parallel to what was proposed earlier with regard to the relationship of mind and matter in the human being. How then are these two hierarchies of active information, the material and the mental, related? Or are there actually two distinct and independently existent hierarchies?

It is being proposed here that there is in fact only one such hierarchy. In this, the more subtle levels, some of which we experience as thoughts, feelings, intention, will, etc., merge continuously with the less subtle levels. And therefore, what we experience as mind is ultimately connected, soma-significantly, and signa-somatically, to the Schrödinger wave field and to the particles. In this way, we can account for how matter at the ordinary level is knowable through what is called mind, and how the latter can affect what is called the soma of the body, and through this, matter more broadly. So we do not have a split between mind and matter in general. As with information and meaning they are two sides of one process, separable only in thought but not in actuality.

This implies of course that human consciousness is not something altogether outside the overall universe of matter. But matter has now come to signify a totality of being, ultimately of a subtlety beyond all definable limits. And thus, it may equally be called mind, or mind-matter, or matter-mind. In this one totality, meaning provides all being and, indeed, all existence.

Dialogue as a free flow of meaning

It is thus suggested that there may be cosmic meanings, beyond any human individual, or even the totality of humanity. But on the other side, human meanings affect not only the soma of the individual who holds them, but also that of other people to whom these meanings are communicated. And vice versa, the being of each individual is deeply affected by the meanings of society as a whole, as well as by those in nature and in the cosmos. Moreover, such meanings are communicated to inanimate matter, as human beings in their work profoundly affect their whole environment, which in turn profoundly affects them. The very essence of all being is thus in the flow of meaning, which is a generalized kind of communication. In this flow, everything enfolds everything and unfolds into everything. It is basically creative, and the appearance in it of relatively fixed forms is a kind of temporary crystallization of meaning, which can, however, 'melt' back again into the flow when the conditions change.

In society, the basic carrier of meaning is culture, which is indeed just shared meaning. (Thus art, literature, science, etc., which are commonly agreed to be parts of culture, conform to this notion.) It is crucial that the forms of culture (as well as those of social organization) shall not rigidify excessively, or else society will fall apart in fragmentation. We may compare this to what happens to a collection of electrons in a metal. They may move together through an organized and coherent common pool of information; or else they may break up into separate groups or even into individual particles, that move according to separate and independent pools of information. When human society as a whole breaks up into separate nations, religions, ideologies, and other groups, then there are many subcultures that largely ignore each other, and so the whole falls apart because there is no common pool of shared meaning. Eventually, this goes so far that, to a considerable extent, each individual seems to have a separate and independent pool of meaning, which may in turn fragment into many sub-pools. Such an individual feels lonely, even in the prescence of others, for without a shared deeper more inward and more subtle meaning, people have only a rather superficial, crude mechanical relationship.

One of the most important reasons why such fragmentation is sustained is that each person, each group, etc., tends to hold rigidly to certain basic meanings, which are in effect non-negotiable. Thus, when people in groups meet, the aim is either to convince the others of one's own position, or to persuade them to adopt it. Very often this leads to confrontation in which no real communication is possible, or at best to agreement, which again is rather superficial.

What is called for here is a genuine dialogue. The word dialogue is based on the Greek 'dia' meaning 'through' and 'logos' meaning 'the word'. But what is signified here is not the word as such (i.e. the sound) but its *meaning*. Dialogue is a free flow of meaning between people. We may use here the image of a stream flowing between banks.

What is essential for dialogue is that while a person may prefer a certain position, he or she does not hold to it non-negotiably. Such a person is ready to listen to others with sufficient sympathy and interest to understand the *meaning* of the other's position properly and is ready to change his or her own point of view if there is good reason to do so. Evidently, a spirit of goodwill or friendship is necessary for this to take place. It is not compatible with a spirit that is competitive, contentious, or aggressive.

If people are able to engage in a real dialogue, then there can be a free flow of meaning, in which there can arise a creatively new common pool, that allows the group to move together in a coherent and intelligent way. This will happen when people are able to face their disagreements without either confrontation or polite avoidance of the issue, and when they are willing to explore together points of view to which they may not personally subscribe. If they can in this way engage in a dialogue that is free of evasion or anger, they will find that no fixed position is so important that it is worth holding at the expense of blocking the creativity of the dialogue itself. If this sort of thing could ever happen on a large scale, it would constitute a revolutionary transformation of the very nature of culture, and even of consciousness itself.

I hope that in the course of reading and discussing the ideas in *The Search For Meaning*, we can not only explore the nature of dialogue as a free flow of meaning, but also, feel encouraged to engage in an actual dialogue of the kind that has been called for here. Thus, we may be able to see in actual fact whether the notion that meaning *is* being is relevant or not.

DISCUSSION

Is meaning being?

Maurice Wilkins: I wonder if you could clarify this statement you made that 'meaning is being'.

David Bohm: Remember what I said about the computer, the DNA, the electron, the pools of information that make the metal into the superconductor, that determine the properties of all matter. If you analyze what I said, you'll find that all these phenomena are produced when a significance *informs* energy. So according to this picture, matter is not a dead thing. It's not anything like billiard-balls pushing each other around. Rather, its structure and form is organized by an *active meaning*, meaning acting within energy. This notion is a kind of extension of our usual notion of meaning which applies in the human world.

Wilkins: I see the drift of your thought but I still find it confusing to say that soma is significance.

Bohm: The point is that *ultimately* there is no separation. In the beginning you can see that significance affects the energy and that affects the soma, right; we first separate them. But then, let's ask the next question: what is the soma? When we analyze the soma it sort of disappears. You see, here's a nice solid table, soma, but according to physicists, chemists and so on, it's made of particles which are moving around. It's mostly empty space but we say that the particles are the soma. But what are these particles? Ultimately you have to look at them with quantum mechanics and then you'll find that they're not at all like what we usually call particles. If you really try to understand what sort of particles they are, you'll find that they are particles that respond to *information*. The difference between an electron and a proton is largely the different way in which each responds to information in the wave-function.

Wilkins: Even if soma and significance aren't separate it doesn't follow they're the same. Can't you say that they are two aspects of the same basis, or that both being and meaning have the same essence?

Bohm: No, I think that puts the essence out somewhere else beyond both being and meaning. It is hard to see what this would signify. I think it is better to say that the essence of being *is* meaning. I have already explained this, both with regard to a human being, and, as I have just said, also with regard to inanimate things, including even the particles of physics, such as electrons. In all these cases, as the meaning changes so does the essence.

Wilkins: Going back to another point in your paper, you mentioned non-negotiable views and the harm these cause in human relationships. But some people might have got the impression that 'here is professor David Bohm, taking the fixed position that being is meaning and meaning is being' (laughter). I mean, I'm trying to understand this, I'm not just being awkward. Intuitively your position seems quite correct, for I can see a number of specific examples of human situations where this 'being is meaning' is appropriate. But would it possibly represent your position better if you would say that to see meaning and being as separate is an appropriate way of looking at things in certain situations, whereas to see meaning and being as one is appropriate in some other contexts?

Bohm: You could say that. I'd like to emphasize that none of the things that I say are meant as a completely exhaustive statement of reality.

Wilkins: So you're not really taking a fixed position although you might have appeared to...

Bohm: Let me put it differently: I'm making a proposal which is to be explored, and I want to put it fairly strongly to attract your attention (laughter). If I put it weakly you won't give your attention and it would be a waste of time.

Wilkins (jokingly): I don't think that's fair on the audience!

Bohm: No, I mean all of us like to put our proposals strongly.

Wilkins: I see your point. But I wonder about the need to see all being and meaning as one. It seems to me that in some of these examples you've referred to it is not clear where the idea of separating them is inferior to the idea of seeing them all as one. But there are other contexts where it clearly is desirable to see them as one — for example, scientific knowledge. If you regard knowledge as separate from its application or implication, then there is no necessary connection between being a scientist who produces the knowledge and being responsible for the application.

Whereas if you regard scientific knowledge as one inseparable process which includes the way in which it is applied, then it is inescapable that the social responsibility for science must be part of the scientific process. This is a point which is very important in the world today. Another example which occurs to me is that I once read an account of a priest who had been asked to work in a prison and he was told: 'go into the cell with the prisoners and do what you can with them'. He realized that he could not very well go in there and talk — he just went in and he said he just had to *be*.

Bohm: That was his meaning at that moment.

Wilkins: So there you have a practical, real human situation where being and meaning seem to be very much the same. But do you agree that the thing can be usefully split up sometimes and at other times you ought to see all as one?

Bohm: What you say is in a way implicit in what I said in my paper, for there are three stages in this matter. Firstly, meaning *becomes* being (and vice-versa). Through this process, meaning and being come to *reflect* each other. But ultimately, meaning *is* being. As with form and content, we make the distinction between meaning and being in order to express our thought. But this distinction does not imply a real difference, it is the way by which we understand one ultimately undivided whole. At the stage in which meaning and being reflect each other, they may be treated as separate. But in the deeper stage, meaning and being have to be seen as essentially one.

As you suggest, one could say that each of these stages is valid in its proper context. However, if we hold onto any one of them too rigidly, we will carry it too far. Thus, it *is* appropriate in a certain context to separate meaning and being. For example, I might say that this table has a certain meaning to me. To you or to a being from Mars, it may mean something else. So in this context we can separate meaning from being, for there are many meanings that are attributed to the chair, but the being of the chair is not directly affected by this.

But suppose we are discussing a particular person's notion

of truth and trying to say that what truth means to that person is one thing and what he or she *is* is another. This would rarely be the case. Imagine, for example, a person to whom truth means that national interest comes first and that you can lie if that is necessary to protect the interest of the state, as Machiavelli said. Or take another person who might say 'no, truth comes first and national interest comes second'. These two meanings of truth give rise to two clearly different states of being, not separable from the whole being of the persons in question.

Wilkins: So are you saying that in thought you can regard the soma and significance as the aspects of one continuous reality but these differences only exist in thought, they are only separated in thought whereas in reality one is the other?

Bohm: Yes. That raises the question about what is the role of thought in trying to describe being. You could say that thought provides a kind of analogy to whatever is beyond thought. An analogy is literally a proportion. You could say that as things are related in whatever you want to call reality, there is a similar relationship or a similar proportion in thought, a proportion not merely being number but proportion as quality. For example, A is to B, as C is to D. So we say that as certain things are related in thought they may be related in the thing. That is the essential quality of thought. But thought is not the thing. Whatever we say anything is, it isn't. It may be similar, but it is not it, it is more, it is different as well. Therefore, whatever reality is, it is inexhaustible. No matter how far we carry this analysis we say it is at most an analogy.

Don Factor: But what does it then mean when you use thought to say that meaning and being are the same thing. Is this still at a level of an analogy or is it something else?

Bohm: There are two points. One is to say 'meaning is being' considered as a formal thought. In this case we say it must provide some analogy. But then we must turn our attention from the ratio in the analogy to the ratio in the thing, whatever is meant by it. The thought will guide us to a correct *perception* if it is a good thought.

Alex Hankey: If one changed it from 'meaning is being' to 'being has meaning', would you object?

Bohm: I think it does not go far enough. If you say 'being has meaning' you could very well say 'it has meaning to me or perhaps to somebody else.' That would make it a fortuitous sort of affair — it happens when somebody comes along that being has meaning. But I am trying to say that meaning pervades being, that it *is* being, both inanimate and animate. I want to propose going further.

Hankey: Meaning for being?

Bohm: Meaning for itself, even. I want to say that ultimately there is nobody to whom meaning is 'for'. Rather, meaning is the basic quality of reality. You see, if we ask 'for whom?' we might say 'it's for me' but I *am* my meanings. If things mean something different to me, I am a different person. If I were born in Nazi Germany, for example, the whole meaning would have been set up in such a way I could readily have said Hitler is wonderful. 'It's all very wonderful, such nice music and marching, it all means a great deal to me. Germany is great.' Then I would be a different person. So for whom is that Nazi meaning a meaning? That meaning *is* the Nazi. That meaning is part of the culture which goes into the person and makes that person.

Factor: If meaning is being in that full sense then where can a change of meaning come from?

Bohm: It can come because meaning is inexhaustible. There's no limit to meaning, you see. All meaning is ambiguous, it depends on the context; as the context changes, so does the meaning.

Frank Archer: Would you say that reality is a relationship between meanings?

Bohm: Well, reality is implicitly held within meanings, yes. Anything we know about reality must be according to what it means to us. Suppose that I say this chair is real. That means that if I push on the chair it will resist, it won't vanish. It will do various things which real things are supposed to do. It's not a figment; figments behave in another way.

Francis Steen: Would you call this the meaning the chair has for itself?

Bohm: No, you can't just say 'the chair itself', for what is it? I think we have to carry this onto the cosmic level, to say that the meaning is the whole. This is close to the Eastern view that matter and consciousness are inseparable, and that there is something you could call a proto-consciousness, proto-meaning or proto-intelligence behind matter. This implies that the mechanical picture of matter is limited, and if you look at quantum mechanics carefully, it is clear that the mechanistic view does not really work properly. Therefore, you are led to a view according to which there is a tremendous whole meaning, and there are sub-wholes of meaning, and so on. And due to these sub-systems of meaning we have relatively independent structures.

Rupert Sheldrake: So you are saying that meaning is being and that soma is also being. If we look at gravity in this way, your model seems to fit very well, because we can look at matter as the soma and the gravitational field as the significance or meaning. Then we have all kinds of particular sub-systems such as solar systems, with their particular meaning and soma-significance. Have you worked your model out in the context of gravitational fields?

Bohm: No, I haven't. I've concentrated on the quantum mechanical side.

Sheldrake: It seems to fit terribly well; I mean everything you've said about the electron and its associated field seems to apply to matter in general.

Bohm: You can look at it that way. The point is that in physics gravity *can* also be explained in a mechanical way, in terms of objects pushing each other through forces. Now, you may provide an alternative way of talking about it. But what is peculiar to quantum mechanics is that the old mechanical way is *not* adequate. That's why I've focused on quantum mechanics.

Sheldrake: Yes, but having arrived at the conclusion that the entire universe, being itself, is meaning, then your view must apply also to gravitation.

Bohm: It will apply to everything. But nevertheless, large scale objects, to a certain extent, have a considerable independence. They are largely following their own pools of information whereas we don't have as much independence at the quantum mechanical level.

Sheldrake: But they're not, though. I mean we know that the moon isn't just following its own pool of information, it's very much related to the sun and the earth, and the entire solar system seems to have just the kind of thing you talked about as a common pool of information.

Bohm: You can look at it that way, but then, it can be looked at the other way. This is an interesting point: physics can be looked at in two ways, either as if it were mechanical or as if it were teleological. The mechanical way, I think, is familiar to all of us; you think of all these planets moving, they are particular objects, moving with their inertia under the force of gravity, pulling and pushing on each other, resulting in orbits — that's mechanical.

Then, another approach was developed by people like Lagrange and Hamilton in the nineteenth century which was teleological, or at least looks that way. In this approach, the motion is no longer seen as mechanical. Instead, it is described by saying that each object moves over a whole period of time in such a way as to minimize a certain function called a Lagrangian. I don't know if you understand that, but you can think of an orbit over a whole period of time and you find that a certain function of this orbit which is rather abstract is minimized. So it looks as if the object is moving in such a way as if it were thinking: 'What shall I do, I'd better minimize my Lagrangian'.

You can look at it that way. It is common in science that there are often two quite different ways of looking at the same phenomenon, two meanings you can give to it. There's no unique meaning there and that's one of the creative features of meaning.

Sheldrake: If, as you seem to suggest, identity depends on meaning, then what about the identity of systems through time. I mean, if meaning is purpose or intention which is directed to the future, would you say that anything, be it a particle, a planet, a plant, an animal or a person, persists in time up to a point, because of this purpose? The meaning which has directed it through time gives rise to a continuation of the soma through time. Therefore the persistence in time actually depends on this purposiveness.

Bohm: Yes, I think that if you pursue this model which I was proposing further than we are able to at the moment, we would come to something like that. We now know that *nothing* persists forever; it is conceived that even the so called fundamental particles like protons are going to decay. Nothing known holds forever, and also if you go into a black hole or into the big bang, everything vanishes.

Therefore, you have to ask what sense it makes to think that some things *persist*. If you are to follow the view that I am proposing, you would say that the persistence of something is a kind of meaning. Its meaning is 'I must continue, I must reach the goal', whatever it might be. The simplest meaning is 'I must go on living' and the more complex meaning is 'I want to change in a certain way'. So you could ultimately say that the persistence of anything was due to a kind of meaning which meant 'keep on going'.

Sheldrake: Or in the case of inertia 'stay where you are' . . .

Bohm: . . . 'keep on moving, keep on doing whatever you are doing'.

Sheldrake: But this would provide a wonderful explanation of inertia. When these principles are applied to gravity or inertia, it seems that one could reframe classical physics and Einsteinian physics.

Bohm: That's an example of saying that the same phenomena can be understood in different meanings. You are quite right, that might be done. Suppose you say 'inertia' — you see, that is merely a word covering your ignorance. For 'inertia' merely says that something keeps on doing whatever it is doing. It doesn't explain *why* it does so. You merely *assume* that it is doing so.

Science must always assume something, and then explain something else with it. So you can start by assuming inertia and explain a lot of other things. But then somebody comes along and says 'Why should there be inertia?' You can always question anything which has been assumed. For example, Newton made certain assumptions and they were accepted for hundreds of years and then Einstein questioned some of them, changed them. But he still accepted inertia. The picture he gave was to say that by first accepting the inertia of matter one could then explain through the curvature of space why there is gravitation. But then, this does not explain why matter has inertia.

But now you come along and say 'I would like to answer that question, I want to have a new meaning'. Then you might say 'maybe matter has inertia, because it has some form of information which is constantly informing it to keep on doing whatever it is doing'. That wouldn't be a final explanation, either, because some day somebody else would ask you 'why should it mean that?'

So the whole point of science is to begin with some assumptions and see if you can explain a wide range of things from a few assumptions. This enables you to *understand* in the sense that far more things are explained than you have assumed.

Hankey: Your suggestion then is that matter is constantly being informed. But doesn't this mean that your model is not only causal but strictly deterministic.

Bohm: Well, it isn't necessarily. You see, this determinism is only relative in the sense that these systems are always open. If you were to take the one-particle system it would look deterministic, but then, as soon as it enters the many-particle system, it depends on a common pool of information. So whatever would determine it as one particle no longer determines it. And this many-particle system can become a part of a yet larger system which has its own pool, and so on. So finally you can say that there's no final determination but really some *relative* determination according to the context.

Steen: Could we consider again your model about the double slit experiment? In what sense can we think about this particle as a self-active system; you're perhaps suggesting it is not merely moving out of its own inertia, for instance.

Bohm: Well, more deeply perhaps even this self-activity depends on a more subtle level of meaning; you see, meaning can never be complete.

Matti Bergström: Are there different sorts of beings, or is the being always the same, without structure?

Bohm: Well, meaning is part of the development of structure, but each structure is according to the meaning. You see, if you take the structure of a molecule according to quantum mechanics, it would depend on the pool of information that is in the wave-function of the whole system. So according to the pool of information you may have one structure or another. Quantum mechanics is now used to explain chemistry as the best theory available. You can either say that it is just a system of calculations and then people use it only to work out the mathematics. Or else, you can try to interpret it, find the meaning.

Now if you propose the interpretation that I have suggested here, you can see that molecular structures are determined by this wave-function which I said is the pool of information. So you cannot understand chemistry, except on the basis of something like information and its meaning. Now this is not commonly known or accepted but I think it's quite a consistent suggestion.

Bergström: But what I asked was whether being has some internal structure or is being always the same being; you see, if meaning is being and there are many different sorts of meaning...

Bohm: . . . then for every different meaning there is a different being, that's what I suggest. Again I want to say that in this area we are not going to come up with final answers; we will propose something and see if it leads to something fruitful which will help to understand. Otherwise we'll drop that meaning and consider another one.

One of the reasons for carrying physics this far is that there are many different meanings that can be given to the same phenomenon, and this requires a creative approach that looks at all of them. In a way you have a dialogue between them, and this may lead on to yet another meaning. The meaning is not fixed, we are not going to end up with a fixed picture of the universe out of this. I hope we are constantly understanding the thing more and more deeply; it is almost like a work of art. You see, meanings of a work of art for the artist are continually different.

When you interpret a physical theory, you are getting the meaning. And physical theories, as I have explained, can often be given a number of meanings. People may prefer one or the other, and they begin to think that's the only one. But as we extend this chosen view we always find that at the edges things are a bit unclear — we interpret these unclarities and try to clarify them. But even this will carry on to a bigger context which eventually wili have its unclear edges.

So you're not going to get a final meaning: the very structure of meaning is such that you cannot reach final meanings.

Culture, creativity and dialogue

Hankey: I'd like to consider your suggestion that meaning is being, in relation to the approach of the Eastern culture, and that of Vedic science in particular. There's a difference there, for while you see consciousness as a dynamic structure, the East emphasizes a more static structure.

But your view is similar to the Eastern notion that meaning is connected to correlations. For instance, in a dictionary, meaning is a correlation of words. Consciousness is something which is intrinsically correlated with itself, it has self-knowledge. It follows that if meaning is connected to correlation, and consciousness has self-correlation, then consciousness becomes something with *intrinsic* meaning. Now, in Vedic philosophy *being* is intrinsically consciousness and so one sees that meaning is being.

Bohm: There are two approaches, but they haven't as yet been gone into here. The fixedness of the Eastern approach may be due to its emphasis on the fullness or completeness of being which results in the suspension of outward action. The West emphasizes the incompleteness of being as something dynamic and transforming, which makes action seem important. Now, I feel that we have to get beyond these two into some creative domain *in between* which is neither one nor the other.

Each culture has its value. There is obviously a high value to what the East is doing and the value of the West was that it produced the tremendous power of science and technology. On the other hand, this power is very dangerous and destructive, and the oriental sense of stillness carried too far was also dangerous.

The important point is that neither approach has actually produced a civilization that is adequate. The East has not only decayed from its original creative state but is now mainly adopting Western science, technology and so on. The West is falling apart in its own way. Each of these cultures has gone to an extreme — perhaps they were originally very similar but then slowly drifted apart. Cultures are meaning, the East has one kind of meaning and the West another. It is the meaning of the West that makes it the West and the meaning of the East that makes it the East. I think that the difficult questions related to these cultural meanings would have to be worked out in a *dialogue*. A dialogue between these cultures would bring us to something new.

The power of meaning is that it completely organizes being. Very subtle cultural meanings have tremendous power over being. Therefore, it requires extreme clarity at these subtle levels and that is where civilizations seem to have primarily gone wrong, in not having that clarity. Maybe a few people had it in the beginning but those who followed began to lose it.

Hankey: But the East doesn't just emphasize fixedness. It emphasizes action and inaction, and inaction and action, which means dynamical fitting into the pattern of all things.

Bohm: That's true, but nevertheless, what has actually happened is that the static thing has become emphasized. You see, nobody has solved the problem of how to prevent the degeneration of the original vision.

Hankey: But the original vision *is* renewing.

Bohm: It is originally new, but nobody has solved the problem of how the vision can be constantly renewed. It becomes more static, more of a habit. The thing becomes, as I was saying, a *disposition* which gradually gets fixed. It gets transmitted from one generation to the other as a disposition, and the people who pick it up don't understand it in the same way as the people who had it, because they are merely imitating the disposition and not understanding the meaning from which it came. They may understand part of it, but not as well as those that came before. Each time it gets a little weaker.

It's this repetition through generations which reinforces the habit to go along with the old ways of thinking and all the old social relationships and the old culture. Especially now, this problem has to be solved if the civilizations are to survive. In the old days you could say 'well, a civilization could die and another one start up' but now with modern technology we may destroy the whole thing. The problem has become far more urgent.

Therefore the key question is: is it possible to have a constantly creative culture? As soon as you set up a culture its meanings become repetitive and they begin to get in the way. Nevertheless, we need a culture.

Questioner: Power gets in the way, too, with the defined power structures. The people in power may not be the creative ones.

Bohm: You see, we automatically assume that anybody must seek power. But if you ask yourself why should anyone want to seek power, and think about it, you can see that very few have achieved happiness through power, while many people have achieved a lot of unhappiness. But what has happened is that the culture has slowly got into the habit of giving great value to power. That is why power excites people and gives them energy and they begin to seek it.

The meaning of power then seems to be tremendously significant. Thinking of having a great power, a godlike power, gives an expanded feeling. The adrenalin flows, the heart beats, everything starts moving, a person finds all his energy directed towards getting power. So he or she becomes like Napoleon or Caesar or somebody. But you can ask why should a person who obviously had great abilities, such as Julius Caesar, have got caught in that trap? It ended up in his assassination. After all, it did not do him any good.

Power is a very subtle meaning which the society has slowly

developed. If you build up a great structure of a state and a person looks at this big structure and thinks he is going to be in control of it, it starts exciting him, it has a great value. But it's an illusion.

What actually has value would be to have a constantly creative culture. Now I suggest that such creativity is related to a constant discovery of new meanings. Generally speaking we start from old meanings and commonly make small changes in them. Sometimes we may, however, perceive a big change of meaning. An idea changes in a fundamental way although, of course, some old features are still carried along, no matter how big the change is.

Georg Wikman: But what is it that really happens when you perceive a new meaning?

Bohm: That's the creative step. If I say that meaning is being and something new is perceived in a meaning, something has changed in being. For example, all the perceptions that took place in science changed the meaning of the world for us and this changed the world. It first changed in the sense that we saw it differently; but science also changed the physical, the somatic level. The entire earth has been changed and it could have changed a lot more, for the better or for the worse. Therefore, at least in my own experience, being and meaning are there together.

And I'm proposing this more generally. So if somebody sees a different meaning to society or to life, that will change society. Every revolution has come from somebody seeing a different meaning in human society. For example, the meaning that some people saw was that of a very static society, where everybody was in his place and the top was overlooking the bottom. Then other people saw a different meaning, according to which people should be equal. That different meaning was the power that generated the change. Then, if people become disappointed, that meaning loses its value and it falls apart. So as long as the basic meaning holds, society will be powerful and healthy, and when that meaning decays society will no longer work.

Paavo Pylkkänen: Earlier you mentioned that it is in trying to convey meanings to new generations that meanings decay. But what would your proposal 'meaning is being' imply to the educational process itself? At least it suggests that a student would *become* all the meanings being presented to her or him, and if these meanings are fixed, the students will end up rigid. On the other hand, if education involved new, creative meanings, the students would become creative because of the very presence of such meanings. Isn't it so that if meaning is being, you wouldn't need to apply meanings, but the effect would be more spontaneous?

Bohm: Yes, I think that if somebody perceives a new meaning he doesn't first perceive a meaning and then try to bring it about but rather, he has *already* changed. You see, it profoundly affects him. Now even in science you can see this. There's the example of Archimedes who, when getting down to his bath, realized that the volume of the water displaced by an object was independent of the shape of the object. It moved him so profoundly that he shouted 'Eureka!', got out of the bath and ran out — at least he is believed to have done so. The point is that people will behave that way when they see a new meaning.

It is thus meaning which gives value — the perception of a new meaning will move people profoundly. People saw the meaning of equality of humanity and of democracy, and that produced tremendous revolutions. Then people saw the meaning of socialism, and it produced worldwide upheavals. Relatively soon people lost those meanings and the society became corrupt — or perhaps as society became corrupt people lost their meanings.

But the power behind all these movements is the meaning. It is not that first somebody sees the meaning and then decides to apply it, but rather, at the *moment* he sees the meaning he *becomes* that power.

Pylkkänen: But then, you could say that when you lose creativity then you don't have the power any more.

Bohm: Yes, when you lose creativity that ceases to happen.

John Briggs: Are you equating creativity with meaning?

Bohm: Well, to a creation of new meaning, a fresh constant perception of meaning.

Briggs: So when you talk about losing meaning, obviously you can't lose meaning because there are other meanings...

Bohm: You can lose the creativity of meaning, and fall back into rigidly fixed mechanical meanings.

Briggs: Could you say something along this line about the comment at the end of your paper, in which you discussed dialogue and meaning. It seems that one direction that you're

taking is to suggest a change in our meaning and culture, a change in the way we behave — obviously we need a big one in order to survive. What's the relationship of dialogue to that?
Bohm: The ordinary relationship of people is that each one holds his or her own views: certain fundamental views are not negotiable and not changeable. For example, take the so-called negotiations that are going on between the East and the West in Geneva — actually most of the basic positions are non-negotiable and only trivial changes are possible. As long as they do it that way it can go on for a million years and nothing will happen.

Therefore, if people hold non-negotiable positions that is a sure formula for destruction, because each one will simply go on until they fight. As von Clausewitz said, war is the continuation of politics by other means. If politics is non-negotiable, then we try to settle it by war. But because of nuclear weapons war is not a feasible way of doing that any more. You cannot possibly use it to solve a crisis.

That difficulty in Geneva is only a magnification of the difficulty which exists in every human relationship from the top to the bottom. In every one of them there is the centre which is non-negotiable. In the individual the centre is the self, and it can be the group, the family, the nation, the ideology, the religion or the urge to make money. In all these cases we have a centre that makes us think 'that's not negotiable, whatever happens I'll defend that'.

The point is whether it is possible for people really to talk. If you now look around and see how people talk in different situations, you'll see that they are holding non-negotiable positions. Occasionally they get into a confrontation and fight, but what usually happens is that they have simply learned skilfully to avoid touching such positions. Therefore the talk is superficial. People are not satisfied with not being able to get anywhere. But if the talk ceased to be superficial we would face the explosions which would come from these non-negotiable positions. So is there any way out of that? I'm suggesting that if it were possible to listen to other positions, this would be a different state of mind. The usual state of mind is not capable of listening seriously to a position that is in contradiction to one's own.
Briggs: Is that because it presumes that its meaning is absolute?
Bohm: Yes, it says: 'this is absolutely necessary'. That is what

is really behind it. This is a disposition. The word necessary comes from 'ne cesse' meaning 'do not yield'. So when something is absolutely necessary the disposition is 'I must never yield'. You get a hard, rigid disposition. It resists everything, it says: 'when you touch that point I will not yield'. But here are all sorts of people having such different points; they all depend on each other and yet they cannot yield.

Briggs: So instead of holding onto our meanings in an unyielding way we could realize that all meanings we have are limited. This is so, because there is always the possibility of moving into a larger context than the present one. In a wider context our meanings might change.

Bohm: Yes, everything is in a larger context. Suppose that I see another position which I detest — that's generally the feeling. Usually I won't listen to it or else I'll fight, or keep away from it. But suppose that I can hold several such positions and say 'ok, I will listen to it, I'll understand what it means'. Usually we don't get that far, we do not see what the other position means, we are rejecting it without even seeing what it means, which has no point. Now if your mind is able to hold a number of positions without rejecting their meanings, then I think it moves into another state from the common state and begins to move more freely without that rigidity.

Briggs: For one thing, you'd be in a larger context automatically.

Bohm: Yes, you're moving away from that rigidity which is preventing creativity. You see, creativity requires a free play of thought to move in any direction which creation calls for. If the mind is rigid it cannot be creative. So any fixed position means the end of creativity.

Briggs: It seems very difficult for anyone to grasp in a somatic way how we tend to hold our meanings absolutely. First of all, we don't attend to that feeling of holding them absolutely, and we don't attend to the difference between how that feels and how it feels when an insight occurs. There are neurophysiological differences between holding onto the old meanings, and finding new meanings.

Bohm: That's quite right. We've had quite a few dialogues with some groups in England, in Israel and in Geneva. Something happened in Israel which was particularly interesting. We were talking about various things, and as part of the flow of dialogue somebody got up and started talking about how irrelevant Zionism was, asking what was the point of it. Suddenly somebody got up explosively and said: 'No, we need it, if we didn't have Zionism, we would go to pieces'.

It developed into something of a tremendous emotional charge, the kind that is very hard to defuse. Whenever anything fundamental like that is questioned, a tremendous emotional charge develops. You may ask, why isn't it there before. In fact it is, but you don't realize how important it is to you; it only comes out at that moment. The dialogue is both public and individual, the feelings of each person are experienced by all who are participating, more and less. You can then see the indissoluble connection between the intellectual idea and the feeling.

You see, Zionism is a purely intellectual idea, it has a certain structure, somebody invented it once — there was a time when it did not exist. Somebody thought of it, and it took hold and great value was attached to it. It was thought to be the solution to all sorts of problems. There had been terrible suffering in Europe and they thought that maybe in Israel they could make a new society. It then built up into a tremendous emotional charge, so that any time it is questioned there's no yielding.

There's a similar emotional charge about capitalism and communism or almost any of the questions that are important. People generally are careful, they see this emotional reaction coming up beforehand and avoid it.

Questioner: We have to bring in the notion of identity when discussing the emotional charge, for it is the extent to which people have identified themselves with these meanings that creates the emotional charge when that meaning is questioned.

Bohm: Yes, but identification is in itself another meaning. Identity means 'I'm always that way'. I take something to mean that I can't be without it, and that's what that thing means to me. Without it I'm gone. This type of meaning is *value*, in the sense that once you identify with something it takes supreme value. To identify with something is the same as to say 'that is equivalent to my life'. So identification is that kind of a meaning. All nationalism is based on meaning, the identification with religion is meaning, the identification with money is meaning — money itself is nothing but meaning.

Hankey: So you're saying that one would lose identification when one stopped projecting meaning.

Bohm: Perhaps in a certain sense. This fixed identification would go, but you would still know where you belong. However, you would no longer feel so attached to certain things that you could never consider changing them.

Questioner: Could dialogue also be used in the way Socrates used it, to break down opinions?

Bohm: I'm not in favour of that myself. You see, I don't think opinion should be broken down; I think opinions must be let go freely. Socrates was obviously far above most of these other people, he could do almost anything he liked with them (laughter). If you look at the various people that dialogued with him, some of the results were not impressive, if you follow them through.

I think something more is needed, let's rather put it that way. If people start to talk and they have not thought about things very much, they are going to come out with a lot of stupid things. If they are simply told that they are stupid, they are going to keep quiet and say nothing and they are not going to think for themselves. Somehow we've got to go beyond this stage so that the confusion clears up and everybody participates. This is difficult, but I think not impossible.

For most of us intelligence is probably blocked by the rigidity of our mind. This rigidity is caused by the fixed meanings that we hold, and the creative intelligence that we might otherwise have is now blocked. Most stupidity, I think, is due to that. So we must question it, inquire into it.

Teemu Kassila: In my experience society is full of meanings and there are always people who try to tell me and others what the true meaning is so that one actually gets quite confused about what is the correct meaning.

Bohm: Yes, I understand — that's why a dialogue is necessary. You see, you pointed out to me that people are trying to tell you what the meaning is; now that is not a dialogue (laughter). In a dialogue you are going through a state where I tell you what things mean to me and you will listen and say what it means to you. I will learn something in this because I see it means something different to you — it will go back and forth. So the meaning will be different at the end of the dialogue from what it was in the beginning.

Archer: Implicit in what you've been saying — and you've also put it explicitly — is that creativity has a high value. It is something that deserves attention. Are you proposing that in the social and cultural dimension dialogue is a means towards creativity?

Bohm: Yes. I am saying that, provided it is a true dialogue, it will release creativity. Take science, for example. It is already admitted that if scientists are constantly talking about their work, attending conferences, publishing, exchanging inform-ation, new ideas arise in a way that can hardly be noticed. It is still very limited, because people are defending their posi-tions and worrying about the financial rewards they are going to get, and so on. But suppose all those pressures were to go; you would have free creativity in communication.

Archer: So really some energy ought to be put into the search for creativity.

Bohm: Yes, dialogue is necessary for creativity in the socio-cultural sphere; that is, this creativity cannot be sustained without dialogue. We may get a burst of creativity but it will not be sustained.

Archer: And you feel there's an urgent need for it — that the state of society really requires and urgent dialogue?

Bohm: Yes. I think society is in a stage where it is fragment-ing, and people are not able to talk to each other — for the most part they ignore each other. Nevertheless, they depend on each other far more than ever before. This cannot go on, we cannot ignore people on whom we depend. Merely to con-front them or to avoid them is not going to work.

Archer: Would you say that, on the whole, humanity has not understood that the world can have a different meaning to different people, and that there is no reason to fight because of these different meanings?

Bohm: Yes, and it's also not realized that there cannot be a final meaning. Thus, there have to be a lot of different mean-ings and we've got to find the relation between them. We have a plurality of meanings, but seek the unity in this plurality, and so on.

You see, the general culture contains the assumption that there's got to be one meaning that is right and the others are supposed to be wrong. The 'right' meaning is absolutely neces-sary and then it doesn't yield to the others. It is just this kind of rigid 'right' meaning that often becomes a wrong meaning, as circumstances change. Culture *is* meaning, and when we have wrong meaning within culture, it is like misinformation.

So we can say there's not only information, there's also misinformation. A virus in the DNA molecule could be called a bit of misinformation, in that it enters the genetic structure and causes the cells to produce more viruses instead of more cells. It's the same way with cancer.

Society, too, is full of this sort of misinformation. We have various ways of dealing with biological misinformation. The best way is by the immune system which recognizes it and gets rid of it, but we have no such system in society. Misinformation accumulates and society gradually decays. You see, the older the society gets, the more chance it has to accumulate all sorts of misinformation and the more it starts to fall apart. The society is blocked because misinformation is held *rigidly*.

Hankey: But there's always renewal.

Bohm: Where's the renewal?

Hankey: The renewal comes from above.

Bohm: But where's the sign of it? You see, we are in danger of entering into a non-renewable situation — it's a fact. I don't think we can count on the above to do it. There's also a statement which probably represents a more Western approach which is that 'God helps those who help themselves' — that 'those who don't help themselves will get no help from above'. So if you are able to help yourself then you will also get the other help.

Hankey: That's certainly true, but it is also true that there is an ultimate meaning.

Bohm: There may be, but suppose you were somebody in a concentration camp in Nazi Germany, you wouldn't see that. All those millions of people who went through all that suffering and were exterminated, as far as they were concerned, except possibly a few of them, it had no meaning. And what would be the meaning of the whole world ending up in nuclear annihilation? The meaning would simply be that humanity was not viable and some other species must take over.

Questioner: Does love have a meaning?

Bohm: Oh yes, clearly it has meaning and it is meaning. But what interferes with it is this hardness, this rigidity of mind. In the intellectual side it comes out as rigidity of thought and on the emotional side as hardness of heart — they are both one and the same thing. Therefore, what is needed is to loosen the rigidity of mind and to dissolve or melt the hardness of heart, and you cannot do one without doing the other. If somebody is not hard-hearted but his mind is very rigid, he will very quickly be in conflict and his love will vanish. Without the loosening of the rigid mind you cannnot love, because sooner or later you'll come to a non-negotiable point with someone, and your love will vanish in the conflict. But I suggest that this rigidity of mind begins to loosen when we see the danger of non-negotiable positions.

Questioner: Isn't it mostly fear that causes rigidity, the fear of letting go of that little world of secure knowledge we've created?

Bohm: Yes, there's a fear of letting go, there's a fear of showing what a fool you are, and so on.

Kassila: So what is it we are avoiding? It seems to me that there is a sensitive area in all of us that we mostly ignore and are afraid to show to others. Sometimes I find it almost impossible to talk about it, and I just feel like crying for that 'being in me'.

Bohm: Behind this sensitive being in us there is some sort of a meaning which has built up throughout the lifetime. It has come from the culture and it produces this fear, resistance and rigidity. There are several ways of approaching this problem. There's the approach of meditation which attempts to deal with this problem at the individual level; and there is the attempt of psychiatry to get at some of this partly by going through childhood experiences. But there is also a third approach according to which a great deal of our anxiety is basically socio-cultural in origin and therefore best approached in a dialogue which is in a socio-cultural context.

Kassila: But what would you say that 'being in us' is?

Bohm: Probably almost nothing — it's misinformation at a central position. It's the same as with the DNA molecule. A tiny bit of misinformation in the DNA can cause everything to go wrong. If there is misinformation at a crucial part of the information that is determining a process, the consequences can be very serious. This can be the situation with the mind. Just a little bit of misinformation, say, in our image of ourselves, can distort the whole mind. We are not aware of it, but I think that our mind is so conditioned by such misinformation that it is frightened even to approach the question whether something is wrong with it.

Kassila: So in that sense we never live in total touch with what I call 'being in us'.

Bohm: Probably not. We are living in contact with an illusory being which is being projected by the misinformation. We have an illusory view of ourselves which is built up largely in a socio-cultural way. Most of our view of ourselves comes from society, doesn't it? For example, the fear of being a fool is a socio-cultural consequence, and also the fear of letting go. So a tremendous part of this fear is socio-cultural in origin. It is socio-cultural misinformation that is transmitted subliminally. Therefore, if we can confront this in a group, we can see the principle and perhaps change.

Kassila: It seems to me that what you have described as meaning could take the same position as God or something supreme had before.

Bohm: Well, then you have to be careful. That's why I said this is a proposal and not a statement of what is true. I'm not claiming that what I say is the truth. It may have many reasons backing it up to make it plausible, but it is a proposal to be explored and not the final truth. As I said earlier, I don't think we can get an ultimate truth out of *any* exploration.

Questioner: But isn't it useful to have a belief in what you might call ultimate meaning. You could then say 'OK, whatever happens, I'm going to be safe, or the world is going to be safe'. That way you can give yourself security in the sense that even if you do something wrong, the ultimate meaning will protect you.

Bohm: Many people have tried that, but sooner or later most of them have lost their faith. Your faith will be tested very much, because things will happen that will make the ultimate meaning look very implausible. If you believe, for example, that there is a God, you might well say 'why has he arranged things in this way — almost anybody could have done better' (laughter).

Now if you could actually discover this ultimate, then, by definition, there would be a true perception, which would be all right. But merely to postulate the ultimate meaning is dangerous, because it leads to the distortion of facts.

What I suggest is that we have to remain with uncertainty. The fear of uncertainty is our basic trouble. Uncertainty is the very nature of meaning and the very nature of being, for meaning is always context-dependent. We do not know the context that might come, and this is why we can never be certain that our meanings will be correct and give us security. So if you cannot live with this fact of uncertainty, some distortion is taking place already.

Questioner: Would meaning and reality exist without consciousness?

Bohm: I don't know. But what is consciousness without meaning? Consciousness *is* meaning. The content of consciousness is meaning, right?

Hankey: But you could also say that the experience of being arises when one stops projecting meaning.

Bohm: That may be so, but we have also got to use meaning or else we will not be able to get together. You see, we are now faced with a situation where people have to create a good society. I think man has several dimensions, the individual dimension, the socio-cultural dimension and the cosmic one. If we cannot live in all these dimensions, I don't think our culture is going to survive. If we don't know how to use meaning properly and in a harmonious way, then our culture is going to fall apart. A few people may have discovered a cosmic meaning, but when the rest of the culture is falling apart, their insight does not make much of a difference.

Briggs: Could you make a distinction between *projecting* meaning which sounds to me like it were a sort of rigid, holding on — I take my meaning, put it out there and impose it on someone else — and *finding* meaning? You seem to be talking about the latter in terms of creativity, as the activity of discovering meanings which is a creative insight.

Bohm: Yes, the creative insight of meaning is the crucial thing and also the creative communication, which means that people can listen to this creative insight and take it up themselves and go on with it. If everybody has got a rigid hold onto his meanings, somebody may have a great creative insight but then the other people won't be able to listen to that person. Then you have to have a battle to impose it, and it all goes to pieces.

Briggs: If someone has a creative insight in a dialogue, there's a process in which other people also have to find that meaning in their own way so that the meaning is the movement itself of the finding of meaning.

Bohm: Yes, every time somebody else sees that creative meaning, it makes a new context and changes the creative meaning in a creative way. So therefore the whole thing never stops. There is a possibility of creativity in the socio-cultural domain which has not been explored by any known society adequately.

I think, again, that the Eastern society tends to de-emphasize the socio-cultural sphere, it has not paid a lot of attention to it. It tends to fall apart in the early stages into family units and things like that. In the West this has been given more attention in places like ancient Greece which emphasized democracy. But insofar as we are trying to do the same thing we have not been very successful.

Hankey: On the contrary, if you look at a place like Indonesia, the first of the five principles of integration means 'unity in diversity' and social justice is another one. Unity in diversity represents precisely that integration which corresponds to democracy in the West.

Bohm: So how is the unity to be achieved?

Hankey: By a common focus of purpose.

Bohm: I don't think that is enough, for then the purpose is fixed. It is essential to have the creation of purpose rather than a purpose that is focussed on. You see, there is no fixed purpose. Meaning is purpose and as meaning develops creatively, purpose also develops. The whole point I'm trying to make is that, in this flow of meaning, purpose transforms *constantly*.

I don't think any society has ever really confronted this properly. For example, you might think of a very harmonious society where somebody at the top organizes it. He or she is a fairly good ruler and, of course, it will gradually decay as the next person is not quite so good, and so on. But that is not the point. The point is that *something new is needed; always was needed*. The fact that we are now approaching a general catastrophe is a challenge. I don't think that any traditional approaches can help us to deal with this challenge.

A Return to Living Biology

RUPERT SHELDRAKE

Introduction

We're used to living in a world that, in the official world-view, has its meaning reduced as much as possible. It's difficult for us to get into the frame of mind of societies where the whole world is saturated with meaning and purpose. These world-views are usually called animistic: the idea is that there are meanings and purposes and motives and goals going on all around one in nature.

This also holds in relation to disease. One example that springs to mind is the tribe called the 'Soras' in India, a tribe in the hills of Orissa, where I had the privilege of spending some time with an anthropologist friend. They have a theory of disease which is different from anything we are accustomed to. It is a very interesting one, and I mention it by way of illustrating how they see meaning and purpose in what happens.

If someone falls ill with a particular disease, like smallpox for example, then it's assumed that this disease is being caused by a 'smallpox spirit' — a spirit which holds in its thrall all previous ancestors and relatives who have died of smallpox. So if you know someone who's died of smallpox, they're living in the place of the smallpox spirit — which is actually (they showed it to me) a group of trees about half a mile from the village, which is where the smallpox spirit lives with the people who've been taken by smallpox. They live there, and have a kind of 'smallpox club'; and if they particularly like you — if it's a husband or a wife or a child that's died of it — they want you to be with them. So if you get smallpox it's because somebody you know who's got smallpox is trying to draw you to that place, so you can be with them. And it's precisely your affinity to the person that means that that dead ancestor or friend is causing a disease in you. And the closer you are to them, the more this is likely to happen. So there is a curious ambiguity of their wanting to draw you to them, and yet their doing you harm; it's precisely because you know them and love them that they're doing this.

Then the Sora have a series of dialogues with the dead, which goes on almost every day through shamans. These dead spirits speak, and say how they're trying to draw you to them. The aim of this whole process, through the shamans and through ritual, is to try to get these dead people to move from their dwelling-places and go into the underworld, with the ancestors. They can get free of these sort of 'clubs' — disease clubs — and join the ancestors in an underground realm. This is done by sacrificing and through annual rituals; it takes several years. Then they're fairly safely with the ancestors, and after a while they become relatively harmless and turn into butterflies. And so, when you see butterflies flying around, these are the liberated souls of the ancestors.

When one is living in that kind of world, the whole landscape has a meaning. There are rocks and trees, and they've all got spirits in them. Everything that happens depends on spirits — while we would say it's just a matter of chance, or just the usual infection by a micro-organism. All these things have an incredibly rich texture of meaning and purpose.

This was of course also the case in our own culture until quite recently. In the Middle Ages there were sacred places, pilgrimages, saints of every kind, angels, demons — a vast range of beings, purposes, and spirits in the natural world, the human world, and the superhuman world. All this changed in the transition in the seventeenth century to the mechanical philosophy, which still underlies much of modern science. And what I want to do is look at this historical process, and then look at what sort of science we would have if science included purpose and meaning. What I'm going to say is complementary, I hope, to what Bohm said above. I'm coming to it from a biological starting point, and he came to it from a combination of Quantum Theory and Krishnamurti, and maybe other starting points as well. So it's in a slightly different language, but I think that there's a way in which it can be translated.

The Aristotelian World View

The first well-worked-out philosophy and science which included the purposes and meanings in nature was that of Aristotle. Nature itself, 'physis', was that self-organizing power that things had in accordance with their own purposes.

Aristotle said that in order to understand any process of change, or anything at all, we need to take into account what he called the Four Causes — not just one cause, but four causes. As many of you know, the classic example he gave, which his followers often used, was that of the sculptor making a sculpture to put in the market place of the town. The *material cause* is the block of stone from which he makes it — without the material he can't make the sculpture. The moving or *efficient cause* is the moving thing that causes the change to happen — and that's the chisel, knocking bits off the block of stone: the moving cause. Then there's the *formal cause* which is the cause of the form — the formative cause if you like. That's the idea of the sculpture in the mind of the sculptor. It's maybe a sculpture of a city councillor or a mayor or a king. Without that form in his mind, merely chiselling away at the block would produce a pile of chippings, which wouldn't be what was wanted at all. So the form is there, but it isn't in the matter, and it's not just in the mechanical impact; it guides the mechanical impact and it shapes the matter. And then there's the *final cause*, or purpose, or goal. The final cause is to have this sculpture in the market place — he's making it for a purpose; he's making it because he has a commission to make it.

In this example, you see that the formal cause — the form of the thing — and the purpose of it are very closely related. People would only give the chap a commission to make this sculpture if it had the right form. If he made a sculpture of a giant butterfly or a caterpillar or something, they wouldn't be very interested.

Aristotle applied this analysis to all living things, and indeed all of nature. In the case of plants, he said that each species of plants has a 'psyche', or a soul, and this psyche is the form of the body; so a dandelion plant has a dandelion psyche, and the psyche, or soul, of the dandelion contains the form of the dandelion plant. When you take a dandelion seed, as it germinates, it moves towards its goal: the goal of the developing seedling is to reach the dandelion form. He called this 'entelechy' — *en* means 'in' and *telos* means 'end' or 'goal'.

The soul, or the entelechy, is what gives the developing system its purpose or goal. The entelechy, as it were, draws the seedling towards it. This is final causation. It's as if the future is pulling or attracting the system towards a goal that hasn't yet happened, and this goal is the form of the organism.

In the case of animals, this kind of soul that gives the form of the body he called the *vegetative* soul. Animals have vegetative souls, which are what govern the development of the form of the animal embryo. We have vegetative souls. When we took our forms in our mothers' womb, we weren't thinking it out, or consulting a human blue-print consciously, or anything like that. The form was taken up through this entelechy of the vegetative soul. In the mature organism, the vegetative soul maintains the form of the body, and is involved in the healing of wounds and so forth.

The *animal* soul is concerned with the movements and instincts of animals. (Of course, the word 'animal' comes from the word 'anima', which means 'soul'.) All animals have their own kind of soul. Again, the instincts of animals have *purposes*: spiders build webs in order to catch flies. We can see purpose in all, or at least most forms of animal behaviour. In human beings, there's a higher kind of soul, which is called the *rational* soul. This is able to understand or comprehend ratios, proportions, harmonies, and reasons. The 'telos' or end of the rational soul is knowledge of God. It's pulled towards an understanding of the underlying unity of things.

What role does God play in Aristotle's system? He's called the *Prime Mover*. When we hear that word, we immediately think of some gigantic fly-wheel or cog-wheel, pushing the whole thing from behind. But that is not how he saw it at all: the Prime Mover was that which caused the whole of nature — and indeed human souls — to move *towards* a goal. The Prime Mover moved the universe through a kind of *attraction* from the future — a kind of attraction towards a goal or purpose. The best modern image of this is in Teilhard de Chardin's concept of the *Omega Point*. This is essentially the Aristotelian idea of the Prime Mover put into modern language.

Well, this view of things was adopted in the Middle Ages, and became the basis of Medieval Christian scholastic orthodoxy. It was taken over and fused with the Judeo-Christian tradition by St Thomas Aquinas. This is what European universities were teaching, right up to the seventeenth century, and this view of things is still being taught today in Catholic semi-naries. But it went out of the main stream in the seventeenth century, when what came in to replace it was the mechanical philosophy. Although of course it's changing, this is still the predominant world-view.

The Mechanistic World View

The primary feature of this world-view is the expulsion of final causes. The whole of nature can be understood *just* in terms of material causes and moving causes: matter and motion — with no goals or purposes.

The soul was eliminated from animals and plants, so they were considered to be literally inanimate, 'soulless'. The rational soul is left as the only survivor of the soul concept, in human beings alone. It was precisely this rational soul that enabled human beings to understand mathematics, and to work out the mechanical philosophy.

What the mechanical philosophy did, in fact, was to put the purpose, the meaning, and the form of the universe *outside* the universe itself. The universe was conceived as a giant machine. And the thing about machines is not that they have no purpose, or that they have no form — they all have pur-poses and forms — it's just that the purposes and forms are external to the machine. They're in the mind of the creator of the machine. So, in a mechanical universe, the purpose and the form were external to the universe. They were in fact inher-ent in the mind of God. This is how Descartes and Newton, and practically all the seventeenth century founders of modern science thought of it. The form was given by the mathemati-cal laws of nature, which were eternal *because* they were in the mind of God.

We're left with a kind of abstraction from the whole. The easiest way to see this process of abstraction inherent in billiard-ball physics is by thinking of billiards. Billiard-balls in reality exist on billiard tables. They normally undergo their mechan-ical movements as part of a game of billiards. The rules of the game, the reason why the balls are being placed there, and the reasons for the impacts that they experience, all come from people playing billiards. And the playing of billiards has a goal: people want to win the game. There are rules which give the game a form. There are purposes — the wish to win — which motivates somebody, pushing with a cue, pushing a ball, so that it then hits another one: then there is a series of actions and reactions according to Newtonian physics.

We can understand these mechanical impacts perfectly well. But we only understand them because the rules and the forms of the whole game are *implicit*. We haven't actually got rid of them; we've simply abstracted the mechanical movements of the balls from them. This is what happened in physics in the seventeenth century, and it provided the model for the whole of science — it still does, as far as most scientists are concerned. It involves a kind of intellectual sleight of hand, because the form and purpose can't be removed — we need them to understand nature — they're simply disguised or put somewhere else.

The crisis became greatest in biology, because of course it's extremely difficult to understand animals and plants — and even more so human beings — without taking into account purposes. Plants are obviously purposive; e.g. shoots grow towards the light. If you say, 'Why is it doing that?', it's growing towards the light because it needs the light to grow. And the roots grow down into the earth — why? — because the roots need coolness and moisture, and so on. It's impossible to think of living organisms without taking into account functions: what's the function of this part? If you find an organism and it has strange structures, the first question you ask is, 'Why does it have this structure?' If you see an animal with a huge claw, you immediately ask, 'What does it use the claw for? Why is it there? What's its function?' And this is in a way saying, 'What's its meaning? What's its purpose? How does it relate to the whole?'

Function *has* to be taken into account in biology. Take another example: the eye. It's possible to study the eye from the point of view of anatomy: cut cross-sections of the eye, look at the way it's organized, study the interconnections of the nerves at the back of the eye; look at the lens, analyse it (it's got lens proteins), find out their amino acid sequences, print them all out in page after page of *Nature* magazine. But the fact remains that the eye, to be comprehensible, can only be understood in terms of *vision*. The eye is for seeing. The eye does not make sense just in terms of these anatomical or biochemical features. We take for granted that it's used for seeing; and, moreover, that seeing is not an end in itself. Animals aren't just going around treating the universe like an art gallery. They're looking out for food, for mates, all sorts of things — they have purposes in the seeing. So this is part of a greater whole.

This is so blindingly obvious that it's taken for granted in biology: you cannot understand living organisms without taking into account purpose. But because the hue and cry in the seventeenth century was all about expelling purpose from nature, getting rid of final causes, there's been a prohibition on the use of the word 'teleology', or 'purpose', in biology ever since. I remember this when I was learning biology at school; it was drummed into us by our biology master that we could never use the word 'purpose' or 'teleology'; that these were forbidden words. We learned at an early stage that although we thought in terms of them, we should use circumlocutions whenever anyone might challenge us. Instead of 'purpose', say 'adaptive value'.

In modern biology, defenders of the mechanistic view (like Jacques Monod) have substituted for 'teleology' — which is bad, being Aristotelian and non-mechanistic — the word 'teleonomy' — which is good. No one has actually been able to explain exactly why it's different, and Richard Dawkins, who's one of the most extreme of the neo-Darwinians (his book *The Selfish Gene* may be familiar to you), has put it very well. He has a glossary at the back of his latest book, and defines teleonomy as 'teleology made respectable'. It's made respectable by Darwinism, and attributed to natural selection.

It is worth dwelling for a moment or two on this transformation, because it helps us to understand what lies behind some of the current controversies. Before Darwin, the idea was that the universe was a machine, designed by God, and everything in it was also designed by the divine engineer. The beautiful adaptations and functions and harmonious workings of the different parts of animals — the way that the bees within a hive all work together harmoniously; the way in which plants and the animals that pollinated them seemed to be so wonderfully harmonious — all these were explained in terms of divine design. God was seen as the designer of the universe, external to nature: an extremely skilful engineer, turning out all these beautifully adapted biological organisms. Their purpose and design was external to the organisms themselves; it was in the divine mind. The purposeful design of living organisms was generally considered to be an argument for the existence of God.

Darwin tried to undermine the force of the argument for design by showing that there was no need to have an external designer. He agreed with the already existing assumption that living organisms were machines, but he said the whole thing could come about by chance and natural selection. Natural selection meant that features of plants and animals were adaptive, because things that weren't adaptive would die out. He didn't explain how the new forms came into being in the first place; that was always ascribed to chance, and it still is in neo-Darwinism. This argument obviously has some truth in it — things that are maladaptive do die out; only things that are fit enough to survive, survive. But it is used by neo-Darwinians to say that purpose can be explained simply in terms of natural selection. There is nothing teleological in nature.

When we come to human beings, the argument becomes slightly more difficult, because human beings are living organisms like others; they're supposed to be machines like others; and, like others, they're supposed to be entirely purposeless — just having adaptive features, favoured by natural selection. It becomes difficult to explain why biologists are doing what they're doing, and what purpose there is in all these theories, and so on. And this then becomes a field of speculation which at the moment is dominated by socio-biology, founded on the 'selfish gene' model.

Modern Challenges to the Mechanistic Paradigm

Let us look at the way in which living organisms are understood. When trying to understand the development of an embryo, or the instinctive behaviour of an animal, it actually is impossible to think of it without the idea of some kind of purpose or goal. When we study development, we find that if we disrupt the developing organism — cut a bit off an embryo for example — the embryo in most cases can still reach the normal form. It somehow gets to its goal, in spite of being interrupted on the way there, or having bits removed. Adult organisms can regenerate lost parts — for example flatworms can be cut into small pieces, and each part can become a new flatworm. So there seems to be some kind of goal or end-point, which the organism in some sense contains and which it moves towards; and it gets there even by abnormal routes.

We see the same in behaviour: if an animal is trying to do something — a dog trying to get to its meat, for example —

and its normal pathway is blocked, it can soon enough learn to get there by going by a different route. And in cases where one leg of the dog has been damaged, by a completely different set of movements it can limp there, and get to the meat anyway. And if the eyes are damaged, so that it can't see, it can get there by smelling. The goal can be achieved by many different routes.

We know this, of course, from human behaviour. If people are blocked from doing something in one way, they very often find ways of doing the same thing another way. The goal is what seems to attract the behaviour towards it, and the entire way of getting there seems to be more like being drawn towards a goal, rather than being pushed from behind according to a fixed set of movements. For this reason, the very notion of purpose — or *meaning* — enters into the understanding of life. Meaning, purpose, and intention, as Bohm pointed out above, are very closely related to each other. The meaning of the parts of the embryo is related to the whole, and their relation has to do with their purpose, the function they serve, in the organism. Each form has a function. Form and function are correlative: the form of the eye is related to its function, the form of the arm related to its function, and so on.

The idea of purpose is necessary in biology, yet it's illegal, because biology is founded on a mechanistic paradigm. The vitalists rejected the mechanistic paradigm, and reintroduced the Aristotelian concept of the soul, or *entelechy*. In the most sophisticated of the vitalist systems, elaborated at the beginning of this century, Driesch deliberately reintroduced the notion of entelechy, because he thought it was necessary in biology. The mechanistic school was locked in deadly combat with vitalism in the first decades of this century. The biological literature is full of polemical attacks on vitalism, and indeed polemical attacks by vitalists on mechanism; the so-called mechanist-vitalist controversy was a dominant feature of biology for many years, but the mechanists won and became the dominant school of orthodox biology.

Having won, it was still necessary somehow to understand the goals or purposes in living things. And what has happened is that the vital principle — the vital factor, or the entelechy — has been reintroduced into biology in a disguised form. It's now called 'the genetic program'. A program is something which has an end or a goal. It's something which is *teleologi-*

cal. Computer programs have purposes (they have forms as well), and they have a kind of specified goal, or end-point. So the idea of the genetic program is that living organisms not only have the *matter* of which they're made up, but also something that *organizes* them: the genetic program. It is of course unclear what the genetic program actually is, but anyway this is what is supposed to give organisms their meaning, significance, and purpose. It's very much an Aristotelian kind of concept, a teleological concept, which has been smuggled back into biology. It's often decked out in the terminology of Information Theory, and talked about in terms of genetic information. Its dualistic nature comes out in the well-known hardware/software analogy, based on computers. The proteins and so on in the cells are the hardware; the program is the software which controls them.

Interestingly enough, a new branch of mathematics has grown up, which is essentially teleological. Modern dynamics is founded on the idea that processes move towards what are called *attractors*. The attractor is defined mathematically in a space, and is the point or 'basin' towards which a system moves. The mathematics doesn't tell you exactly how it gets there; it just says if something starts off here, even though there is a certain amount of chaos and indeterminacy, it will move towards this attractor. So it enables the *evolution*, as it is called, — the unfolding — of systems to be understood in terms of mathematical models based on contending attractors. From the point of view of the developing system, the attractor lies in the future, and it is a point (or a state) towards which the system is attracted. Systems may have more than one attractor. There is a kind of unstable attraction sometimes, where it's attracted to one, but may jump to another. This kind of mathematics can be modelled on computers; one can actually see these trajectories working themselves out.

This form of maths was adopted by C.H. Waddington, an important biologist, who thought that living systems could be understood in terms of their movement towards attractors. He called the way in which a system would develop towards an attractor a *chreode*, a pathway of change, the attractor being the end-point. Detailed mathematical models of development, using this notion of attractors, have been developed by René Thom, the French mathematician. This teleological mathematics of development is quite unlike the traditional kinds of maths used in Newtonian physics.

The idea of morphogenetic fields was put forward for the first time in 1922. These fields inherited many of the qualities of Driesch's *entelechy*. They have an end-point or goal; they guide the system towards this end-point or goal. They co-ordinate the parts of a system, and help to explain its holistic properties. The *chreodes* that Waddington was talking about are pathways of change within morphogenetic fields. Morpho-genetic fields are invisible organizing factors which contain within them goals or future states, towards which develop-ing systems are moving. They are holistic organizing principles.

In my own development of this concept, I suggest that the form of the morphogenetic fields is determined by the form of previous similar systems. This influence of like upon like is what I call *morphic resonance*. The form of the fields depends on what has happened before, and so there's a kind of built-in memory in them.

On the one hand these fields are related to future states — they have the effect of attracting systems towards future states, giving goals, meanings, and purposes. On the other hand they're related to the past, because the structure of the fields, and indeed the future goal, depends on what's happened before in similar systems. So they're inherently related to time, and the future and the past are both essential to the nature of morphogenetic fields. We understand the future and the past psychologically in terms of *desire*, which relates to the future, and *memory*, which relates to the past.

Concluding Remarks

I think that this view of things fits well with what Bohm said above in terms of soma-significance. The energy of something, or the matter — the substantiality — is organized by fields (he would use the term *Implicate Order*) which co-ordinate the parts and give them their meaning in relation to other things. There's an interplay of energy and fields, which means that everything can be understood both in terms of the organizing fields that give it its meaning in terms of the larger whole, and in terms of the system itself, in terms of its material or energetic side. And these together — as he was pointing out — seem to ena-ble meaning and matter to be understood in relation to each other, without having a kind of psycho-physical parallelism.

One of the ancestors of the morphic fields is the Aristotelian 'psyche'. One way that one can translate 'psyche' is by the word 'mind' — psychology is the study of the psyche, and it is usually taken to mean the study of the mind; we often use 'psyche' and 'mind' interchangeably. From this point of view, there's a kind of mind — not necessarily a conscious mind — in animals and plants, and indeed in molecules and crystals, and I would say in atoms as well.

So we get back to a kind of animistic (or perhaps one could say neo-animistic) view of the world: seeing things as organisms, with meanings and purpose. This reconnects us to the animistic world-views which are common to practically all religious traditions, primitive and advanced. The mechanistic world-view is something which perhaps only a minority of people even in our own culture believe, and even then, they only seem to believe it during working hours. I think we may come to see mechanism as an abstraction from the way things are, just as the billiard-balls are an abstraction from the game of billiards. Perhaps it will come to be seen as an aberration in the history of science, rather than as the very basis of scientific rationality, as many people still seem to believe.

PART TWO

Meaning and the Human Being

Medicine and David Bohm's Theory of Soma-significance

LARRY DOSSEY

The grandest effort of modern medical science, that of designing an approach to the health of man that is totally objective, has failed. Today we are forced to acknowledge that not only can atoms move the mind, (changes in our biochemical state can change the quality of thought, e.g.) the mind can move atoms too (a commonplace event demonstrable in any biofeedback laboratory). The distinctions between mind and matter are less serviceable than ever before, and when they are employed they must be used with profound qualification and metaphorical emphasis. This paper will thus argue, in the context of Bohm's theory of soma-significance, that absolute distinctions between 'the psychological' and 'the physical' have no ground any longer in our fundamental observations.

Yet this does not mean that surgery does not work or that immunizations are no longer effective — but that when we go looking for *either* 'the mental' *or* 'the physical' in the complex processes of health and illness we cannot find them. For the mental is inseparable from the physical, tied to it in unending loops of interdependence that defy dissection and categorization of either into independent states.

Deficiencies of Current Models

If these observations seem hyperbolic, perhaps a brief glance at a commonplace description found in a standard medical school textbook will illustrate the current state of affairs. In the figure on the following page the relationship between the 'pumping force' of the heart's main chamber, the left ventricle, is related to the E.D.V. — the end diastolic volume or, roughly speaking, the size of the left ventricle before it begins its action of pumping blood into the aorta and into the body.

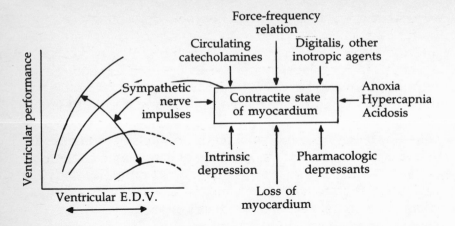

Diagram showing the major influences that elevate or depress the inotropic state of the myocardium (top right), and the manner in which alterations in the inotropic state of the myocardium affect the level of ventricular performance at any given level of ventricular end-diastolic volume (bottom left).[1]

This is an elemental relationship and has been studied extensively for decades. As the figure illustrates, as the E.D.V. increases so does ventricular performance — up to a point, that is. But beyond a certain size or volume at the end of diastole the heart cannot respond with greater work and its performance begins to decrease. At this point the ventricle cannot respond to the increasing work demand and a pathological state results, called heart failure.

Also illustrated are the known factors that determine the contractile state of the myocardium, or how well it can meet the challenge of pumping more blood: drugs, oxygen and carbon dioxide content in the blood, blood pH, the actual amount of heart tissue (affected by heart attacks and other forms of structural damage), 'intrinsic depression,' stimulus from the body's sympathetic nervous system, the amount of catecholamines in the blood (adrenalin, e.g.), and the heart rate. An overall view of these factors and the accompanying illustration and commentary suggest that the entire process is an objective affair describable in utterly mechanical ways. Nothing could be farther from the actual state of affairs.

What is *not* shown in the illustration is the multitude of ways that the psyche-emotions, feeling states, attitudes, states of consciousness, etc. enter in. For instance, 'circulating catecholamines,' so succinctly alluded to, is a factor that is intimately affected by emotion. Fear, anxiety, or tranquility and serenity affect this factor. The same can be said for 'sympathetic nerve impulses,' the discharges of which are tied, hand-in-glove, to one's psychological state. Even 'loss of myocardium' is not objective, for many heart attacks are well known to be provoked by behaviors, emotional predispositions of certain types, and specific choices such as smoking or eating high cholesterol diets. 'Pharmacologic depressants' do not enter the body on their own; these pills and potions must be taken by a human being. They must be considered and thought about and consumed for some reason. Even the biochemical states such as 'anoxia, hypercapnia, acidosis' are related to the psyche: the choices of cigarette smoking or physical exercise are two obvious ways in which 'the mind' affects these 'objective' indices, and the heart rate (in the 'force-frequency relation') is one of the most obvious factors illustrating the effect of states of consciousness.

One could take almost any illustration of 'physical' function from modern medical texts and make similar statements. Examples could be multiplied *ad nauseum*. On the surface the examples do appear straightforwardly objective, but on close examination the objectivity breaks down.

It is no use to try to dismiss the role of the psyche by saying that its effects are present but that they are trivial. In fact, they are far from it. In many cases they may make the difference between life and death. This has been demonstrated by one of the leading researchers in the phenomenon of sudden cardiac death, Harvard's Bernard Lown (the inventor of the defibrillator). Lown has shown that mental-emotional states are primary factors in the so-called 'fibrillatory threshold' of the heart. This is, roughly, the likelihood of the heart to undergo fatal ventricular fibrillation in the event of a premature ventricular beat. The lower the fibrillatory threshold, the easier it is for an irregular beat to trigger this usually terminal event. And what lowers the threshold? Among other things, emotions: fear, anxiety, depression, fright. Even positive emotional states have been associated with ventricular fibrillation: joy, elation, ecstasy. So profound are these interactions that Lown has stated that the ordinary view of the heart as a mechanical force-pump, well insulated from our emotions, is fundamentally flawed:

> The heart and vasculature have been viewed for too long as
> a self-contained system . . . extracardiac factors . . . have a role
> in the genesis of sporadic, paroxysmal ventricular arrhythmias
> as well as ventricular fibrillation. . . . Psychologic stresses, even
> of brief duration, profoundly reduce the threshold for ven-
> tricular fibrillation and result in major ventricular-rhythm dis-
> orders.[2]

This view is an echo of William Harvey, who first put the study of physiology on firm footing by demonstrating the circulation of the blood:

> For every passage of the mind which troubles men's spirits
> either with grief, joy, hope anxiety, and gets access to the heart,
> there makes it change from its natural constitution or temper-
> ament, pulsation and the rest. . . .[3]

Even the most cursory reading of the history of medicine discloses, of course, that at times various persons have viewed the relationship of mind and body as an intimate association. As an example, Avicenna, one of the most influential figures in the history of medicine, stated 10 centuries ago:

> The imagination of man can act not only on his own body but
> even others and very distant bodies. It can fascinate and modify
> them; make them ill, or restore them to health.[4]

Indeed, the history of medicine is littered with ideas pointing to such intimate relations between mind and body and, even, between the minds and bodies of different persons. Professor Bohm's contention that there is a connection between the physical and the mental is part of this lineage. But it is more, and it is separated from postulates such as those of Avicenna in the most profound ways.

Deficiencies of Historical Models of Mind-Body Interaction

If we closely examine Avicenna's observation, certain conclusions can be drawn that apply as well to almost all models of how mind and body are related. There is a strong suggestion of concreteness in his use of 'imagination' and 'body.' Imagination seems to be a thing, as does body, on which the imagination acts. This imagination is something that has broad powers: it can 'fascinate' and 'modify', *make* 'them' ill or restore 'them', the 'distant bodies', to health. There is *work* going on here, things acting on other things. We are in a world of objects, a universe of things in which the doer and the deed and the done-to are paramount factors.

Throughout the history of medicine this mechanical flavor has come through whenever psyche and soma have been juxtaposed. Not even the psychosomatic theories of our own time have escaped this fundamental characteristic, for we have been bedeviled in our attempts to think non-mechanistically. The thingish nature of mind-body theories is a fundamental fly in the ointment, for it has created a paradoxical dilemma of referring to a thing (the mind) that cannot be seen or specified in the usual ways of referring to things, in contrast to the body or soma, which *can* be so specified. And, what is worse, such theorists have been left in the awkward position of trying to explain how this ethereal thing can act on something material, the body. Because of such difficulties no current notions of mind-body interaction have proved satisfying.

The Theory in Perspective
The theory of soma-significance proposed by Professor Bohm is immediately separated from all such theories in the most unambiguous way:

> The notion of soma-significance implies that soma (or the physical) and its significance (which is mental) are not separate in the sense that soma and psyche are generally considered to be; rather they are two aspects of one overall indivisible reality.[5]

He goes further:

> By such an aspect, we mean a kind of view or a way of looking. That is to say, it is a form in which the whole of reality appears (i.e., displays or unfolds), either in our perception or in our thinking. Clearly, each aspect reflects and implies the other ... .[6]

Professor Bohm's theory of mind-body relationship, then, is at the outset fundamentally a departure from the traditional ways of discussing this association: it goes beyond the notion of substance and of independent entities exerting energetic effects on each other — qualities which have characterized, and ultimately sabotaged, the various forms of mind-body interaction that have come down to us. Again:

> We are proposing to look at soma and significance [in a way
> in which] we regard them as two aspects introduced at an
> arbitrary conceptual 'cut' in the flow of the 'field' of reality
> as a whole. These aspects are distinguished only in thought,
> but this distinction helps us to express and understand the
> whole flow of reality.[7]

No current theory of mind-body interaction is so explicit in
introducing the concept of reality as an unbroken whole, for
they remain tied to the supremacy of thing-and-substance.

Order and Organization as Key Elements in the Theory of Soma-significance

> To bring out how soma and significance are related, we first
> note that each particular kind of significance is carried by some
> somatic order, arrangement, connection, and organization of
> distinguishable elements. ... Modern scientific studies
> strongly indicate that such meanings are carried somatically
> by further physical, chemical, and electrical processes into the
> brain and the rest of the nervous system, where they are appre-
> hended at higher and higher intellectual and emotional levels
> of meaning.[8]

Here another key difference of Bohm's theory emerges: the
notion that the 'carrier' of significance or meaning is 'order,
arrangement, connection, and organization of distinguishable
elements.' We here go beyond the notion of substance into
something that is physically intangible and which might be
roughly thought of as 'information'. This, in my view, is one
of the key distinguishing characteristics of Bohm's theory, one
which empowers it as an explanatory principle for the relationship between mind and body.

Relationship to the World Outside in the Theory of Soma-significance

One of the features of Bohm's theory that clearly sets it apart
from the traditional psychosomatic idea is stated as follows:

> One can see that ultimately the soma-significant and signa-
> somatic process extends even into the environment. ... even
> relationships with Nature and with the Cosmos are evidently
> deeply affected by what these mean to us. In turn, such mean-

ings fundamentally affect our actions toward them, and thus indirectly their actions back on us are influenced in a similar way. Indeed, insofar as we know it, are aware of it, and can act on it, the whole of Nature, including our civilization which has evolved from Nature and is still a part of Nature, is one movement that is both soma-significant and signa-somatic.[9]

We are tied, thus, hand-in-glove, to the world: its manifestations enter as meaning at increasingly subtle levels in us, and these meanings affect our soma at more manifest levels. Yet it is to be continually emphasized that we are not dealing in this world with collections of objects but with unbroken processes, 'an unbroken flow of soma-significant and signa-somatic process,' as Bohm emphasizes.[10]

The idea that we are not ultimately separable from nature is a distinctive feature of Bohm's theory that deserves special notice. Whitehead's observations were similar. He made use of the idea of man's oneness with the world in developing his own process philosophy. Whitehead stated:

> . . . neither physical nature nor life can be understood unless we fuse them together as essential factors in the composition of the 'really real' whose interconnections and individual characters constitute the universe. . . . Scientific reasoning is completely dominated by the presupposition that mental functionings are not properly part of nature . . . this sharp distinction between mentality and nature has no ground in our fundamental observation . . . all [the] functionings of nature influence each other, require each other, and lead on to each other. . . . The human individual is one fact, body and mind. . . . We are in the world and the world is in us.[11]

A particularly attractive expression of this view has been put forward recently by the nuclear physicist, Jeremy Hayward, in his book, *Perceiving Ordinary Magic:*

> Mind is not a 'something' separate from nature. It is identical at various levels of order with all of nature, not solely with individual brains. It emerges as a characteristic of processes of nature at a certain level of evolution. It is therefore futile to look for evidence of mental process as located purely in the brain of an individual organism. We must look for such evidence in the entire network of patterns of interaction which that organism has with its environment, or which a group or society of organisms has with its environment.[12]

Moreover, the view of Gregory Bateson about man's connectedness with the world should not go unmentioned. Bateson has influenced Bohm, as he implies, and Bateson has said,

> The individual mind is immanent but not only in the body.
> It is immanent also in the pathways and messages outside the
> body.[13]

The implications for a model of health and illness are profound. Normally, we suppose the genesis of illness is one-way: we are healthy until we are beset from without by hostile forces. There is no give and take between ourselves and the world. It is the 'things' that are 'out there' that eventually do us in: viruses, bacteria, auto accidents. Even those that come from inside us — heart attacks, e.g., or strokes or cancers — are really external processes, not really us, but something essentially foreign which do not belong to us: invaders or hostile events. This way of thinking has engendered the idea that the human body is essentially an outpost in a foreign territory and that it will eventually be overrun by the enemy. What a refreshing contrast is Bohm's notion of unbroken flow and process in which the essential features are *relational*.

Meaning in Clinical Medicine

In clinical medicine Bohm's idea of the importance of meaning has particularly striking relevance. Let us consider the chief cause of death in the industrialized Western world, coronary artery disease. Based on work done by Rosenman and Friedman, it has been shown that so-called Type A persons — those who have a pronounced awareness of time and who seem dominated by a sense of urgency — die more frequently at an earlier age than their more relaxed Type B counterparts. Originally it was felt that it was the behavior itself that was the key factor, with the cascade of physiological changes it engendered — the neural and hormonal changes that are well known to accompany anxiety and emotional agitations. Yet, when the original psychological test patterns were examined more closely, even more prominent than the pathological time-awareness was the *hostility* and *cynicism* demonstrated by the test subjects.[14] What, may we ask, did the world *mean* to these persons? — to emphasize Bohm's approach. Whatever the meaning, it involved hostility and anger. It is a psychological attitude everyone has seen: the person who is incensed because the traffic light turns red; at the restaurant the waiter never arrives on time and cannot please, no matter how hard he tries; and on and on. In this situation, *meaning*, via the signa-somatic feedback that Bohm describes, surfaces with a vengeance. It is clear from such examples that in clinical medicine we are not dealing with trivial philosophical matters.

This is not a rare example. Recently, Schleifer and colleagues have demonstrated that the immune system of the body—the T- and B-cells that protect against invasion by micro-organisms and which defend against the development of cancer — stop working during the weeks and months following the death of one's spouse.[15] A trivial observation? Probably not, since the death rate in surviving spouses in the first year of bereavement is two to four times that of the age-matched, married population.[16] It would appear that the meaning of the world that is felt by the bereaved person shifts drastically at such a time, and that it is the signa-somatic process we are seeing in this situation.

As Bohm points out, the meaning of any particular event is an individual matter. And in clinical medicine, too, one cannot assign a value to any event a patient experiences, as one might do for the hemoglobin level or the blood pressure. A particularly vivid area wherein the uniqueness of the *meaning* of life events crystallizes into actual medical problems is in the problem of cardiac arrhythmias, where the clinical spectrum ranges from asymptomatic irregularities of the heartbeat to sudden death. Lown has expressed the uniqueness of the meaning of life events in this setting:

> . . . the predisposing psychologic condition is subjective, not readily measurable, uniquely individual, and derived from a complex weave of past experiences and diverse processes of psychologic conditioning. The factors triggering arrhythmia may appear to be innocuous stimuli to the clinical observer but *in the particular patient* gain their currency and strength from *symbolic meaning* deeply enmeshed in a prior conditioning matrix.[17] (Emphasis added.)

To even suggest that disease or illness has meaning is generally considered an absurdity in modern medicine. All illness is taken to be bad, and the goal of the healing endeavour is to eradicate it without thinking further. There is no place in this reflexive position for the possibility that illness may have hidden messages or subtle meanings to convey, or that the perceived meaning may play as crucial a role in some illnesses as a bacterium or a virus.

Bohm's theory allows meaning to come to the fore. It does not demand an automatic response *against* illness, which is our usual strategy in health care in which we react to the *least* subtle connotation of illness, that of physical derangement. More subtle levels of meaning may exist alongside the physical aberration — levels that can shed light on the disease process and transform it from something that is malevolent into something that can be seen, at higher levels of understanding, possibly, as a positive event.

This theme has been taken up by many seers, among whom was Rilke, who observed,

> Perhaps everything terrible is in its deepest being something helpless that wants help from us. ... Why do you want to shut out of your life any agitation, any pain, any melancholy, since you really do not know that these states are working upon you? ... If there is anything morbid in your processes, just remember that sickness is the means by which an organism frees itself of foreign matter; so one must just help it to be sick, to have its whole sickness and break out with it, for that is its progress.[18]

Consciousness: What Is It?
But, then, if this 'everything' does indeed have meaning, and if, as Bohm has stated, meaning is ultimately tied to 'mental', is the world itself conscious? What is to separate Bohm's vision from pantheism? He is explicit on this point:

> ... consciousness as we know it is not being attributed to nature. Rather, the suggestion is that both nature and mind *as we experience it* (which has somehow evolved in nature) share a basic overall process which is an extension of soma-significant and signa-somatic activity. [As a result] there is no absolute distinction between [mind and matter]. Rather, there is only one 'field' of reality as a whole, containing the universal but relative distinction between generalized soma and generalized significance (which as we recall are not separate entities or substances, as would be psyche and soma). What we call 'matter' is then *encountered* wherever the somatic side of this universal and fundamental distinction is the major factor and what we call 'mind' is *encountered* wherever the side of significance is the major factor ... perhaps both sides ultimately meet at 'infinite' depths, on a ground from which the whole of existence emerges.[19] (Emphasis added.)

Particularly intriguing is the way in which Bohm uses the term consciousness. Nowhere is it explicitly defined. (This is no mark against Bohm; no one else in the history of Western philosophy has totally succeeded, either, in the attempt.) Whatever consciousness is, it is pervasive, something found in nature at large with which it shares a 'basic overall process.' And it seems tied to the fact of experience. Fundamentally, it is not a 'thing.'

This view is strongly reminiscent of the position of the American philosopher, William James, who in 1904 published an essay with the startling title, 'Does Consciousness Exist?' Up until that time almost everything in accepted philosophy in the West hinged on the idea that the subject/object and knower/known distinctions were fundamental. In a stunning burst of originality James cut through these assumptions:

> [Consciousness is] the name of a nonentity, and has no right to a place among first principles. Those who still cling to it are clinging to a mere echo, the faint rumor left behind by the disappearing 'soul' upon the air of philosophy. [There is] no aboriginal stuff or quality of being, contrasted with that of which our thoughts of them are made. [There is] only one primal stuff or material [out of which everything in the world is composed. This stuff is] pure experience.[20]

If I interpret Bohm's concept of consciousness correctly it lies very close to that of James — as do the perspectives of Whitehead, Hayward, and Bateson, as we saw earlier. It is important to realize that these observers are not resolving the question of 'what is consciousness?' by the facile act of defining it out of existence, rather, they are denying that consciousness is a thing. Each of them would, I feel, acknowledge that the event called 'knowing' is the most ineluctable fact of existence for each of us; and 'experience' and 'encounter' are words used by Bohm to allude to the origin of 'knowing' and to suggest the transcendence of the duality that James initially criticized.

Intention and Action
Yet, not all of the signa-somatic and soma-significant processes spell doom for us, as the above examples might imply. Indeed, in Bohm's theory these processes are the springboard to active

participation in bringing about health. Bohm states, 'an intention generally arises out of a previous perception of meaning or significance of a certain total situation.'[21]

Having perceived a meaning or a significance, then, we can *act*. This is a marked distinction from the older psychosomatic theories. In them, there was an emphasis on psychosomatic *disease*, but almost never on health. There was a distinct flavour of guilt and punishment implicit in the theories: it was always the poor body that was being punished for the transgressions of the mind, always on the receiving end of anxieties, neuroses, depressions, psychoses, fears, etc. Not so in Bohm's concept; for action, intent, and motive flow from perceived meaning, and these actions can be enlisted in the cause of health. Again, these are not discrete events but part of a single process: Meaning and intention are thus seen to be *'inseparably related, as two sides or aspects of one activity.'*[22] (Emphasis is Bohm's.) And, 'Meaning unfolds into intention, and intention into action, which however, has significance, so that there is in general a circular loop of flow.'[23]

Yet it would be inaccurate to impute to ourselves the power to *always* stay healthy through capitalizing on the circular loops of meaning and intention and action. Unfortunately, we tend to do just this, supposing that through the most vigorous, robust activity we can forestall and prevent illness and otherwise think, exercise, diet, or relax ourselves into some nirvanic state of healthiness. Bohm warns us against such quick conclusions:

> Intentions are commonly thought to be conscious and deliberate. In fact, one's ability consciously to choose or to determine his intentions is very limited. For the deeper intentions . . . generally arise out of the total significance, in ways of which one is not aware, and over which one has no control.[24]

But we are not helpless, for we 'discover' our intentions in an ongoing process wherein we observe our own actions. Or, as Bohm says, we can 'display' our intentions and their expected consequences through the imagination, through writing, miming, and the like. From such a display we can modify our intentions and actions as we go along, and 'this process can continue to ever greater degrees of comprehensiveness and depths of inwardness. . . .'[25]

This description suggests a particularly refreshing aspect

when applied to health care. We have become attracted to a way of thinking in matters of health and illness in which we juxtapose 'problem' and 'cure' in a one-to-one ratio; e.g., the cure for a strep throat is penicillin. A hopelessly damaged heart can be fixed by a cardiac transplant. This is perhaps a hold over from the 'magic bullet' thinking that characterized the hopes of the earliest discoverers of antibiotics: in theory, they presumed, it should be possible to find a specific, single agent for every known infectious disease. This linear form of thought contrasts mightily with Bohm's. The former is rigid and inflex-ible; the latter is circular, with feedback loops and increasing degrees of 'comprehensiveness and depths of inwardness.' Bohm, for example, might not have us say that the proper intention on perceiving a headache would be to take aspirin; he might propose that there is further meaning than pain that is implicit in the headache. 'Headache' might be seen as 'process' in which its meaning might unfold with time — and whose character, the pain itself, might also undergo the most profound alterations (either ceasing altogether or getting worse).

This example was in fact related by a practitioner of medita-tion. When his meditation teacher walked by it was obvious that the young and inexperienced practitioner was in pain. 'What is the matter?' the master asked. 'I have a headache; I cannot concentrate,' the novice responded. 'Wonderful!' the master responded. 'Are you *learning* anything?'

In this example the master went beyond the ordinary way of judging illness as something, by definition, to be rid of. Ill-ness may have a greater meaning. It takes its meaning from the whole in which it is embedded and enfolded, a whole that includes health in its various gradations and expressions. We cannot say that it is wrong to intervene, that the novice medi-tator would have been wrong to take an aspirin — but that there is meaning that is immanent in all events, including pain.

The Imaginal Realm in Medicine
In our reaction to illnesses, then, Bohm carves out a place for the imagination and for processes within our minds that are not fully conscious. We cannot know the full meaning of a health-event by its superficial appearance; indeed, we cannot even know our full intent toward the event by utilizing our conscious mind. In view of these limitations, then, *some* use

of the imagination would seem to be required if we are to understand the meanings of health and illness and how we should regard them. It is perhaps because we have lost touch with this imaginal realm of illness that we seem to experience less and less a sense of health when, our technology assures us, we should be experiencing more and more. Something has gone out of our experience of health and illness, something which, I feel, might be reinserted by allowing the 'greater degrees of comprehensiveness and depths of inwardness' to have their way.

This modern dilemma has been described by the psychologist, Tom Moore:

> ... Modern medicine, having chased the gods out of disease, has lost an imaginal consciousness of illness. It has left modern man with physical material to be manipulated, whereas in an imaginal context it could lead consciousness through 'rites of passage,' deepening the quality of experience, initiating the psyche further in its own labyrinthine mysteries. The tradition which holds that disease manifests divinity and calls for a religious response deserves a modern hearing, so that the psychological passages that disease signals and embodies might be discovered.[26]

I dwell on this point for I think it has led to many of the great excesses of medical therapy of our day, such as the unending 'wars' on certain diseases that are plied with such muscular singleness of purpose that in some instances they come eventually to seem inhumane (the fanaticism in developing and installing artificial human hearts is perhaps the most widely known current example). For when it comes to illness and being uncomfortable we seem to have lost all capacity for ambiguity, for supposing that maybe, just maybe, there could be hidden messages and meanings to illness that could not be apprehended by a quick scan of the *fact* of the illness as such. In matters of health we eschew ambiguity. We want to be rid of pain and illness, and the sooner the better. But there are 'depths of inwardness' that may not be discovered if this single-minded approach is blindly pursued. Lewis Thomas has described a similar situation with regard to our use of language, a situation where ambiguity seems as essential as in our experience of illness:

> Ambiguity seems to be an essential, indispensable element for

the transfer of information from one place to another by words, where matters of real importance are concerned. It is often necessary, for meaning to come through, that there be an almost vague sense of strangeness and askewness. Speechless animals and cells cannot do this. . . . Only the human mind is designed to work in this way, programmed to drift away in the presence of locked-on information, straying from each point in a hunt for a better, different point.[27]

Content, Context, and the Necessity of Ambiguity

The ambiguity inherent in our experience of the world is, of course, not confined to matters of language nor of health and illness. It invades all human experience and even areas of knowledge that are frequently assumed to be free of it, such as modern physics. Bohm says,

> It is not commonly realized . . . that the quantum theory implies that no such 'bottom level' of unambiguous reality is possible.[28]

And,

> . . . there is no unambiguous context-independent 'bottom level' of reality in physics, beyond the phenomena themselves. Indeed, the whole question of what is to be meant by terms, such as 'electrons,' 'quarks,' etc., is inseparably bound up with the forms to which we have chosen to give emphasis . . . So, the higher levels that depend on meaning and what is hoped to be the 'fundamental' level (e.g., of particles) are bound together, in a way that cannot be disentangled.[29]

And the situation in physics, of the dependence of meaning of experimental results on context, although negligible at the ordinary level of experience, nonetheless extends qualitatively to the domain of the everyday:

> The kind of situation described . . . is . . . what is pervasively characteristic of 'mind' and of meaning. Indeed, the whole field of meaning can be described as subject to a distinction between content and context, which is similar to that between soma and significance, and between the subtle and the manifest. That is to say, *there are two aspects that are invariably present, at least implicitly, in any attempt to discuss the overall meaning in any given situation. . . The content is the essential meaning. . . but any specifiable content is abstracted from a wider context, which is so closely connected with the content that the meaning of the former is not fully defined without the latter.*[30] (Emphasis added).

And what is the limit to the context Bohm suggests? There is none, for

> ... to suggest such an idea is to extend a notion similar to that of meaning to the whole universe. For it is implied that each feature of the universe is not only context dependent in a fundamental way, but also the grosser manifest features will in general depend significantly on the subtler aspects.[31]

The roots of illness, then, in Bohm's vision, would seem to be considerably broader than the terrestrial plane on which we experience them. The meaning of health and illness extends ultimately to the entire universe.

This feature of Bohm's theory would, it seems, do much to restore the imaginal, religious quality to our concepts of health and illness. Illness goes beyond its associations with terrestrial bacteria, viruses, cholesterol obstructions in coronary arteries, and cancers of the colon; these are only 'the grosser manifest features' of illness that are seen only from a limited, physical, earth-bound context. But meaning can come from larger contexts than our immediate surroundings, even from the entire universe.

Bohm's notion that meaning and context are tied together in such a way that they cannot be separated in our experience is consistent in many ways with information about human visual perception. It is well known that the information we glean from the world is highly context-dependent and has surprisingly little to do with 'the world out there.' There *must* be context, it seems, for us to see anything at all. In fact, it is so essential that we *create* context. One sense of the meaning of context is 'background' or 'contrast.' The human eye is constantly in motion, moving dozens of times a second, creating a moving panoply of what is external to it. Without this movement we would be visually impoverished. For retinal impressions to be perceived we require this motion which creates a contrast or context. Stasis is a kind of antithesis of context, for it implies fixity and an unchanging sameness. So, just as meaning is context-dependent in Bohm's theory of soma-significance, our physical visual apparatus depends similarly on context.

The biologist, Davenport, has expressed the situation:

> If we examine the experience from which our knowledge of the world arises, we can see that they consist of various types

of differences. Without difference, there can be no experience. The experience of difference is basic to our notion of existence, the latter being derived from the Latin *ex sistere*, which means 'to stand apart,' i.e., to be different. ... The foundation of any valid epistemology must be the recognition that, since all properties must be experienced as difference, the physical world exists for us only in terms of relationships. ... Recognition of the nature of the experience that underlies our knowledge is important for the realization that physical reality does not exist before us as an object of study but *emerges from our consciousness during our changing experience within nature.*[32] (Davenport's emphasis.)

This situation is reminiscent of the ambiguity that Lewis Thomas believes to be necessary for language to have its fullest meaning. From several perspectives we seem to come to the same point: what is perceived — whether a meaning, language, visual stimuli, or anything else — is dependent on the context in which it is perceived.

The Shadow Side of Health
Thus, the theory of soma-significance allows a place in our experience for contrast, ambiguity, and events that seemingly oppose each other. Just as the North and South Poles of a magnet (one of Bohm's examples) define each other and are incomplete without each other, the so-called oppositional qualities of health and illness also define each other. One cannot exist without the other, for each provides the background or contrast against which the other can be sensed. From this perspective, then, the commonly espoused goal of perfect health makes no sense and is not only an epistemological impossibility, it is not even desirable — since to banish all illness would be the equivalent of banishing our knowledge of health.

Unlike current models of health, which make room only for the desirable events of life, Bohm's model allows for illness as well. In so doing it provides for a richness of human experience that has been all but banished by our fanatical concerns about achieving perfect health. The philosopher, Huston Smith, expresses the fuller view that is allowed by the theory of soma-significance:

> If anything, a realized soul is more in touch with the grief and sorrow that is part and parcel of the human condition, knowing that it too needs to be accepted and lived as all life needs

to be lived. To reject the shadow side of life, to pass by with averted eyes — refusing our share of common sorrow while expecting our share of common joy — would cause the unlived, rejected shadows to deepen in us as fear, including our fear of death. ... The peace that comes when a man is hungry and finds food, is sick and recovers, or is lonely and finds a friend — peace of this sort is readily intelligible; but the peace that *passeth* understanding comes when the pain of life is not relieved. It shimmers on the crest of a wave of pain; it is the spear of frustration transformed into a shaft of light.[33]

In Bohm's proposal we find a new way of conceptualizing our place in the world. In his theory it is no longer possible to invoke such rigid distinctions as seer and seen, subject and object, and 'the world out there.' A new way of seeing is called for, which has been described by the philosopher of science S. Toulmin:

First and foremost, [we] must set aside all the absolute distinctions that were by-products of seventeenth century theory (mind and matter, physical and psychical, etc.), since these represent false and needless antitheses. ... This means posing all problems having to do directly with intellectual and perceptual capacities in terms of the total relationship between our sensory systems, our brains, and the environment with which we have to deal — which includes the conceptual patterns we inherit or acquire.

We may call the resulting explanation mechanistic [or physicalistic or reductionist ...] if we please, but this no longer matters. Once the Cartesian [and Newtonian] antithesises have been cleared away, we achieve nothing by asserting that our systems are material, physical, or mechanical — for these adjectives no longer have any opposites...[34]

Conclusion

Medicine has for three hundred years looked to physics for its models and frameworks. This reliance has, until now, assured us that the mechanistic, classical descriptions of man in which mind and consciousness play no part are sufficient. Yet from within medicine itself has come information that cannot be explained by such an approach.

Still, however, we are bereft in medicine of an adequate model of the human being. Perhaps Bohm's contribution will help remedy this deficiency, for the theory of soma-significance contains an inclusive model of mind-body interaction which medicine can use to interpret its own observations. The impact of the theory on the health professions is potentially enormous — as is, I feel, our debt to Professor Bohm.

Illustrations of the Confusion of Mind and Body in Clinical Medicine

One of the most celebrated areas in all of clinical medicine where the interaction of mind and body are currently being debated is the problem of cancer. Do emotions, attitudes, states of consciousness, and psychosocial influences make a difference in the origin or the prognosis of the disease? Stringent stands are taken by researchers on both sides of the fence, and as yet a consensus has not emerged.

As a typical example of the rhetoric involved, the following citation is taken from a study which purported to show no influence of psychosocial factors. (Examples could as easily be found from the literature contending the opposite case. The point is to illustrate the either-or, mind versus body, forms of thought that influence *both* those who favor the powers of the mind and those who deny such.)

> Our study of patients with advanced, high-risk malignant diseases suggests that the inherent biology of the disease alone determines the prognosis, overriding the potentially mitigating influence of psychosocial factors.[35]

From the perspective of Bohm's theory of soma-significance, what can the 'inherent biology' of a disease possibly mean? For in the theory the material world does not stand in isolation from mind and cannot therefore act 'alone.'

And in the editorial that accompanied the above article in one of the most prestigious medical journals in the Western world, the following comment arose:

> One frequently-cited study ... reports that the death rate among people who have recently lost their spouses is higher than that among married people. ... [Some] have been quick to ascribe the finding to grief rather than to, say, a change in diet or other habits.[36]

Again from Bohm's perspective we can ask how, conceivably, 'change in diet or other habits' arise, unaffected by thought, emotion, and states of consciousness. These changes do not inflict themselves on one out of the blue, and to ascribe an increased death rate among bereaved spouses to changes in habits hardly banishes the effects of consciousness. In fact, one may insert an extraordinarily lengthy chain of intervening variables (see diagram, p.102), but we should not be misled into thinking that in so doing we have annulled the effects of mind.

Bohm's theory of soma-significance overcomes these mutually exclusive ways of analyzing the origins of health and illness, because no ultimate primacy is being attributed to either mind or matter as separate, independent entities. And until such a conceptual leap is managed in medicine we shall continue to wander about, asking the perennial question: Is it mind or matter that is most influential in any given disease process?

Examples

Examples from three states — (a) chronic illness, (b) hyperventilation syndrome, and (c) cardiac arrhythmias — illustrate how the theory of soma-significance can be visualized in actual operation:

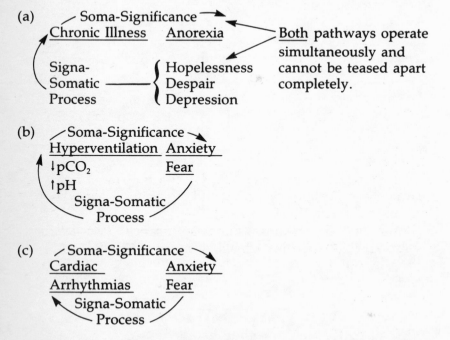

These common clinical examples illustrate Bohm's contention that,

... both nature [the disease entity illustrated on the left] and mind [the reaction to such illustrated on the right] share a basic overall process which is an extension of soma-significant and signa-somatic activity.[37]

But nature and mind, like the poles of a magnet, are only conceptual conveniences. There is only the 'field' of which each partakes, and which unites them both.

It might seem that the soma-significant and the signa-somatic processes might involve us in an unending, downward spiral toward increasing illness: e.g., illness generates fear and anxiety which perpetuate greater illness in a vicious cycle. But this is not invariable. There is always the chance for new meanings to be discovered, even in the experience of illness. A bad beginning does not always guarantee a bad end. New meanings can arise among the direst situations that can serve a corrective action, and to which we attach the words: homeostasis, health, and wisdom.

References

1. Braunwald, E. et al., in Isselbacher. K. J., et al. (eds.). *Harrison's Textbook of Internal Medicine*, New York, McGraw-Hill, 1980, p. 1031.

2. Lown, B. and Verrier, R. L. 'Neural activity and ventricular fibrillation'. *New England Journal of Medicine*, May 20, 1979, *294*:21, pp. 1169-70.

3. Whitteridge, G. *William Harvey: an anatomical disputation concerning the movement of the heart and blood in living creatures*, Oxford, Blackwell, 1976, p. 11. (Cited in *NEJM*, December 7, 1984, *311*:23, p. 1521.)

4. Regardie, I. *The Philosopher's Stone*, St. Paul, Llewellyn, 1970, p.90; (Quoted in Severson, Randolph, 'The alchemy of dreamwork: reflections on Freud and the alchemical tradition,' *Dragonflies*, Spring, 1979, p.109.)

5. Bohm, D., 'The theory of soma-significance,' *Personal Communication*, p. 1. (See his *Unfolding Meaning*, RKP, 1987.)

6. Bohm, pp. 1-2.

7. Bohm, p. 4.

8. Bohm, p. 4.

9. Bohm, p. 11.

10. Bohm, p. 10.

11. Whitehead, A. N., *Modes of thought*, New York, Macmillan, 1968, pp. 156-165.

12. Hayward, Jeremy. *Perceiving Ordinary Magic*, Boston, New Science Library, 1985, p. 214.

13. Bateson, G., (Cited in Hayward, p. 214.)

14. Williams, R. B., Jr., 'An untrusting heart'. *The Sciences*, September/October, 1984, pp. 31-36.

15. Schleifer, S. J., et al., 'Suppression of lymphocyte stimulation following bereavement', *Journal of the American Medical Association*, July 15, 1983, *250:3* pp. 374-377.

16. Kraus, A. S. and Lilienfeld, A. M., 'Some epidemiological aspects of the high mortality rate in the young widowed group,' *Journal of Chronic Disease*, 1959, Volume 10, pp. 207-217.

17. Lown, B., deSilva, R. A., Reich, P., and Murawski, B. J., 'Psychophysiological factors in sudden cardiac death,' *The American Journal of Psychiatry*, November, 1980, *137*:11, pp. 1325-1335.

18. Rilke, R. M. *Letters to a Young Poet*, (Trans. M. D. Herter Norton) New York, W. W. Norton, 1954, pp. 69-70.

19. Bohm, pp. 25-26.

20. James, William, in Russell, B., *A History of Western Philoophy*. New York, Simon and Schuster, 1945, p. 812.

21. Bohm, p. 12.

22. Bohm, p. 13.

23. Bohm, p. 13.

24. Bohm, p. 14.

25. Bohm, p. 14.

26. Moore, Tom, 'Images in asthma,' *Dragonflies*, Spring, 1979, pp. 6-7.

27. Thomas, Lewis, *Lives of a Cell*, Toronto, Bantam Books, 1974, p. 111. (Cited in Smith, Huston, *Beyond the Post-Modern Mind*, p. 87.)

28. Bohm, p. 20.

29. Bohm, p. 22.

30. Bohm, p. 23.

31. Bohm, p. 25.

32. Davenport, R., *An Outline of Animal Development*, Reading, Mass., Addison-Wesley, 1979, p. 192.

33. Smith, Huston, 'The sacred unconscious', *Beyond health and normality*, (eds. Walsh, R. and Shapiro, D. H.) New York, Van Nostrand Reinhold Company, 1983, pp. 269-270.

34. Toulmin, S., in Foss, L. and Rothenbert, K. *The Second Medical Revolution: from a biomedical to an infomedical model*, in publication.

35. Cassileth, B. R., et al. 'Psychosocial correlates of survival in advanced malignant disease?' *New England Journal of Medicine*, June 13, 1985, *312*:24, pp. 1551-1555.

36. Angell, Marcia, 'Disease as a reflection of the psyche,' *New England Journal of Medicine*, June 13, 1985, *312*:24, pp. 1570-1572.

37. Bohm, p. 25.

Meaning and the Living Brain

MATTI BERGSTRÖM

Introduction

There is a widespread confusion about human values and about the sense of meaning in our lives. The scientific method now available does not include the concept of value nor of meaning. It does not ask 'Why?' or 'What for?' These are questions practically forbidden in the positivistic empirical science. Only the question 'How?' is allowed, which means that only that which exists in time and local space is supposed to be real.

When such a method is applied in brain research, the brain becomes a physical system. All processes in the human brain are understood as mass-trajectories in time and space. Our concept of a human being becomes that of a physical system. Such a system does not ask a question 'Why?' or 'What for?' It only asks questions of the type 'How?' Consequently, the brain does not search for answers concerning the *meaning* and *value* of its own behaviour.

Physiologists, whose aim in studying brain functions is connected with medical problems know, however, that a human being cannot live without asking 'Why?', or asking what is the meaning of his doings and the value of life. We could say that meaning and value are the qualities of a *living brain*. These attributes do not apply to a scientific, physical brain.

There is an apparent discrepancy between these two concepts of the brain. This discrepancy ought to be solved since the present scientific view alone does not help human beings to find a way out of the huge problems facing humanity. The question would then be how to define values and meaning in brain function.

In the following, we are presenting on the basis of empirical brain research, a view of the living brain. This view includes the concepts of value and meaning. At the same time we shall show how there exists a new way of looking at the *mind-body problem* so that no conflict arises between psychological and physical views. It seems that a solution of the psycho-physical problem is possible only if no contradiction exists between these views (Bergström 1978).

In this article, we shall first give a description of the place of neural systems and the brain in nature as a whole in order to understand the world of neurons, and why the brain exists at all. Then we will describe the brain as a system, in order to give an idea of its working mode. After this we shall describe the brain's 'self', the 'I', and connect these concepts with the mind-body problem. Additionally, it will be shown how the brain interacts with the environment. Finally, some problems concerning human society will be treated in the light of brain function.

It will be concluded that there is an urgent need to realize that the question about the nature of meaning and values is not only a philosophical question but is also related to our brain and the environment.

The place of the nervous system in nature

It is difficult to understand the intrinsic function of the brain if we do not know which role the neural tissue in the animal organism has in nature as a whole. Why do nerve cells and the brain exist?

Because of the ability of nerve cells to convey electrochemical signals along their long branches, the nervous system can effectively connect distant parts of the organism. In this way it can efficiently take part in the control and regulatory functions. The high velocity of the signals and the accurate wiring and coupling of the branchings make it more efficient than the primitive hormonal regulative systems.

But what was it that made the nervous system first appear on the earth in the sea environment of the Precambrian age, and later to develop to the extent we now find it in animal nervous systems and in the human brain?

The most plausible explanation is that the species with a nervous system had an advantage to those without one. Natural selection favoured not only a brain as such, but also the large number of nerve cells in the brain and the large number of branchings and contact organs or synapses between the cells.

Such an increase in the number of brain cells, or in what could be called the *substantial capacity* of the neural system, was not very important in the homogeneous water environment of the Precambrian sea. But it did become much more important later, when the organisms 'climbed from the sea to the land' and had to evolve in the dry environment of the earth, which was energetically very different from the sea.

In the sea there were no noticeable and sudden energetic differences. For example, in the depths of the sea the changes in light and pressure were gradual. But life on the land provided a totally different energetic environment, most notably because of the force of gravity. The nervous system had to be able to control in a new way the posture of the organism, and above all, it had to be able to adjust the posture very quickly during movement.

It seems that the increase in the number of nerve cells and the associated increase in the *signal capacity* of the brain, took place simultaneously with the increase of the environmental demands due to the land environment. Natural selection favoured those organisms which could survive in the new situation. In order to cope with the quick energetic changes of the environment (e.g. due to gravity) , the animal species needed a better behavioural capacity. This was provided by the increase in the substantial and signal capacities of the brain.

A comparison between the mental and the behavioural capacity of an animal suggests that the psyche is somehow connected with the number of substantial and functional neural elements, the synapses and the neural signals. A larger brain consists of a larger amount of synapses and signals and it has a larger mental capacity. There are zoologists (eg. Rench, Horridge and others) who have considered this parallelism. It remains to be investigated how the connection is established.

The nervous system originates in the same embryonal ectodermal plate as the skin. Thus we should not be surprised that the primary function of the brain is the same as that of the skin: to adapt the organism to the environment. As the environment differentiated more and more, because of the varying energetic conditions of the dry land, the adaptive functions had to grow more efficiently. At last, the 'neural skin' grew into a brain with its efficient ability to mediate interactions between the organism and its environment.

When speaking about the brain we can use Claude Bernard's

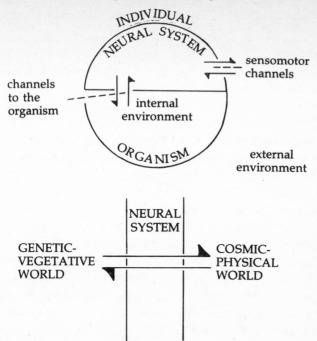

Fig. 1 *The place of the neural system (brain) in nature between our external and internal environment.*

concepts 'milieu interieur' and 'milieu exterieur'. The brain can be viewed as a boundary (Fig.1) between these two separate worlds: the inner world of the organism controlled by the genetic forces, and the outer world controlled by the cosmic, physical forces. In spite of our considering both forces as physical, there are considerable differences in their effects. The genetic force preserves the past history of the species in the organism whereas the cosmic force acts mostly as the actual effect of the physical environment upon us. The brain and its inherent capacity, which we usually call the 'psyche', can be characterized as a bridge between these two worlds. The situation is a 'dialectic' one and the psyche acts as a 'moderator'.

In order to understand the 'boundary world' which is our brain and thus ourselves, we have to look at the structure of the neurophysiological 'signal space'.

The neural signal space
A vast number (up to 10^{18}) of nerve signals are constantly circulating in our brain. It is interesting to look at the 'world'

of these signals in itself, independently of the other processes in the brain.

In the neurons under consideration at a specific time we can experimentally determine on the one hand the *amount* of signals and on the other hand, their *order* (in space or in time). Even if we cannot measure the amount and order of the signals in the whole brain, we can, in principle, measure them in limited regions. It is from this concrete experimental basis that we can abstract the concept of *neural signal space* which has two degrees of freedom, the amount and the order of signals.

There are certain advantages in describing the neural functions as occuring in such a signal space. The space itself is an abstract one, and can be considered as consisting of two dimensions which we know from Cantor's set theory, the cardinal (amount) and ordinal (order) dimensions. The dynamics in such a 'Cantorian space' becomes interestingly one which can be treated mathematically in the form of a 'set dynamics'. Since this dynamics would also be a dynamics of our psyche it is no wonder that Cantor considers his set concepts as being realized in the human mind (the existence postulate of Cantor), a fact which we seem to have forgotten.

In fact, sensory physiologists (see eg. Reenpää 1962, Hensel 1966) constantly emphasize that the subjective content of a perception consists of the 'intensity' (amount) and 'quality' (order) in time and space. This is in accordance with what Cantor, too, thought about human mental contents. These contents are apparently macrostate contents of the neural signal space, representing the behaviour of neural networks as a 'wholeness'.

On the other hand, as was shown above, the state of the neural network (a brain) can, in principle, be specified at each point of time in the cardinal-ordinal space. So there exists the possibility to define both the physiological and the mental events on the same ground in this neural signal space. This can be compared with David Bohm's idea that mind and matter have the implicate order in common, and that this similarity in basic structure enables us to understand their relationship. (See also Arleta Griffor's 'The Mental and the Physical', this volume.)

The brain can thus be briefly and generally described in the following way: It consists of a large amount of (cell) units, whose state is determinable in the two-dimensional (order, amount) space which is 'occupied' by nerve signals. This space fulfills the same criteria as the number space, whose co-ordinates are the ordinal and cardinal dimensions. With neurophysiological measurements we can, in principle, unambiguously define (experimentally) the so called *microstate* of the brain (i.e., the state of the nerve cells).

The concepts microstate and *macrostate* are commonly used when describing the behaviour and properties of gases in physics. The microstate of a gas is specified by the positions and momenta of the individual molecules (statistical mechanics), and the macrostate is described by such quantities as pressure, volume and temperature (thermodynamics). Could we use this as an analogy when discussing the brain, and what would the macrostate of the neural microstate be like?

The above analogy has been one of the guiding factors for my own work in neurophysiology. If we are looking at the brain and the mind as a physiological system, then I think it is reasonable to suppose that the macrostate of the brain is the psyche.

The macrostate quantities of the brain (Bergström 1972) differ, of course, from those of other physical systems, such as gases, because the basic elements of the systems are different. But it is interesting to note that the concept of neuronal entropy ('disorder') corresponds to entropy in physics, and so does the concept of information, when used in a way Brillouin uses it.

When looked at in the above way, the mind-body problem seems to reduce to the problem of the relationship between the macro- and microstates of systems. This does not mean that the mind-body problem will be solved. The advantage is that the problem can be carried to the context of systems analysis, and thus, as it were, closer to our usual scientific concepts. But we must remember that concepts such as the micro- and macrostate of the the system are not unproblematic, nor is the relationship between them.

Without going into the details here, it has been shown that it is possible to calculate the macrostate behaviour for a neural network, if we start from its elementary, microstate function. In fact, the same macrostate function is obtainable for neural systems by two independent ways, i.e. by 1) direct 'measurement' of the subjective, psychological state (by asking questions from people in experiments) and by 2) theoretical calculation of the macrostate from the microstate. This strongly supports the following thesis: *'The psychological state is a macrostate of the same system of which the physical state is a microstate'* (Bergström 1986).

In another connection (Bergström 1975) we have also shown that the well-known empirical psycho-physiological Weber and Stevens functions may be derived theoretically by calculating the corresponding macrostate functions from the microstate of neural nets.

Thus, we may conclude that the psycho-physiological relation is a relation between the macro- and microstates of neural systems. This solution preserves the thermodynamic rules in the mind-brain interaction.

The mind-brain problem
In the light of the above we can now understand the dualistic-interactionistic view of the mind-brain problem presented by Popper and Eccles (1977) and Eccles (1987) in a new way. The interaction between the psyche and the neural system can be seen as an interaction between the neural macrostate and microstate.

The view of Popper and Eccles is, however, incomplete, because it does not explain the interaction between mind and brain in terms of the thermodynamic theory. For the macro-microstate relation this is no problem since the interaction between these states is well-known (Prigogine 1976) and can, in principle, be well measured. In fact, this is just what the psycho-physiological measurements do.

Regarding the view presented by Sperry (1973), we can understand that his description of the psyche as a 'molar, holistic and emergent' property of the brain, is a description of the macrostate. Also, the example of the 'wheel rolling downhill', which Sperry uses in order to describe the relation between mind and brain, is a description of the macrostate (rolling wheel) in its relation to the microstate (its atoms).

On the other hand, the macro-microstate aspect of the psycho-physiological relation makes understandable the identity view of the mind-brain relation. After all it is the same system (identity) which relates to itself.

For an interaction between psyche and matter to take place,

certain statistical conditions have to be fulfilled. One interesting feature is that one and the same macrostate (psyche or the subjective state) allows for a number of different microstate (neural signal) configurations. This means that the psyche is relatively free from the organic processes. This is also supported by the well-known Lashley effect of injury of neural tissue: only a statistically significant loss of neural tissue affects the behavioural state of the brain.

The macrostate property of the psyche makes it understandable that the mind cannot be localized, not in space nor in time: a macrostate is the 'whole system'. It also makes it understandable that the causality between mind and brain is a statistical one (compare with the 'Wahrscheinlichkeits-Implikation', or the probability function between the stimulus and the subjective sensation which was pointed out by Reenpää 1962).

The brain as a dipole system
On the basis of empirical work on the development of the central nervous system, the brain can be viewed, from the systemic point of view, as a core-shell system. This has concentric central reflex-circuits and it consists of two poles (see Bergström 1969 and Fig. 2). It includes the primitive *entropic power generator* of the brain-stem and the highly developed *information generator* of the cerebral cortex. The two generators inter-

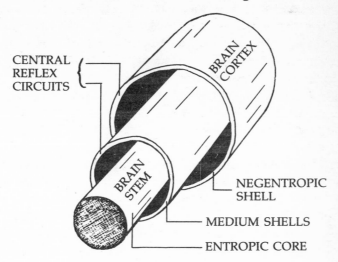

Fig. 2 An entropy model of the brain with a non-ordered, entropic core and ordered, negentropic shells.

act (see Fig. 4) and control behaviour, including language and speech. The brain-stem discharges mainly non-ordered, non-informatory nerve signals towards the cortex and the cerebral cortex discharges informatory, ordered signals towards the stem. The effect of the power generator can thus be defined as entropic, that is, it conserves disorder. The information generator has a negentropic effect, which means that it conserves order, information. The power generator is also known as the reticular formation.

The sources of the signal-flow from the entropy generator are the vegetative system and the non-specific part of the sensory channels. The latter includes in particular the primitive sensory modalities which feed signals to the brain-stem. To these sources belong the stretch muscle proprioceptors which are driven by the gravitational force. This force, thus, is a precondition for a proper function of the brain-stem entropy generator and of the consciousness. The information content which derives from genetic sources and from the environment via specific sensory channels, feeds into the cortical information generator. The adequacy of these sources and adequate transfer capacity of the corresponding feeding channels are prerequisites for the efficient operation of the generators and, consequently, of the behaviour of the individual.

The described physiological system of the brain forms the basis for mental functions. The effect of the entropy generator is expressed in the appearance and intensity of mental activity or consciousness. This in turn is a prerequisite for different types of behaviour such as cognitive functions, speech and movement. The physiological basis for this is the integrative effect of the random discharge of neural impulses on the cerebral cortex. The effect of the information generator appears in the informatory content of our psyche (hereditary and acquired information) with which we control our behaviour. It also gives the informatory content of language and speech. Its physiological background is a highly-structured columnar system of the cortex.

We can see that language and speech as such, without the integrative power of consciousness, do not have any meaning for the brain producing them. We shall later see how this meaning arises in connection with the 'value production' in the brain, caused by the consciousness potential.

The brain's two generators can be seen as the material rep-

resentations of the dimensions of Cantor's set theoretical space
(Bergström and Hari 1976): the entropy generator serves for
the amount (cardinal) and the information generator for the
order (ordinal) dimension. The resulting number space of the
brain takes shape in the interactive field between the two generators of the model. It is this space which acts as the final source
of the behaviour of an individual. It consequently can be called
the world of our 'self' which receives influences both from the
primitive entropy generator in the form of consciousness (the
reticular arousal function) and from the highly developed information generator in the form of sensory stimuli. In this 'self'
the 'dialectic interaction' between the primitive and developed
parts of our brain is realized. The 'self' also acts towards its
environment through behaviour.

We could thus say, for the sake of our discussion to follow,
that the brain has three separate organs: one for producing
consciousness, another one for representing material objects
in space-time, and a third one which integrates the two others,
and which we experience as the 'self'.

So when I hereafter speak of 'matter' or 'physical' in the
context of the brain, I refer to the ability of the cortex to *represent*
material objects and their space-time co-ordinates. Likewise,
when I talk about 'mind', 'psyche' or 'consciousness', I refer
to the *activity* of the brain-stem as a *necessary* condition of consciousness. (It may not be a *sufficient* condition for consciousness; perhaps consciousness has a more subtle aspect which
goes beyond the 'manifest', physiological process. But I will
not discuss this interesting question here, for my primary concern in this article is the interpretation of the *physiological* aspect
of consciousness.)

So 'matter' refers to the representation of material objects
in the cortex and 'psyche' or 'consciousness' refers to the
activity of the brain-stem. The 'self', then, refers to the *interaction* of these two brain processes — in this sense the self is
between the 'psyche' and 'matter'. The 'self' refers to a third
type of brain process which arises when the brain-stem activity
('psyche') and the cortical activity ('matter') meet.

Although this way of talking about 'psyche' and 'matter'
may be a little unusual and thus confusing, it also helps to
emphasize how different types of physiological processes have
particular characteristics which seem to correspond to particular mental phenomena. In this presentation, I am, of course,

discussing in terms of the brain, and thus the words 'psyche', 'matter' and 'self' all refer primarily to processes of a 'living brain'. But naming these processes in the above way helps to suggest just what type of mental phenomena may be associated with a particular type of brain activity.

The value of specifying the use of the terminology at this point was suggested to me by the editor of this volume, and the above definitions grew out of our discussions.

'Self', the 'Third' between consciousness and matter

Thus, in the brain there are three distinct regions with clearly different physiological tasks: the brain-stem, the cerebral cortex and the intermediate interactive fields. The brain-stem regulates the conscious 'tonus' (arousal state) of the brain, the cerebral cortex differentiates this tonus according to the physical co-ordinates of the matter, the interactive field combines the actions of both and feeds the resultant to the behavioural channels. This is physiology.

If we consider the mental phenomena that may be associated with these physiological events, then the intrinsic psychological factor has to be sought in the brain-stem since it is the physiological source of consciousness. Without it no psychological activity is possible. Also, signal-flow which the brain-stem sends is (almost) devoid of any representative space-time structure. It activates the target brain areas and integrates them into one unified process.

On the other hand, the material characteristics in terms of space-time structure have to be sought in the cerebral cortex. Without cortical sensory activity no perception of physical matter is possible. The signal-flow from the cortex 'down' towards the brain-stem exhibits an ordered structure which it has abstracted from the objects that have been observed. This order is a real microstate, a material order which represents elementary objects in time and space.

The third component in brain physiology is the interactive field between the stem and the cortex. We have called the field as the 'self' by virtue of its central position in *controlling* the behaviour (sensory and motor). We also described the physiological signal space where this self 'exists' and pointed out that this space is empirically measurable as a cardinal-ordinal number space.

The self represents the brain's *selective capacity*. It either treats the elementary functions so that they form wholenesses, or it treats wholenesses so that they are broken up into elements. The self integrates and differentiates brain function freely, according to its needs. The self is thus in between 'mind' and 'matter'. This reminds us of Descartes, who also had the notion that there was something in between mind and matter, namely God. Of course, our view is very different from that of Descartes. For example, he thought that mind as pure thought is totally immaterial, whereas we consider mind to be represented by a brain process. But it is interesting to note that Descartes also thought there was a third factor, even if he had very different reasons for postulating it. (For Descartes' view, see Arleta Griffor's paper 'The Mental and the Physical', this volume.)

A kind of 'betweenness' characterizes the 'self' also in our usual life. We feel the needs of our physical organism, like hunger, thirst, etc., and have to fulfill them in the outer world. We also feel our psychological needs, eg. love, fear, etc., and have to cope with them. There is always present our inner mental environment and our outer physical one. The inner 'things' are, for the self, as real as the outer ones, but they do not consist of information like the outer things. They are shapeless, holistic and emotive 'entities', and have an immediate connection with values such as good or bad.

C.G. Jung said that some inner things, like emotions, are connected with physiological (vegetative) processes whereas abstract 'feelings' exist 'which do not change the physiological conditions' (Jung, 1968). These 'feelings' might correspond to the brain's self, which has the ability to experience the emotional needs of the inner world and to select among different types of informational programs etc. from the outer world in order to satisfy its needs.

The self has apparently an evaluative ability, that is, it is possessed with a kind of 'value-capacity' and 'meaning'. Interestingly, when Jung considers that abstract feelings are free from physiological functions, he says that 'feeling (German 'Gefühl') is a function of value'. He also connects this function with 'abstract thinking'.

It thus seems that the brain's self is connected with our free thinking and evaluation, in which we can choose any purpose, meaning or target for our sensory or motor behaviour, or thinking.

The Darwinistic dynamics of the selective brain

It is an interesting question to ask just *how* the selective operation in the brain's self works. Selection, understood in connection with 'value', is certainly among the highest categories of human psychology, and is linked with such areas of the human mind as creativity, motivation, evaluation, emotion, channelling of interest, aesthetics, ethics, morality and meaning. Since all these are connected with the topic of this book, which is meaning, it is relevant to examine here the principle of selection in the brain.

The physiological dynamics of what happens in the brain during the interaction of the generators is in principle the same as that of Darwinian natural selection (Bergström 1980, 1982 and Fig.3). The information discharged by the information generator is subject to random changes, as is the genetic material in nature. In nature this random element derives from cosmic radiation or chemical errors; in the brain its main source is the brain-stem entropy generator. This random generator of the brain is able to give rise to 'mutations' — or variants — and 'errors' in the more or less stable information structures of the brain. These stable structures, originating from the stable environment, genetic sources, the 'cultural inheritance' (compare 'memes' by biologists), memory etc., are also operative as subjective concepts.

Continuous variation of information is thus possible in the brain, and gives rise to new and unpredictable types of information (Fig.4). The psychological counterpart of this could be called true creativity, in which the new information is unpredictable and cannot be logically deduced from the old. This is a possible explanation of the capriciousness of our thinking and the unexpected production or creation of entirely new ideas.

For the new, randomly-produced matter to take over in the brain, it must compete with other information, especially the old, stable kind. This competition is a genuine struggle for survival, a 'natural selection', analogous to the way new species struggle for survival in nature. The struggle which takes place in the brain is for *synaptic space*, in which the new configuration of information must gain a foothold in order to be reproduced, and thus survive. (For 'physiological competition' in neural systems, see eg. Hyvärinen 1982 and Edelman 1987).

This is a genuinely Darwinian struggle for living space: a case of *neuro-Darwinian selection* (Bergström 1980). Information

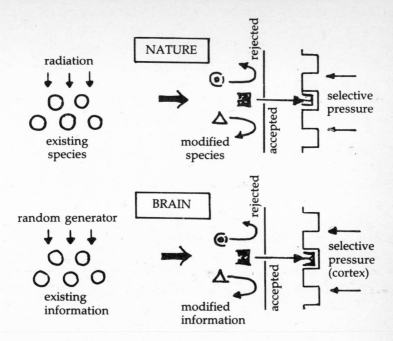

Fig. 3 The Darwinistic principle operating in nature and in the brain.

which has strength and vitality, and has the potential to control the behaviour of the individual successfully, survives the struggle. The criterion of selection is, in the first hand, the social and/or natural environment. The ultimate criterion in the outer environment is the cosmic world. This selective pressure is exerted via the information generator, which represents the environment and also the influence of genetic and cultural inheritance.

The criteria for a new 'idea' to live in the brain and to spread to other brains are thus the same as for a new animal species to continue its life: 1) the ability to fight, 2) the ability to reproduce and copy and 3) the ability to adapt. But in the context of the brain, the Darwinian *natural* selection is only a secondary phenomenon; the primary process occurs in the individual's 'self' which controls the outer behaviour.

The crucial element of the process is the constant battle waged in the brain between various information structures. Psychologically speaking, this may correspond to the competition between thoughts and ideas in our mind. We know that not all thought consists of the logical processing of the old infor-

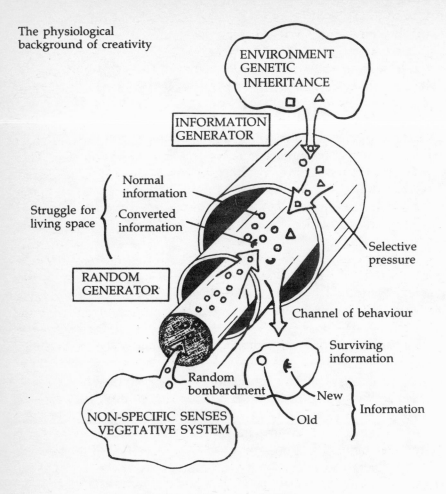

The physiological
background of creativity

ENVIRONMENT
GENETIC
INHERITANCE

INFORMATION
GENERATOR

Normal
information

Struggle for
living space

Converted
information

RANDOM
GENERATOR

Selective
pressure

Channel of behaviour

Surviving
information

Random
bombardment

New

Old

Information

NON-SPECIFIC SENSES
VEGETATIVE SYSTEM

Fig. 4 The physiological background of creativity.

mation, which is the dynamic mode of the information generator. If what happens in our mind is produced by our brain, then the brain has to be able to create new, unforeseeable meanings in our minds.

A world of possibilities

In the brain, in the interaction field between the generators or in what we called the 'self', the two streams of signals from the generators meet. The one coming from the primitive brainstem conveys to this interaction field the potential of the consciousness, and the other one, from the cerebral cortex, conveys the informatory pressure. The first stream acts more or less chaotically and carries disorder, while the other acts deterministically and carries order.

Let us now ask where does a new and unpredictable information or an idea come from. Where is it before it appears? It must be somewhere, if we apply our usual, causal, way of thinking here.

It is apparent that the 'new', before it appears in the 'self', exists in a *potential* form in the signals flowing from the entropy generator and being responsible for the consciousness. This potential form might have some relation to the 'implicate order' of Bohm (1980). There are also new efforts made in looking for hidden structures in entropic and chance-like phenomena.

The 'consciousness potential' of the entropy generator is, physiologically, a 'possibility potential' where all the unrealized but possible ideas and thoughts of our brain and spirit are stored. Since 'possibility' is the original meaning of the word 'tempus' (time) and since it is consciousness that reveals to the 'self' its existence experience (the physiological arousal function), the possibility potential of our consciousness is a 'storehouse' of our existence in time. Here, in the 'conscious-

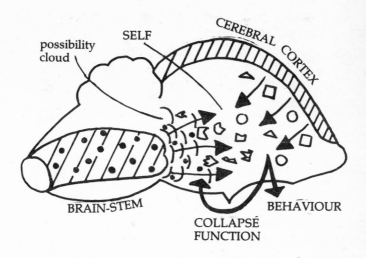

Fig. 5 Circulating information in the networks of the brain (the 'possibility cloud') from which a part is selected for external behaviour of the individual.

ness potential', existence or being is 'devoid of any temporal connotations' (see Prigogine and Stengers, 1984, about this topic).

In the interaction field of the brain the effect of the consciousness appears as a 'cloud of possibilities' (Fig.5). This cloud contains informatory signal material of all kinds, old and newly-created, inherited or acquired, including more or less chaotically or primitively shaped signal streams ('primitive' here refers to MacLeans's 'reptile brain' (1958)).

For the probability function (Bergström 1957) of the brain's mental self and the interactive field there also exists a *collapse function* which forces the probability function to collapse when one possibility is actualized. The mechanism which underlies the collapse phenomenon might well be the 'neuro-Darwinistic' neural selection process which was described above.

Let us assume that the *conscious* behaviour of the brain's self is governed by the *subconscious* probability function. We might have here a neurophysiological mechanism serving as the material background for certain known psychological events. It is possible that Jung's archetypal influences (or Sheldrake's morphic fields) act through this probabilistic process; at least these influences are *consistent* with the view of brain considered here. It is possible that the reason why children often do not feel themselves separated from the environment is because they 'live' in the possibility cloud of their brain and project a kind of 'virtual space' to the outer world. They see the physical space through some kind of 'possibility spectacles', which makes them experiment and play with the things they are surrounded by. In fact, they live many lives at the same time. This ability, also common among artists, is a true creative ability. We can view the brain's ability to create possibilities, or its creative phantasy, as an immense resource. It may be the source of all development and it is our challenge to make proper use of this resource.

The catastrophe function of the brain
The above collapse function of the brain can also be connected with the ability of the brain to create new and unpredictable information: the brain both creates and destroys. How can these two contradictory processes be put together? And what is the purpose of such a 'machinery' which produces new ideas but also builds up catastrophes?

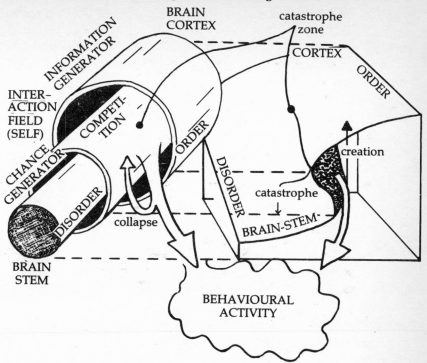

Fig. 6 The 'catastrophe-creativity-cycle' of the brain producing order and disorder.

The catastrophe theory (Thom 1975) has been applied to brain function especially with situations appearing in aggressive behaviour. Here, sudden changes occur in the emotional states which can be explained with this theory. An example is the jump-like change in the state of a threatened animal between escape and attack.

It is possible to use the catastrophe theory also for the collapse function (Fig.6) since it occurs suddenly (in fact at the same time as an action is initiated) and also since it includes a well-describable change of an ordered state into a disordered state in the signal space of the brain. Interestingly, when looked at in this space, creativity, too, is a jump-like process and occurs in the opposite direction: a change of a disordered state to an ordered one. (see Fig.4). The creativity and the catastrophe form a kind of envelope surrounding the interactive field between the generators, the field we called the 'self'.

We may look at this mechanism as a kind of genetically built-in machinery, a catastrophe-creativity machine which is respon-

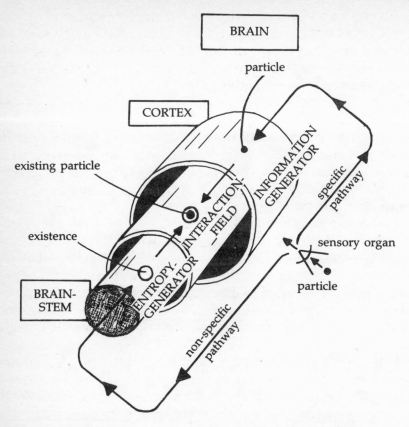

Fig. 7 Observation of an external object by the brain. The combination of the 'objective message' and its 'existence'.

sible for the 'birth' of new ideas and the 'death' of old ones. Presumably catastrophe and creativity are constantly alternating. They regulate the sleep-awakening cycle. This conclusion can be drawn on the basis of a biomathematical study by Pohjavirta (1971) concerning neural transmitter kinetics in the brain. The changes in the transmitter functions exhibited similar jumps in two opposite directions, as seen in Fig. 6 (in the 'catastrophe zone').

The tight union between creation and catastrophe tells us that creativity has a very high price in our life: it has always to be paid for with destruction, the birth with death — always, everywhere.

In fact, there is a structure in the language which mirrors the creativity-catastrophe function (Bergström 1986, 1988) and that is the verb. Transitive verbs always describe a conflict between two states: consider the sentence 'I go out'; it is a conflict between 'being in' and 'being out'. The latter state is created and the former destroyed. Verbs are natural tools in our language for creative activity. But the price is here also the destruction of something.

How the brain interacts with the environment
In order to get an idea of how the brain is connected with its outer environment we shall now look at a situation where the brain *observes an environmental object*. This is an especially interesting situation because observation is a fundamental component in our physical world-view.

Let us consider what happens when the brain of a physicist observes a single particle in an experiment. The particle is acting as a stimulus at the sensory-motor border of the brain (Fig.7). The receptors convey the information along the so-called specific sensory pathway to the corresponding sensory area of the cerebral cortex. Here, a coded message about the particle is represented by a certain signal configuration in a set of neurons.

It is important to note that at this point the message is not yet being observed by the researcher whose brain is in question. For a conscious observation to take place an additional process is needed: the sensory process also has to convey signals representing the particle along the so called non-specific pathway to the brain stem (in fact other routes also exist). Here the signal configuration encoding the spatio-temporal features of the stimuli is *mixed* so that only a message that 'something exists' remains.

At this stage, when there is one message situated in the cerebral cortex and another one in the brain-stem, the brain has no knowledge of the position, time specification or the existence of the particle. It only has a feeling of an 'existence as such' of which it can say that something 'is'. It is similar to the feeling one may have in the morning before waking up fully: a sense that something 'is', without knowing 'what' is, or 'where' or 'when' it is. In order for the brain to observe the existence of the particle, the two messages have to interact. It is only then that an ordinary, empirical *observation* of the external environment has fully taken place.

In summary, *without* the 'existence factor' generated by our brain-stem, the object does not exist for us and cannot be described by us in any way. *With* this factor operating it exists for us and can be described.

There obviously is a strange paradox in the behaviour of the brain in an observation situation: the particle does not 'exist' for the brain as a particle just by being represented in the cortex. In order to exist it needs an additional factor, the existence factor, generated by the brain-stem. But, becoming existent, it disappears as an individual, separate particle. Since consciousness integrates cortical elements into a collective whole, a macrostate, we may say that the price of a particle to become existent for us is the *loss of its singularity* and the necessity of becoming included in a *collective* whole (the existence paradox).

A singular 'one' does not 'exist' for the brain. If it exists, it has to belong to a collective 'whole', say, a number system. The integrated whole is the only phenomenon that we can be aware of. It is also evident that no physical, spatio-temporal specifications apply to the existence factor itself. All such characteristics stem from the cortical, non-conscious part of the observation. This can be interpreted so that the psyche itself (the conscious aspect of which is existence) does not include physical time or locality. These belong to the non-existent, cortical part of the observation.

When the brain is connected with its environment, it must be able to select that information which applies to a particular environmental situation from the vast number of available pieces of information. This calls for an efficient system of selection in order to make it possible to classify information according to its value and meaning in each specific behavioural situation. Such a system is in fact known to exist in the brain (see e.g. Hyvärinen 1982), although its precise location and operation have not yet been established. The control of behaviour can be illustrated by the following expression (Bergström 1980):

$$V \longrightarrow I \longrightarrow E \longrightarrow M \qquad \text{(expression 1)}$$

V = selection (value), I = information (knowledge), E = energy (power) and M = matter (environment)

In our generator model of the brain, the selective system is situated in the interactive field between the generators. Thus all that has been said above about this field, of the 'self', applies to this selective system and to the selective or value capacity inherent in it.

The most important aspect of the value capacity is that physiologically it cannot be considered as information since it controls information: it is able to place information into scales of preference. It seems that in every behavioural situation the brain sorts out its informatory resources and uses that part which is considered as the most useful for the situation in question. But since the brain knows this only with a certain probability it places additional informatory 'programs' in second, third, and so on, position in case the first one happened to fail in achieving the wanted result.

In the brain function there are yet other signs pointing to the possibility of the existence of a neural 'force' inherent in the value capacity, the nature of which is unknown to us. One finding comes from Sperry's observations (see eg. 1973) on the 'pictorial', 'holistic' and 'simultaneous' type of processing in the brain which has been assumed to be connected with our aesthetic abilities. These abilities, again, resemble evaluative thinking according to art researchers (eg. Ansermet 1973, on music) and also concepts such as morality, ethics (see also Bergström 1988) and emotions. There is one 'meaning' or value foremost in our life as a species, and that is *survival* in the frame of natural selection.

The brain's action has the purpose of optimizing the selective pressure of the external environment so that the new-born ideas may persist in the brain. The selective pressure has been manipulated by us in many ways by our having created a cultural and technical sphere around us. To this belongs also the active part of our scientific experimentation. We are thus helping our own survival.

But again, we have another environment *inside*, in which we also have to survive. The 'self' has to live between two environments, the outer and the inner, and so it has to act in both.

The possibility of the brain's self to act towards its inner, mental psychological world puts Darwin's theory of natural selection into a new light: The dynamics of evolution is determined not only by the survival of the fittest in the selective pressure of our outer, surrounding world but also by an *overall survival*, including not only the fittest but also the weakest, in the 'holistic, collecting pressure' of our inner, psychic world.

In fact, Darwin also thought that a unifying force operated

in evolution, but he used this primarily to account for the fact that different evolutionary forms are collected into classes and species.

The new type of survival dynamics we proposed above is realized in the integrative and unifying capacity of the brain-stem generator, which physiologically determines our consciousness. The 'holistic pressure' does not separate fitter from weaker, nor refuse some and accept others, but merely collects together (note the 'possibility cloud' in the brain) and accepts all.

This activity of the brain towards its deeper, purely mental regions or towards the inner environment of the self shows itself also in the outer behaviour. It exhibits itself in a greater consideration in charity, love and other 'holistic' and collective characteristics around one (also stressed by Wallace 1890). It also includes an open mind for 'mysticism' and 'belief'.

In this manner the brain has the ability to 'manipulate' its inner environment as well. Probably the human brain is most developed in this ability, but to some extent all brains possess it — especially species living in social groups.

We may also have, in the brain functions described above, a firm ground to believe that peace in the form of a collecting, unifying and holistic activity in our society is possible after all. In fact, our one-sided trust in the Darwinian theory has been an obstacle against this kind of belief: neurophysiology may help us here!

Behind the axioms
Let us now briefly consider what kind of brain process could underlie the selective or value capacity.

It is only when value has been selected or created that the logical apparatus of the information generator is put into action for a consolidation (confirmation) of the created value. The value acts as a kind of *axiomatic force* from which the logic of the behaviour is developed. But behind these axioms (values) is a world operating with the irrational laws of fight, competition and collection. This is the brain's self, and it is in this world that we must search for the process behind our value capacity.

In order to describe the world, let us define a new quantity for neurophysiological purposes. We could describe this quantity with the world 'enaxy' (Bergström 1986), coming from the greek word $\varepsilon\, \nu\, \alpha\, \xi\, \iota\, \alpha$, meaning 'something which produces or results in value' (or has value). This quantity was denoted in expression (1) with V (value), and it describes a change in the capacity of information (entropy) to perform effects on the energy. In order to describe fully a behavioural phenomenon, we have to define its mass (matter), its energy, its entropy (information) and its 'enaxy' (value).

The future of the brain society

The new vision of man and his behaviour which is given by modern brain research stems from the fact that there exists an entropy source providing the brain with a chance-like activity. This changes our view of our mental behaviour, which we have thought to be a more or less logical process with certain errors and disturbances in some special situations and stages of individual development, as in childhood and during old age. This view is incorrect and should be revised according to the physiology of the brain.

What the classical view has taught us is that we are rational beings and that the highest mode of this rationality is the one implied by the scientific view about man and his world. Here we seem to have forgotten that there are other categories of human performance than those based upon observed facts which we should take into account. But the classical view has already had its effects on us, which has led to the present type of brain society which is an 'information society'.

The present society, just like each individual human being, has evolved from a more primitive stage. In the individual the organic and energetic level is maximized first, then the informatory control, and last, after puberty, the value level (approximately, at the same age the society gives us the right to vote: a sign of maturity is the ability to evaluate the social situation). In our modern society we are leaving behind the stage in history when the primary task was the investigation and maximization of energy resources; instead, we are now engaged in maximizing our information resources. We seem to believe that information is all that we need, and do not understand that we should develop our value system.

Therefore our educational systems and institutions are set up to maximize the information content of the brain of students in schools and universities. Our philosophy of education is information-centered. But an information-centered view of man neglects the importance of the value-capacity. This may have disastrous effects especially in the education of children, since the brain at this stage may not develop the cells necessary for the mental activity of evaluation.

It is possible that whole generations of children will develop a deficiency which can be called *value-invalidity*. This deficiency means a lack of ability to see things as a whole and to evaluate them, to see alternatives and select among them. The possibility to grasp the wholeness of a situation is a prerequisite for the full understanding of the meaning contained in the selection and evaluation situation and for getting an insight into it. People who suffer from such a deficiency are dangerous especially if they possess great amounts of information and energy (capital and power) since they cannot use these resources adequately: an inhuman technology results.

Thus, an information-centered view can be seen as the cause of many problems we are faced with in modern society: inhuman technology, pollution and disturbance of ecological balance, danger of primitive and destructive energy-type war, mental imbalance and aggression. My intuition is that immaturity at the moral and ethical level of behaviour control is part of the deficiency of the value capacity of the brain.

A direct effect of such a deficiency is that the integrity of society is disturbed and we no more have a sense for the right values or the meaning of our life. Also, and especially, we are no more able to produce new values for the control of the rich amounts of information and energy we are about to be in possession of. The lack of this ability 'devaluates' our information resources, which become useless. This is a true sign of a deficiency in 'enaxy', the force inherent in value: the information about nature produced by science is not effective for its original purpose, the protection of nature; it thus has no value.

My feeling is that if we are to have a healthy relationship to the world we have to abandon our individuality and 'melt' into society and nature. In this way the world constitutes an integrated whole, in which we are not a 'part' or member (see above about micro- and macrostates) but in which we are only 'it', the collective. This means that ultimately we *are* humanity, living and non-living. This is what the meaning of our life is.

We can understand why information at present is considered to be so important in our world. It is probably because there was a time, when we did not understand our environment and when our unknown surroundings posed a danger for human beings and evoked a fear in us. At this time our brains had to protect themselves against the fear of this unknown with an 'antibody', which is information (Fig. 8). Now, in spite of the fact that protecting ourselves against the dangers of nature is not the central concern of our life anymore, we still continue with the storing of information in our brains so that it is the only prevailing education in school teaching. Just as the hunting instinct is still active in some people, even if it is not needed anymore, there is an 'information instinct' still active in us which is not a prerequisite for our life at the present time.

We can expect that a human race overloaded with pure knowledge and lacking the value-capacity and a sense of meaning cannot prevail in natural selection. The future 'mental species' of human beings has to be a 'value-species' (Fig. 9), which has the necessary vital, collecting and creative force to select a safe way of living for us. The 'info-species' will not survive

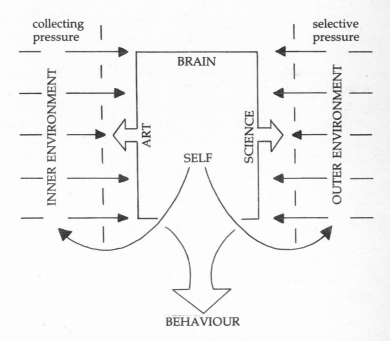

Fig. 8 Natural selection and collection operating in the brain's self. The neurophysiological background of art and science.

because it suffers from 'value-invalidity'.

At present, there is another unknown which poses a danger, and this is the unknown of our 'inner world', our psyche. It evokes also fear: fear of inner 'demons', which we do not understand. We have to protect ourselves with an 'antibody'. This time information does not help, since the unknown is not of spatio-temporal form. It is of a more subtle shape of 'wholeness' and something which is 'existence' and 'everlasting' and 'everywhere'.

The 'antibody' here is the arts: music, painting, literature etc. The arts protect us against the inner unknown and the great artists of each time with their creations protect us from the demons of our inner environment. We do not sing only for pleasure, nor do we compose only for beauty; we also sing

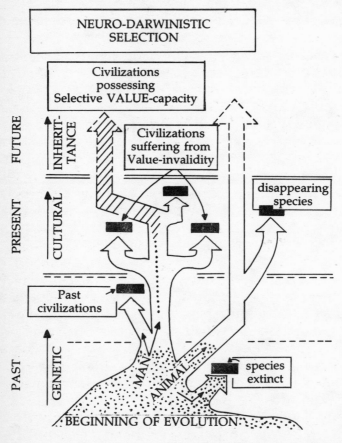

Fig. 9 The 'neuro-Darwinistic selection' and genetic and cultural inheritance.

to our children in order to save them from their inner fear; we sing psalms in order to protect ourselves from the demons of unknown death. Great composers create music against the fear of their time; the young create heavy metal rock music in order to chase away the fear of an uncertain future in a primitive way, like primitive tribes chase away dangerous reptiles and beasts in the jungle by scrambling pots. Correspondingly, science protects us from the unknown or the demons of our outer environment nature. There is here a 'symmetry of fear' (see Fig. 8), which is a reflection of the symmetry of the self as given by the structure of the brain.

With this symmetry of our self, we are able not only to change our external selective pressure but also our internal 'collective pressure', in order to survive. There operates not only the 'natural selection', emphasized by Darwin, but also a 'divine selection', with collecting forces acting upon us from the deep unknowns of our soul.

Already the Greeks (Anaximander etc.) had a similar insight into the basic structure of the whole universe, a structure which is congruent with the brain structure: *Apeiron*, the unlimited, *Peras*, the limit and the *Peperasmenon*, the limited, the latter resulting from the interaction of the first two. In the brain, too, there is in the brain-stem the unlimited (entropic, conscious potential, the amount or cardinality, the existence itself), in the cerebral cortex the limit (negentropic, informatory process, the order or ordinality, the non-existent limiting material) and finally, resulting from the interaction of these two, the *self* in which the unlimited conscious and existence potential appear in the limited space-time form of human behaviour.

And in fact, in the smallest atoms, as well as in the big stars, there always seems to exist the same basic design (Bergström 1982a): innermost there is a nucleus with non-ordered, entropic power, and outermost there are ordered negentropic shells and structures. And also in our basic theories, such as Cantor's set theory, there is a non-ordered fundament, the cardinality, and an annex, the ordinality. And in physics, there is entropy, and on top of it the ordered negentropic phenomena. It seems as if the same architect had been at work everywhere. Or, do we merely see the structure of our own brain everywhere? Is it so that wherever we look we leave behind us a 'brainprint', just as the thief during the night leaves a 'fingerprint' after him, without knowing it.

In Eastern thought all this is represented in the principle of Yin and Yang, the two principles doomed to be together, and yet separate: a principle which can never be satisfied, but which constantly *wants* to be satisfied. In the brain's core this will appear as a non-directed consciousness, and in the cortex as a space-time-directed attention which is evoked by the brain-stem arousal. This 'will' seems to be the meaning everywhere, within our brain, as well as in the outside world where this brain lives and where it creates and destroys ideas and produces new values which are a precondition for our future existence. In doing this the brain has to ask the question 'Why?' and not only the question 'How?' Understood in this way our brain is a living and meaningful brain and not merely a physico-chemical system of the type represented by the present 'value-invalid' scientific view.

The view of our brain presented here may serve as a starting point for a new understanding of man in his world. The logical mode of brain function belonging to the scientific method of today has to be combined with the creative mode belonging to the values and to the selective and collective ability of the brain.

In as much as the theologian in his 'theory of God' looks at the greatest wholeness, so the physicist looks at the smallest non-divisible particles: the two of them stand with their backs against each other — like a Janus face — looking in opposite directions and not understanding each other's language. And in between stands the ordinary man, confused and trying to bring these two together. This is the paradox of today.

Literature

Ansermet, E., *Die Grundlagen der Musik*, R. Piper & Co, Munich, 1973.

Bergström, R. M., 'Die Mitberücksichtigung des Subjekts im Sinnesphysiologischen Messakt, *Acta Phys*, Scand, Suppl. 41, 1957.

Bergström, R. M., Über das Wahrnehmen der Zeit als Wahrnehmen der Bewegung. Ann. Acad. Sci. Fenn. Ser. A. V. Medica. 106/2. 1-25. 1964.

Bergström, R. M., 'An Entropy Model of the developing Brain', *Developmental Psychobiology* 2(3), 139-152, 1969.

Bergström, R. M., 'Neural micro- and macrostates', *Advances in Psychobiology*, Vol. 1, pp. 53-93, Eds. G. Newton and A. H. Riesen, 1972.

Bergström, R. M., 'Entropic properties of the neural signal space', *Proc. of the XII Meeting of Soc. Physiol*, Pol, Gdansk, 1975.

Bergström, R. M., *On the Mind and Physiology of the Brain*, (in Finnish). WSOY Juva, 1978.

Bergström, R. M., 'Brain physiological aspects on behaviour and communication', Report of EASE 80, *The Finnish Association for Special Education*, 1980.

Bergström, R. M., 'Brain, behaviour and aging', *Geron XXIII Year Book*, 1980-81.

Bergström, R. M., 'The Brain, Alcohol and Creativity', (in Finnish with English summary), *Alkoholipolitiikka 6*, 1982.

Bergström, R. M., 'Neurodynamics and development of behaviour', *Tutkijaliiton julk*, sarja 18, 1982a.

Bergström, R. M., 'Mind-Brain interaction: consciousness as a neural macrostate', *Finnish Artificial Intelligence Symp*, Vol. 1, pp.42-63, 1986.

Bergström, R. M., 'Music and Living Brain', *Acta Philosophica Fennica*, Vol. 43. (*Essays on the Philosophy of Music*, Eds. Rantala, V., Rowell, L., Tarasti, E.) 1988.

Bergström, R. M., and Nevanlinna, O., 'An entropy model of primitive neural systems,' *Intern. J. Neurosci*, Vol. 4, pp.171-173, 1972.

Bergström, R. M. and Hari, R., 'An Application of set theoretical concepts to neurophysiology', *Proc. of the II National Meeting on Biophysics and Biotechnology*, Espoo, 1976.

Bohm, D., *Wholeness and the Implicate order*, Routledge & Kegan Paul, London, 1980.

Bohm, D. and Peat F. D., *Science, Order and Creativity*, Bantam Books, Toronto, 1987.

Brillouin, L., *Science and information theory*, Academic Press, New York, 1963.

Descartes, R., 'Meditationes de prima philosophia,' in *Ausgewählte Schriften*, Verlag Philipp Reclam jun, Leipzig, 1980.

Eccles, J. C. *The effect of silent thinking of the cerebral cortex in the brain-mind problem*, Ed. B. Gulyas, Leuven University Press, Van Gorcum Assen/Maastricht, 1987.

Edelman, G. M., *Neural Darwinism — The theory of neuronal group selection*, Basic Books, Inc. Publishers, New York, 1987.

Hensel, H., *Allgemeine Sinnesphysiologie, Hautsinne, Geschmack,*

Geruch, Springer-Verlag, Berlin, 1966.

Hyvärinen, J., *The parietal Cortex of Monkey and Man*, Springer-Verlag, Berlin, 1982.

Jung, C. G., *Analytical psychology: its theory and practice*, Routledge & Kegan Paul, London, 1968.

Lindroos, F., Riittinen, L., Veilahti, J., Tarkkonen, L., Multanen, H., Bergström, R., M., 'Overstimulation. Occipital/Somesthetic Cerebral Cortical Depth, and Cortical Asymmetry in Mice', *Devel. Psychobiol*, 17(5), pp.547-554, 1984.

MacLean, P., 'Contrasting Functions of Limbic and Neocortical Systems of the Brain and their Relevance to Psychophysiological Aspects of Medicine', *Am. J. of Med.*, Vol. 25, No. 4., pp. 611-626, 1958.

Pohjavirta, A., 'Model, for the dynamics of large instabilities in dense neuronal nets', Dissertation, Techn. Univ, Helsinki, 1976.

Popper, K., Eccles, J., *The Self and its Brain*, Springer Verlag, Berlin, 1977.

Prigogine, I., 'Order through fluctuation', in *Evolution and Consciousness*, Eds. Jantsch, E. and Waddington, C. H., Addison-Wesley Publ. Co, London, 1976.

Prigogine, I, Stengers, I., *Order out of chaos*, William Collins Sons & Co. Ltd, Glasgow, 1984.

Reenpää, Y., *Allgemeine Sinnesphysiologie*, Klostermann, Frankfurt, 1962.

Sperry, R., 'Lateral Specialization in the surgically separated hemispheres', in *The neurosciences: third study program*, M.I.T. Press, Cambridge, Mass., 1973.

Thom, R., *Structural stability and morphogenesis*, (translated by D.H. Fowler) W. A. Benjamin Inc, 1975.

Wallace, A. R., *Darwinismen — en framstellning af teorin om det naturliga urvalet*, Fahlcrantz & Co, Stockholm, 1890.

Making Meaning
DAVID SHAINBERG

Consider the following experiments:

> Meltzoff and Borton blindfolded three-week-old infants and gave them one of two different pacifiers to suck on. One pacifier had a spherical-shaped nipple, the other had nubs protruding from its surface. After the baby had some experience feeling (by touching) the nipple with its mouth they took the blindfolds off and set the two nipples side by side. The baby looked more at the one it had just sucked. (Stern, D., 1985, p.47).

This experiment suggests that the baby formed a notion of the whole nipple out of the touch experience and that he was able to use that notion to identify the nipple of choice when he saw it rather than touched it. Apparently he knew that the nipple was constructed in a certain way. With that knowledge he could then know the overall characteristics of the object and he could use his visual sense to determine the identity of the preferred nipple when he went to choose again. Such discrimination points out the baby's capacity to make a meaning. It is interesting too that once the baby had made the meaningful construction of the whole he could then, within that knowledge of the whole, perform a cross-modal transfer of information. That is, he transformed an experience of touch into visual knowing. Thus the meaning seems to provide him with the structure to process information of one mode of sensing into data that has relevant connection with other data. Second:

> Infants can be trained to suck to make something happen. It is done by placing a pacifier with an electronically-bugged nipple — that is, one with a pressure transducer inside it in the infant's mouth. The transducer is hooked up to the starter

mechanism of a tape recorder or slide carousel, so that when
the infant sucks at a certain specified rate the recorder goes
on or the carousel turns over a new slide. In that way the infant
controls what he hears or sees by maintaining some rate of
sucking. Sucking was used to determine whether infants are
especially interested in the human voice in preference to other
sounds of the same pitch and loudness. The infants did so
prefer. There are other such experiments to show that infants
will suck to bring the picture into focus (Stern, D., 1985, p.39).

These events suggest that infants, with their very primitive
and undeveloped nervous systems, already seek an order in
their experiencing. Perhaps it is incorrect to say the infant
'seeks' as that might imply a subject self that has some idea
of what it wants to achieve. It seems more to the point that
the basic matter of the biological system is inherently acting,
'choosing', a form of order, a direction we call meaning. Meaning in this case is a sense of a coherent whole that the infant
has already constructed and attempts to match. The infant system seems to develop awareness of such wholes and makes
distinctions between one whole and another. In the first experiment the infant's conception of the whole seems to grow from
the 'capacity to know' such wholes. In the second it seems
that the infant prefers a known order, a focus that he has come
to appreciate. He has the capacity 'to choose' that particular
whole.

We shouldn't really be so astounded to find this order and
ordering in the infant, it is after all present everywhere in the
universe. If we look around at the cosmos, at nature, and at
all the biological systems we find there is an order wherever
we turn. In fact this order in nature is a given. It forms the
basis of all life. This order is evident in the shape of the infant.
He has two arms, two legs, a coherent metabolism, etc. This
order (and ordering) is there when the infant looks at the nip-
ples because looking is itself a part of the order of relationship when it establishes connections. But also the order is there
in the fact that the nipple is made of material which is in some
structure and that man has constructed it in the shape which
imitates the natural form nipple. It is an organized form and
therefore order. We also find form (active forming of connections, making order) in the human voices which the infant has
already heard.

Thus life is whole-making, witness the various species, the

individual autonomous organisms; witness the plants, and the various solar systems. Human beings display the action of whole making in the shapes of their bodies, the metabolism of their system, the activities of perceiving and other aspects of their life. It could be said that the various modes of perceiving establish connections of human beings to other human beings and to the world. Establishing those connections makes for, among other things, the creation of larger wholes of language, culture, and government, forms of relationship which make wholes. Their creation displays the making of meaning which is basic to human life.

In the process of making larger wholes the smaller units are combined. But in order to combine these smaller units they, the basic elements of existence, must be appreciated as wholes which are unified in and of themselves. How a human being comes to an awareness of such basic elements is difficult to state because the process is undoubtedly a complex of many processes. On the one hand there is the movement of perception which makes wholes; but also the structures of nature have inherent organizations, invariant structures. The tree, for example, is organized into a form with certain characteristics. So is the horse, the dog, and other animals and plants. These invariant structures in nature are also present in the structure of our nervous system, and are also ordered into specific forms. There is a relationship, perhaps we should call it resonance, between what is there in nature and what we find in our instruments, vision, taste, hearing, etc. Everywhere we turn there is an organization into whole forms and this is the meaningful way in which matter is assembled. As part of our further organization of these perceptions we give the unique and nonunique wholes names and that places them in relationship to other forms that have names. Thus things connect to other things through language, they have a relationship and a meaning that we identify as culture, and culture, as well as ideas, forms into unified constructions with certain specific forms.

The discovery that our bodies are one separate entity establishes the meaning of being a person in the context of relationship to other persons. This awareness spontaneously arises in an infant out of the continuum of his sensations. These sensations, as we have noted, are the response of the nervous system to the various invariant or ordered forms in the environment. But it could also be said that sensations articulate the relationship between these invariances of the nervous system and those invariances represented by any form in nature. Sensations are the registration of differences. So they give information which Bateson (1972) defined as differences which make a difference.

The whole-making that occurs in establishing that we are our one body is then an ordering of differing perceptions: we 'see' in the mirror that our body is one thing over time. We see that other people's bodies are similar to ours and that they remain the same over time. All this we garner with our visual, tactile, proprioceptive and other sensations. We note that our body is different from the other bodies in our environment. Through our appreciation of the arms, legs, trunk, and face that hang together we connect experientially and we know that our body is the same as these other bodies but also that we, like those others, occupy the separate space. We have many different feelings in many different contexts, yet these feelings have a common element, the invariant element, of being registered as one event in our body.

Another element in the realization that our body is separate is the factor of memory. With different perceptions there is not only the establishment of a memory of what has occurred but also there is simultaneously the arousal of memories of previous experiences. Although the memories are of different events they all also have this invariant aspect of being known as personal experience. They are known to be constituted by elements of events in this one body that we recognize as having the common piece with other experiences known in this way. Correlations are made between any current experience and the past and as a result the conception develops that not only are these sensations occurring as a registering of being, they are also seemingly events of one body, one self-entity that exists through time 'having' these experiences. The context is created as a life of 'me' or 'I' and it connects all of these events.

That is to say that first there is a state which we best describe as an ongoing eventing, sensations which are the registering of relationships and appreciations of whole forms. There are memories which happen out of both sensations and the creation of a whole, and there are memories of the process of being which the organism 'happens through'. Out of all this there is a change of concept. First, there is simply the experience of these sensation events and then the process shifts into an ordered conception in which the organism starts 'thinking of itself' as both being and owning its sensations. Being and owning sensation builds up a notion that a thing that can do such things is an entity, a self, that is separate. It also, in a subtle way, separates this self from those elements which constitute its process. Perhaps this process is further stimulated when in the course of human development the child is constantly addressed by name. When care-taking persons emphasize that the child is an entity, this self, with this name, which is doing this or that behaviour, they support the gradually developing idea that there is a separate self which is different from its experience and different from others.

This self is seen as having these experiences rather than being constituted by these experiences. Certain physical qualities, certain ways of responding, and certain images establish who and what this self is and can do. These elements and many others unite to construct the identity of self. The process of experience is felt in part to be creating the self and in part as happening to the self which exists through time.

The formation of the sense of our body and our self is an example then of *making a meaning*. It is a meaning that grows out of that grounded active ordering of sensuous presence that the basic form of self is made. How we feel in an ever-changing world of experiencing is established in the process of making body and self. When sensuous experience is lived, known, and felt to be a harmonious part of living capacity we come to have a sense of our body and being as something that grows inherently from experience. The sensations are known as something to trust but more deeply 'our capacity' to find forms that connect and work in the world is established through the harmonious operation of such experiencing; then we trust our capacity to make meaning in all the moments and situations that make up life. When such harmony exists between self-identity and sensuous experience the self that emerges is aware of the relationships between the sensations and the notion of self that emerges moment by moment out of the sensation. It is apparent to such a self that it is created out of the events of being and that its notions of owning and having these meaning-making events is another order of experience.

The relationship of this body-self to the world and to other bodies emerges and changes within limits imposed by the constraints of given structures. Trusting to sensations conveys the nature of connections in the context of relationships. In this trust we depend on their inherent spontaneous action. This spontaneous action by the nervous system and general ordering of biological process explores the ways things of the present are connected to old experience and other aspects of the present life.

More often than not, however, we observe that human beings are particularly prone to lose the spontaneous creative meaning-making. We see that we become fixed in modes of behaviour which are governed by memories, ideas, and concepts. We do not depend on our spontaneous creative capacity to organize new events. We do not make meaning in an ongoing manner. We look to the past mode of behavior and those past modes are plans of behavior that have worked in the past to bring order and pleasure. So on meeting a new moment we look for similarities to some earlier situation and relate the new moment to those past times rather than engaging that moment from the sensations that it brings up at that present time. That is to say we depend on our self-identity and its ideas of meaning that have arisen in previous experience. That self has fixed notions of what is right for the self and what is possible for it to feel and know. With these rules stored as a program of how to be, the self protects itself from the uncertainty that comes when we approach a new situation without preconceived notions. The self seems to 'think' it knows before events, the meaning of events. Our question is then why do so many of us lose this capacity to make meaning? Why do we fall into habits and ruts that lean on old meanings rather than embrace the moment? Why are we so afraid to discover the meanings in our lives at any moment?

In the human mind thought is the extension of the process of perception that orders those perceptions into concepts. The mind uses these ideas to guide it in future behavior. The ideas form a matrix which structures the relationship among the perceptions. For example when we first see a bird we form notions of the general characteristic of birds. Gradually we form a concept of what a bird is, and from there we often take parts of the birds we see and compare them to the concepts of bird that we have in mind. From there we determine that the parts of the things we have sighted represent the whole we have come to call bird. Thus the meaning of those particulars is bird.

Or we might find that while certain new perceptions indeed do match the bird concept there are others that do not so fit and we determine that it is necessary to revaluate what we see. Perhaps these are entities that are like birds in some ways and not like birds in others; or perhaps the things we see are a different variety of bird and we have too narrow a concept of what a bird is. We move from fragmentary perception to the idea of bird and back to perception.

In the sphere of the objects in the world the concepts that we develop, as for example with the notion of what a bird is, are no problem because a bird does remain through time as a flying phenomena that has two wings, a tail, a beak etc. The basic structure remains the same and from it we can enlarge our notions of bird to include the different varieties of the type of animal we are considering. We could say the same for trees, rocks etc. The different particulars have the same basic shape and the differences can be compared to the deviations from the standard models.

But there is a difference in human relationships where the process is always changing at a very rapid rate. A human being in relationship with another human being is called upon to change and respond to changes in relationship. There is always the possibility in human relationships to make new moves which change the structure as a result of the events that occur. As a result the fixation into any particular image of the relationship stultifies the situation. It denies the new feelings that arise and as a result blocks the changes and the responsiveness to the present changes in feeling that occur. Such fixation creates a lack of attention, a blandness or lack of faith in the importance of the ongoing relating process of human beings.

The tendency to fix on images and thoughts comes about in part because of the nature of the human nervous system and its particular development in human infants. As we noted, under the best of conditions the child might be able to develop a faith in the process of the brain to meet the new moments and to make meaning as the need arises. To think, that is, 'standing on his feet'. Again, it probably would be more accurate in such instances to say the brain develops a faith and remains capable of such direct participation. It sees and understands relationship and spontaneously appreciates its position in these relationships.

A young child lives in an uncertain and developing world. He responds, reacts and resonates in his engagement with the world but his co-ordination and integration is quite imperfect and he is dependent on those around him to assist him in his interactions with the diversity of the environment. This incomplete development decreases gradually but as we know the operations of the nervous system are sensitive and thus are more or less always incomplete and available for new movements. In the young child though the state of incompleteness and sensitivity is ever present as so many new perceptions are flowing in his life at all times. When the capacities for language and thought appear they provide a new tool for manipulating this uncertainty. They enable the child to move into the human domain and this provides an avenue to make connections to the whole. Language and thought are ways to make meaning and to some extent their way is to enable the child to connect to fixed meanings as they exist in human community. The community offers many set notions of what experience is and what things mean so the language and thought encourage a kind of deterioration in the child's sensitivity to his own meaning-making process.

Thought and language are actions in the nervous system which express the ways things connect. But they are also stored in memory as are images and concepts. When human beings depend on memory they bring in ideas and ways to engage the moment that do not call for the active thrust of making meaning. In such action we do not operate from the active thrust that the body had generated in direct sensuous motoric perception. The direct perception occurs but these actions and images are referred to the models of the past that are stored in memory. There are associations of one thought to another, recognition of one perception fitting with thought and then relationships of thoughts, and comparisons between thoughts. All these processes guide the ordering activity of being away from the active process of connecting to a more passive process of using connections based in memory. Thus thought and language, the process of thinking and developing connections, arrived at before the immediate moment, protect the brain from the vicissitudes of perceived events but from such a questionable good fortune the brain is cultivated to lose the ability to meet the moment as it applies past results to the present.

When a child is anxious, or for some reason does not have

a secure sense of his capacity to meet the moment or to experience his own flow of making meaning out of his sensation, these new abilities to use thought and language help him avoid the anxiety and meaning in the moment. For example, the child senses that he operates as the one body and as the self that seems to repeat itself in each moment. Then that concept of self and of body become forms in consciousness which assume a static and fixed identity and the child depends on his self-concept and his memory/idea of being his body. Rather than constructing his sense of what is happening fresh in the moment, the child comes into the life process with set ideas of who and what he is. Thought and language, and concept formation, helps him because he doesn't have to remake himself every moment and it gives him some security from day to day to depend on who he is. But at another level he comes to feel he can depend on the thoughts and memories of his self rather than on his sensuous participation in the day to day experience that is his life.

When the child is faced with uncertainty in his family he may, for example, find that certain action brings about an ordering of the discomfort. It might not have been action that arose out of his present moment or his own sense of what he was registering as important for his own movement as an organism in the world, but it was action that had the meaning of doing what the mother or father needed and thus made the situation less anxiety-provoking for him. It is a subtle distinction we are making here, but at the core of the child's perception is the understanding that what is important is to be determined in terms of the other. He knows that this situation is uncomfortable and that he is out of order with the context in which he lives and that he can bring about relief of his anxiety through the other. The meaning in this situation is in terms of the other and is not related to how he feels in his relationship in the world.

In one set of experiments a mother was first encouraged to support her child's enthusiastic interest with a very positive response and when she did the child was visibly able to go on with his involvement. Then the mother was told to be only half-hearted in her response to the child's interest and when that happened the child looked as if he didn't understand what was happening. Perhaps he felt he had been deceived (Stern, D., 1985, p.150). Such experiments point out how important the mother's response is to underline the child's responses. When one watches a young child develop it is incredible to see how he looks to the mother for the validation or creation of meaning. He might for example feel something cold and then look to the mother to see if it is right for him to have this experience. That is should he be afraid and cry, or can he see it as something to laugh or integrate with. These experiments also show how different it is for a child when his context favors his spontaneous unfolding interest. He is able to follow those sensuous events and make meaning. But when the situation in which he lives does not fittingly support his making of meaning he adjusts to make meaning in ways which organize the whole in more harmonious ways. For many children this means learning to form a meaning which solidifies the anxiety and demands of the care-taker. In such situations, however, the child comes to feel that he is unable to deal with the uncertainty of the sensuous experiences of living in his environment and he must assuage them. As a result of this 'successful' development in his human relationships the child forms an idea about how to be with other people that leads to his thinking that certain behaviour will provide pleasure and safety in life. If he remembers this and acts accordingly he will not feel the uncertainty or anxiety that he has felt when he simply depended on his ability to meet the moment. And he will have moved another step away from the development of his capacity to make meaning.

It is also true that under such difficult circumstances the child makes a meaning of human relationships. He finds that one set of behavior produces comfort because it fits with other people's needs and that other behavior gives pain because it is discordant with the other's needs. So he concludes that it is always better to act the way that gives pleasure rather than the way that gives pain. The nature of the behavior that gives pleasure is governed by the structure of his family where more often than not the individuals are more interested in their needs than his. Often this leads to a system that opposes his listening to his particular rhythms and desires and forces him to make his meaning 'to-fit-in-with-the-system'. He finds that if he doesn't act in certain ways he is left alone to feel the normal insecurity and anxiety that growing into his new being entails. He gets no support and it can easily happen that his sensations do not order into meaningful whole relationship with others. This is experienced as anxiety and it moves the child to order himself in ways that are not disordered. He tries hard to find the right technique for living which will relieve the pain. There is gradually a sense that he must make the right moves to find the right way to be in his family.

The child who is faced with such a situation doesn't get support to go through the tensions that spontaneous flowing sensations involve. Sensuous experience does not automatically flow into smooth order, it may go through different orderings and connections with uncertainty as to how it will come into form. A child needs support to try out his experiencing and may even need real help and patience to survive the awkward trials and errors going through such making of meaning. Instead of such help the difficult family situation makes it uncomfortable for the child to go through such moments. Then the child develops the ideas of what is right to fix the uncertainty with which he is faced and orders the uncertainty of his sensuous moments directly into the order he seeks without going through the process of practice that develops a capacity to make meaning. Perhaps the facility of his thought and language seduces him and it is so much easier for him to form concepts about what should be, and applying these immediately solves the problems of uncertainty brought on by direct experience. Perhaps he senses an easy way out of the anxiety by merging with what his family needs. In any event what is most pertinent for our discussion is that the human being becomes dependent on his thought processes and loses touch with his meaning-making.

It is characteristic, for example, that the child creates one or another concept, an ideal, of what would bring pleasure in the human situation he encounters in his family. Then he generalizes this operational judgment to include all human relationships and assumes that he should act in the ways called for by that program with all human beings. As part of such an assumption he realizes he must become and be a certain type of person. Thus he moulds himself into a creature who would act in those ways because they relieved the fears and anxieties he felt in the world. He feels annoyed if he feels anything that shows he isn't that way. Or he is all the time feeling he should be a certain way. In a very strong way his concept of what is right is what guides his life. The idea, the concept of this self, what Horney (1950) called an idealized image, guides what he is because he feels driven to become the safe condition proposed by his ideas. Eventually the various characteristics which he has found work best toward reducing his anxiety in the world are combined into an idealized image of himself and that image becomes the self he feels he must be. His being, that is his sensuous experience, is governed by a thought and he does not live from or in the process of making meaning. On the contrary he lives as if the meaning is in the ideal and the solutions to the uncertainty of being are given in the plan of what he already knows to be 'right'.

An adult person under the influence of his ideal about how to be does not attend to his capacity to meet other human beings in new ways. He relates to them as if they were what his thought governs. He acts with them according to old form and meaning, and acts out of that conceptualization of the whole. In this way the making of meaning in the mind is not something that changes or that grows from any active engagement in the world. It is a meaning that is brought from the past or is carried around as the way to be and the human being, living from the isolation of his vision of life, imposes the meaning on the world.

But it could also be argued that what we are presenting here is basic to nature. It could for example be said that the repeated use of memory to guide the present is another example of nature's way. Nature is constantly repeating structure. Thought can be seen as operating like DNA in that it takes the matter of perception and fits it into old forms. DNA guides matter into programs of becoming that are repeats of genetic structures. Those genetic structures to be sure represent combinations of the old forms and thus create new shapes and patterns out of combinations of old elements. In a sense our question is how caught is the human brain in the material habits of nature, in the old ways of forming in nature, and how far is it capable of going beyond the material structures of which it is constituted. Is the combination of the matter of the nervous system in interaction with the variety of forms in the universe a possibility for new and creative behaviors that goes beyond the conservativeness of thought? To what degree is the human brain able to go beyond its material constitution?

The fact is that the human mind tends to fall away from making meaning into the use of old meanings or into the combination of old meanings. Thought and memory, often expressed in concepts, are the guides for most of human living. Active possibilities that arise in the present are constantly bypassed or lost in human life. Human beings follow the dictates of the programs but these programs are not developed out of the current making of meaning. Most human beings, caught by the operations of thought, live their lives to confirm the ideas of their system rather than to discover their meaning as it develops. They find relationships, work, and entertainment which completes their idea of what they should be doing and becoming in order to find the security they need. They feel a need for success, for love, for power, or what have you, in order to fulfil their ideal image of what it is important to be. They live in a sense after the fact — based in needing to accomplish a particular goal.

At the core of human being is a *lack of faith* in making meaning. Human relationship, which offers such a possibility for extending beyond the inertia of thought through its possibilities of flow and connections, is lived instead as a way to confirm the techniques for finding security. Under such auspices as the search for security human beings and our self are considered to be known. We know about ourselves, we know about each other, so there is no reason to discover any meaning beyond the forms we have already conceived to be at the core of human connection. The meaning is established in the thoughts and ideas that precede any relationship so there is no reason to enlarge the possibilities in relationship or to realize that the active movement in the flow of relationship could expand our vision of what human life could be. Indeed we see that many people do not put much value in human relationship. They focus on their work, on 'outside' phenomena, or on what they produce. They think that large movements such as their influence on a group of people or purveying ideas is the central fact of life. They do not ask whether in so doing they are living in a whole-hearted and direct way, nor do they ask if the purveying of ideas or the ambition they embody actually leads to transforming human life. In one dialogue group, for example, several members kept requesting that we have a seminar about the meaning of the word dialogue or of the process of dialogue. They seemed more interested in knowing about dialogue than they were in actually talking to each other. In actuality they did not want to attend to the active transformations that were going on between the human beings in the group in each moment because they are too caught up in the movement of thought to allow the happening of such moments between people to affect them. It could be argued that discussing the question would have been an opening into questions of the moment but at that point it did not seem that such an abstract discussion would touch on what was happening in between the people, it seemed more in the service of avoiding those kinds of interaction which would be active in the moment of contact.

In dialogue with another human being or many other human beings there seems to be a possibility for a breakdown of the limitations that thought imposes on each of us. When we talk in groups or with another individual we see that other people are as caught by the thoughts they have as we are. At such moments we see mirror images of ourselves in the isolation and egocentricity of the other person and simultaneously realize that self-involvement, isolation, domination by thought, and a loss of presence in the present is common to many people. Often in dialogue it is clear that the other person is not responding to what is happening to and between us at the moment. It is clear that we too are attempting to mould the situation into things we know or that we are reacting in ways which come from a repetition of old ideas or patterns. As this becomes clear it simultaneously is awareness of the operations of human consciousness and an insight into the fact that we are not moving with the experience of the moment. We are not making meaning at the moment and are afraid to do so. If we leave such insight alone and let it act without again falling into the repetition of old patterns we become aware of the anxiety about being in the present with other people and that that anxiety comes because we are afraid to await the meaning-making events.

Sometimes the relationship in dialogue group or the love of another human being can at that moment enable the unfolding of the flow, that would make it possible to engage in experiencing the sensations and presence allowing active meaning-making to occur. Such meaning can only occur when we are able to happen in the present, to live our lives as they unfold in front of us. As we discover new things in the direct sensuous moment we make meaning rather than confirming ideas that are already formed. The operations of the human brain seem to be one of the most unique forms in nature because it is able to reach beyond the inertial and repetitive functions of thought and memory which are indigenous to its material nature and to operate in the present in a spontaneous mode.

We observed that human development often leads to a lack of faith in the capacity of the brain to actively engage in the present. But it seems too that where there is a breakthrough or break-up of this thought form which guides the behavior and undermines the faith of the brain in its own capacities there is the beginning of the healing of this essential distrust of meaning-making. As this occurs in human relationship it is also possible that the brain will have less tendency to depend on the old forms of thought and to be more available for the instant engagement that is involved in making meaning. Thought could then operate differently as an extension of the awareness of new perception in the moments of change.

References

Bateson, G., *Steps to an Ecology of Mind*, Ballantine, New York, 1972.

Horney, Karen, *Neurosis and Human Growth*, W.W. Norton and Co., New York, 1950.

Stern, D., *The Interpersonal World of the Infant*, Basic Books, York, 1985.

PART THREE

Philosophical Explorations into Meaning

Beyond Cezanne's Mountain: Exploring the Activity of Meaning

F. DAVID PEAT

Without meaning life would simply not be worth living. Indeed, people have been driven to suicide and to other bizarre and destructive acts by a sense of meaninglessness in their lives. A state of profound depression, in which all drive and creativity vanishes and human relationships wither away, is felt as an almost tangible void, lacking all meaning, within the centre of a person's existence. Indeed when society itself begins to lose its meaning then its cohesion breaks down and more and more individuals are driven to crime, violence and mob behaviour.

While meaning may be particularly difficult to define and pin down, it is clear to everyone that its absence is immediately recognizable. For example, to stand before nature and experience only a sense of emptiness is the most frightening of fates. Clearly what are generally taken to be the very highest achievements of civilization are all concerned with the response to meaning. The poet, painter and composer begin their art out of a deep sense of meaning. And through the artist's skills, perceptions, experience, intelligence and depth of feeling something new is able to flower. Meaning therefore becomes not only the ground and origin of a work of art but also lies at the heart of its inner structuring and its manner of being. But this expression of meaning is not confined to the artist alone for it becomes the expression of a whole society. The great Gothic cathedrals are today seen as a manifestation of the whole medieval society in which everyone, from peasant to the nobility, took an active, physical role in their construction. Clearly, in the medieval world art was both the source, the expression and the sustainer of meaning. Indeed the great stained-glass windows at Chartres, for example, provided a doorway from the everyday world into the transcendental. Meaning therefore was one of the key factors which cemented society together and gave it its generative power.

While meaning can always be apprehended directly within the implicit levels of our experience it does prove difficult to capture or to point to in any explicit fashion. This extreme difficulty in defining and talking about meaning sometimes gives us the feeling that meaning is of such an ephemeral nature that it will vanish in the hard light of reason. However to attempt to come to terms with a Bach Cantata, a speech by Shakespeare or a painting by Cezanne is to realize how meaning always plays a powerful, active, generative and structural role. It is of course possible to make an intellectual analysis of any work of art and discover the formal relationships that can be unfolded from it. It may even be possible to excavate something of the creative process that is characteristic of that particular artist. Yet it is always the case that some essence escapes such analysis. While the internal logic of the work may be exposed there is always something more deeply enfolded that can only be captured in the infinitely subtle levels of the mind. How often, for example, has this writer stood before the paintings of Paul Cezanne and asked himself why Cezanne returned again and again to the same motives: a group of bathers, a bowl of fruit, Mount Sainte-Victoire. It is only at the level of an active, enfolded meaning that one begins to appreciate how, week after week, month after month, Cezanne would push around tiny areas of colour on the same canvas, always experimenting, never satisfied, moving at first in a hesitating, tentative fashion and then with great boldness and confidence. In looking at such paintings, meaning no longer appears ephemeral but intensely active, as it plays its generative role. Meaning seems to lie outside the purely subjective realm and hints at an objective dimension in which the divisions between internal and external, mind and matter, reason and spirit are transcended.

Does this suggest that meaning must be thought of as a formative and active principle that functions within nature? Does it play its role not only within our subjective experience and the creation of works of art but also, for example, within the proper functioning of the human body and even the structures and transformation of inanimate matter? Indeed could it be that what we know as inanimate matter is in fact the explicate form of something far deeper and of potentially infinite subtlety which has its origin in some unknown ground that involves meaning?

The notion that meaning may play an active role within the universe is clearly one that is ripe for investigation. The psychologist Carl Jung and the physicist Wolfgang Pauli suggested that mind and matter have a dual, complementary nature. Indeed the term *synchronicity* was proposed to describe the meaningful conjugations and patterns involving both these aspects. For Jung and Pauli, mind and matter grow out of a common ground in which meaning plays a significant and active role.[1] More recently David Bohm has proposed that meaning and information play active roles at the quantum level of matter. This idea is currently being investigated in terms of certain 'active information' that determines the quantum mechanical outcome of atomic events.[2] Within Bohm's *causal interpretation* of the quantum theory therefore, meaning appears to play an objective role.

Meaning has also come to represent the indivisible unity of mind and body which has so long been a feature of Eastern thought. More recently such an approach has been recognized within orthodox Western medicine. The role of the immune system, for example, in maintaining the body's proper functioning and in preventing disease is beginning to become a topic of serious research. Here again meaning plays an active role in generating subtle patterns of wholeness which then unfold across the mind and body into healthy action. But without such active meaning, it appears, the body becomes susceptible to disease and the whole essence of the individual is compromised.

But all these studies are only in their infancy and, for the most part, still lie outside the mainstream of what is considered to be serious research. Nevertheless this present publication clearly shows that some serious interest is now being generated in the whole question. One area of particular interest to this writer is the possibility of discovering a deeper unity between the arts and sciences, and, for that matter, philosophy and religion, by discovering the common, generative role that meaning plays within them. David Bohm, for example, has suggested the possibility of levels of feedback and cyclic activity that exist between the explicate, implicate and superimplicate orders. Something analogous also exists within the field theory, or second quantized version of his causal interpretation

of the quantum theory. In this case the movements of unfoldment and enfoldment of explicate forms out of the implicate
order has its origin in the active information associated with
the underlying quantum field. This information is likewise conditioned by the explicate structures that arise in the quantum
environment and, in this way, active information flows in a
cycle between the various explicate, implicate and superimplicate levels.[3] A similar activity also takes place in the work
of a painter, and for that matter other creative endeavours,
in which the unfolding of meaning into art takes place both
internally, through perception, thought and feeling, and externally, in the physical interaction of paint and canvas.

As the painter confronts the growing work it constantly feeds
back into his or her consciousness as fresh perceptions and
new layers of meaning. These in turn unfold themselves into
the physical activity of painting. The result is a whole process
of artistic expression, a single dynamical whole whose meaning stands beyond any simple analysis. While the work itself
may have its origin in the initial creative act of perception, its
meaning is constantly growing, transforming and developing
in fresh ways that ultimately unfold out of the scene itself, the
personality of the artist, the whole history of art and the society in which the artist inhabits. The meaning of the work of
art therefore grows out of its generation and is constantly
changing and transforming. Moreover this activity continues
when the work is viewed, for rich levels of meaning are generated within the dynamic flow of perception between painting
and spectator.

Meaning is therefore clearly and indissolubly linked with
creativity. Meaning is not a fixed and static thing, such as that
which is normally meant by, for example, information, it is
dynamic and fluid, constantly generating and transforming
itself out of its own activity. A key issue which emerges is therefore how such active meaning is to flower and blossom in the
life of the individual and, indeed, in society at large. In certain highly-creative periods of civilization a strong and subtle
sense of meaning must have been shared by most of the population. That explosion of creative energy that characterizes both
the Renaissance and the Classical age in Greece, must clearly
have pervaded the whole society. Active meaning must have
been enfolded within each individual and likewise have
unfolded across the society at large. Within such creative

periods each person would have experienced a strong sense of the meaning of the age which became expressed in great works of art, literature, theatre, music, legislation and fresh social organizations.

In a sense such products of civilization were the realization, or unfoldment, of underlying active meaning. Of course none of these societies were ideal. There was considerable poverty, violence and disease during the Renaissance and the citizens of Athens saw nothing incompatible between their new-found democracy and their attitudes towards women and slaves. Nevertheless the positive side of their society, the dynamic sense of its meaning, still comes down to us today.

Our modern age is, however, less strongly imbued with a sense of meaning. Great works of art and literature have certainly been created in the twentieth century yet they no longer appear to serve an active, integrative function within society as a whole. Prejudice, fear, aggression and violence have always been with us but in our more complex, technological age their effects have become magnified and more threatening. Clearly the search for a generative, healing activity of meaning is the key issue which faces the world today. But where is such meaning to be found and how is it to be fostered?

Such questions are by no means easy to confront, particularly when the traditional forms, values and beliefs all appear to have lost their power and vitality. Clearly something new and creative is called for in which society and each individual is willing to face the unknown. In the beginning this will require greater communication and dialogue between people who must learn to work and explore together in a spirit of openness and goodwill, and who are willing to acknowledge and face the fear and anxiety that the events of this century have generated into the unknown. Possibly this publication may spark off and encourage each of us to make that first step into the infinite realm of meaning.

References

1. Peat, F. David, *Synchronicity*, Bantam Books, New York, 1987.
2. Bohm, D. and Hiley, B.J., Foundations of Physics, *14*, 255, 1984.
3. These issues are discussed also in Bohm, D. and Peat, F. David, *Science, Order and Creativity*, Bantam Books, New York, 1987.

The Mental and the Physical

ARLETA GRIFFOR

In this paper we will consider how the notion of the implicate order can help in clarifying the relationship between mind and matter.

It is important to note that Bohm's proposal of the implicate order as the order of matter is actually a change from what is usually meant by matter. That is, the implicate order is not another description of the *same thing* which Descartes described as extended substance, but rather, it is a new way of understanding what matter *is*. Consequently, with this change in what is meant by matter, we may expect a change in what is meant by the relationship between matter and mind.

Descartes' claim concerning mind and matter

Descartes' attempt to formulate how mind and matter could be related was based on his way of understanding what mind and matter were supposed to be. That made the task particularly difficult. He assumed that the whole of existence can be fitted into two separate compartments of extended substance and thinking substance. Extended substance, or matter, he defined as existing in space in the form of separated objects. Thinking substance, or mind, did not exist in space, nor did it involve spatial extension and separation in any way. And so the division between mind and matter seemed quite radical, exclusive, and exhaustive.

Having established the division, Descartes set out to formulate how mind and matter act on each other. That there is a kind of interaction in the sense of thought leading to a physical action and vice versa, was no less evident than the apparent fundamental difference between extended and thinking substances. The question was, how could such basically distinct substances interact, if it was postulated that the world consisted only of these two distinct modes of existence. Of what could a link between them possibly consist? Without any kind of link that could bridge the ontological gap between the mental and the physical, the issue of their interaction remained entirely unintelligible.

One of Descartes' solutions to the problem was to propose the pineal gland as a point of connection of mind and body. During his lifetime the function of the pineal gland was unknown, and so at least it was not certain that the gland was not the point of connection. However, such a solution was not satisfactory, since it only moved the problem from one place to another. The question remained concerning how the pineal gland, being extended substance, was connected with thinking substance. Another solution which contemporaries of Descartes found to be consistent with his philosophy, was to regard god as a link between the extended and the thinking realms of existence.

Perhaps the problem of connecting the mental and the physical would not arise, if in the first place Descartes had not defined had them as distinct substances. It is however interesting to note that his own approach forced him to establish this division: it was a logical consequence of his conviction that he had found a way of distinguishing knowledge which is certain from that which is not.

The issue was that Aristotle's map of the universe was revealed to have some serious flaws, not being able to account for the new discoveries about matter which came with Copernicus and Galileo. Because of that, Aristotle's authority ceased to be the criterion of truth. Descartes' attempt was to establish another criterion of the credibility of knowledge than the authority of Aristotle.

Indeed, he believed that he had discovered the general criterion of truth in the particular way he had arrived at the truth of the 'cogito', i.e., the truth of the proposition: 'I think, therefore I am'. This proposition was known clearly and distinctly. Descartes then came up with the notion that whatever is known clearly and distinctly is at the same time true. From that he only needed to go one step further in order to establish the 'truth' of the division between the mental and the physical. Since the thought *'what I think about* is different from *the act of my thinking'* seemed for him clear and distinct, he concluded that *thinking substance* is different from *what the thought is about*.

Of course, one could still question whether man's clear and distinct ideas were not, nevertheless, deceptive. Descartes' way of securing these ideas was by means of proving the existence of God who was not a deceiver. Such a god had therefore no intention to deceive man by implanting in him clear and distinct ideas which would be deceptive. In this way, Descartes' criterion of truth was guaranteed by God.

There are, however, doubts as to whether or not Descartes was arguing in a cycle here. He 'proved' the existence of God using the criterion of clearness and distinctness, but on the other hand, God established in such a way was supposed to guarantee the truth of this criterion.

In other words, one cannot see a logical need to maintain Descartes' argument, which got him trapped into the double framing of reality, causing in this way the split of the whole of existence into two ontological species of extended substance and thinking substance. This was evident even for the contemporaries of Descartes, since they tried to improve his structure in various ways. However, the division between the mental and the physical remained in power in spite of its questionable logical status, dominating science and ordinary thought up to the present day.

Regardless of the logical status of Descartes' rationalizations, which were supposed to justify the difference between mind and matter, the postulated difference fitted both the ordinary experience and scientific knowledge of matter very well. It is clear that, as long as matter matched Descartes' definition of extended substance, its relation with thinking substance — if any — had to be provided in terms of some additional ontological order. A co-ordinate system that Descartes imposed on the realm of matter was not suitable for describing the thinking realm of existence. There was no common quality that could provide a reasonable basis for the relationship of the two substances. The notion of bringing in God as a link between the substances was a typical way to deal with the issue which apparently had no intelligible solution.

However, we may suppose that the situation changes if matter ceases to be understood as extended substance. In this sense we may say that a new way of understanding what matter is makes it possible to consider again the relationship between mind and matter.

The implicate order as the basis of the relationship between mind and matter

Concerning the implicate order, it is of key significance that it applies not only to matter, but also, to consciousness. As Bohm indicates[1], the activity of consciousness can be regarded as being basically an enfolding-unfolding activity.

One can see this, for example, by being aware of how consciousness is activated in response to sense perception. The perception activates memory, and gives rise to thoughts, feelings, intentions to act, etc., which unfold into further activities of consciousness. These activities involve not only yet more thoughts and feelings implied by those to which the original perception gave rise, but also still further perception which enfolds again.

It is clear that one may begin not with perception, but with a thought, feeling, or with any other aspect of the mind's activity, being aware of how all of these aspects enfold, imply, and pass over into each other. For example:

> The thought of danger unfolds into a feeling of fear, which unfolds into words communicating the feeling, and into further thoughts... Thoughts and feelings also enfold intentions. These are sharpened up into a determinate will and the urge to do something. Intention, will and urge unfold into more action, which will include more thought if necessary. So all the aspects of the mind show themselves as enfolding each other, and transforming into each other through enfoldment and unfoldment.[2]

That both matter and mind can be discussed in terms of an unfolding-enfolding activity, that is, in terms of the implicate order, may help us to understand how they are related. That was not the case with the Cartesian order (i.e., the co-ordinate system) which was suited to discuss only the extended realm of existence. The thinking realm was established somewhere beyond the Cartesian order, without an intelligible connection with whatever was accounted for by this order.

Bohm's suggestion that mind and matter are both in the implicate order, changes the situation in that it points to something basically common in these two apparently separate realms of existence. One may therefore reasonably suppose that the implicate order can be considered as a means of expressing consistently the relationship between mind and matter.

What is there to be related?

Before we go into the question of *how* the mental and the physical could be related, it is important to note that Bohm's view entails an essential change in *what* is to be related, when we talk about the relationship of the mental and the physical.

It has already been mentioned that the implicate order brings about a change in what is meant by matter. However, yet another feature of the implicate order has to be emphasized in the present context. This is that the implicate order is essen-tial to what things *are* in that it is a dynamic unfolding-enfolding activity, inseparable from all the forms which are generated by this activity, unlike the Cartesian order which applies 'externally' to pre-existent extended things that are independent of it.

To say that matter and mind are in the implicate order means that their basic structure is grounded in the whole of the unfolding-enfolding activity. In other words, both matter and mind are inseparable aspects or forms of this activity. The question of their relationship would therefore be the question of how the mental and the material forms of *activity* are related within the common context of the universal activity of unfoldment and enfoldment, or, how they are related within the overall structure of the implicate order. This is clearly different from the question formulated by Descartes; namely, how two distinct and independent forms of *substance* can be related.

This leads us to the question: what is the nature of the overall structure of the implicate order?

The self-organizing nature of the implicate order

In the present context it is of key significance that the implicate order can be regarded as a self-organizing activity. The self-organizing nature of the implicate order is emphasized in Bohm's causal interpretation of the quantum particle theory extended to the quantum field theory. In this interpretation he introduces the notion of information that is objective and active.

Since the notion of active information is crucial for understanding the self-organizing nature of the implicate order, we will consider it in the context of Bohm's interpretation of the quantum theory. However, as will be shown later, this notion has a much broader significance which goes beyond the context of physics.

As he proposed in his initial interpretation, each elementary particle can be considered as inseparable from a quantum wave that satisfies Schrödinger's equation. Both particles and their waves are assumed to be physical actualities. The important point is that a new kind of activity is displayed in the way in which the particle is affected by its wave. Namely, the wave *does not act mechanically* on the particle. That is, the particle responds not to the *intensity* of its wave, but to *the form*. As Bohm puts it '...the electron moves under its own energy, but the information in the *form* of the quantum wave directs the energy of the electron.'[3] In other words, the self-active particle can be said to be guided in its movement by the *information* content of the wave function. Since the information content of the Schrödinger wave concerns the entire context of the particle, it follows that the behaviour of the particle cannot be consistently separated from the whole of its relevant environment[4].

For the many-particle system, the wave function of the system cannot be represented in the ordinary three-dimensional space (which is done for the one-particle case) but has to be represented in a multi-dimensional space. Each point of this multi-dimensional space corresponds to a configuration of the entire system of the particles. In this way the wave function of the system depends on the positions of all the particles. The activity of each particle of the system is therefore guided not by its 'private' information, but by a common 'pool' of information contained in the wave function for the whole system[5].

We can say that in the case of the many-particle system, the activity of each particle reflects the state of the whole system. It should be added that by the activity of the particles we understand here not only their movement, but also their capability to enter into connections with each other. In other words, not only the *form of movement* of the particles, but also the *form of the connection* between them depends on the state of the whole system.

Extending the causal interpretation to the quantum field theory, Bohm gives up the notion of the particle as the basic actuality, and takes instead the field. This is because in the quantum field theory particle-like manifestations can be regarded as certain phases of the unfolding-enfolding movement of the field.

These particle-like manifestations, together with their order of movement and interaction, arise as the effect of a super-quantum field on the original field. This situation is similar to the quantum particle treatment where the form of the activity of particles arises as the effect of the quantum wave on the particles. In other words, the multi-dimensional superquantum field represents an information content which guides the activity of the three-dimensional field. However, in the present context not only the *activity* of particle-like manifestations, but also their *creation, sustenance and annihilation*, can be said to be guided by the information contained in the superquantum field.

The important thing to note is that both the original field and the superquantum field are forms of the implicate order. The original three-dimensional field represents the first impli-cate order, and the superquantum multi-dimensional field represents the second implicate order that is of a more subtle nature than the first one[6]. The causal interpretation of the quantum field theory can therefore be understood in terms of two interrelated implicate orders. As Bohm says:

> In principle, of course, there could be a third, fourth, fifth im-plicate order, going on to infinity, and these would correspond to extensions of the laws of physics going beyond those of the current quantum theory in a fundamental way. But for the present I want to consider only the second implicate order, and to emphasize that this stands in relationship to the first as a source of formative, organizing and creative activity.[7]

As noted earlier, the relationship in which the second impli-cate order stands to the first one, is not of a mechanical nature. The second implicate order acts on the first in the sense that it informs the self-active movement of the first implicate order, organizing it into manifest structures of the explicate order.[8]

As in the quantum particle theory, we deal here with the notion of active information[9], that is, information that gives rise to a certain activity. This activity to which information gives rise, Bohm calls *meaning*.

For example, in the case of a many-particle system, the mean-ing of the information content of the wave function would be the explicate order of movement and interaction of the par-ticles. In the context of the quantum field theory, the mean-ing of the information enfolded in the superquantum field would signify the whole activity of the first implicate order.

In other words, the meaning would signify here the enfolding-unfolding activity of the first implicate order, in which particle-like manifestations and the order of their movement and interaction are generated.

Since both the wave function and the superquantum field are forms of the implicate order, it can be said that in both examples meaning signifies the activity of the unfoldment of enfolded information. This would imply that information itself can be seen as meaning. For if we suppose that beyond the first and second there is a third, fourth, etc., implicate order, the information enfolded in the second implicate order can be regarded as the meaning of a more enfolded information content of the third implicate order, and so on.

When we deal with the many-level structure of the implicate orders, we can therefore discuss the self-organizing activity of this structure in terms of meaning, leaving out the notion of information. Such an approach seems to be particularly suitable when considering the activity of mind.

The signa-somatic and the soma-significant aspects of the activity of meaning

Discussing the activity of mind in terms of meaning, Bohm considers two aspects of this activity, the first one being the enfolding or *soma-significant* activity, and the other being the unfolding or *signa-somatic* activity[10].

An example of the soma-significant activity is the way in which sense perception takes place. In the act of sense perception the significance of a somatic structure (such as a printed page, a structure of sound, an image, etc.) is being apprehended. That is, the significance of a given somatic structure is being encoded into somatic processes (i.e., electrical, chemical, etc.) of the organism. These somatic processes have further, intellectual or emotional significance. This significance is, however, also encoded in some more subtle somatic processes of the brain and the nervous system. These more subtle somatic processes may in turn be significant for still more subtle, or more enfolded forms of significance, and so on.

What Bohm suggests further is that there is no need to assume any limits to the possible depth of enfoldment of this soma-significant activity. That is, it may extend indefinitely beyond any specifiable level of meaning. Although the example of the soma-significant activity concerns sense perception, it is clear that perception of significance is not limited to sense perception. It can take place at any level of meaning, and it may involve quite subtle forms of mental activity[2]. In other words, what is suggested here is that an indefinite depth of inwardness is possible in our mental processes.

The signa-somatic aspect of the activity of meaning calls attention to the somatic unfoldment of significance. For example, whatever structure of significance is present as the content of consciousness at a given moment, it organizes the subtle somatic processes of the brain. These, in turn, organize or inform the less subtle somatic processes of the body. Finally, the original structure of significance unfolds as a manifest activity of the body which affects the environment. In this way, the signa-somatic activity extends into the environment.

In fact, we may say that the structure of our environment, that is the structure of the world in which we live, is for the most part the somatic result of various forms of significance that constitute the 'information content' of human consciousness. We should, however, note that the soma-significant activity of perception includes perception of new meanings. These new meanings, when somatically actualized, bring about new material, cultural, social, etc., forms of human life. In other words, the overall structure of meaning is capable of indefinite extension, both in the 'enfolded direction' of ever more subtle meanings, as well as, in the 'unfolded direction' of manifest actualizations. This implies that, at least in principle, mind is capable of going beyond any specifiable level of subtlety of meaning. This capability of going beyond any level of meaning, Bohm points to as the essential feature on which *intelligence* is based.

It is clear from the above discussion that 'soma' and 'significance' are relative notions. The significance of a somatic structure is conceived in a more subtle somatic form, and so on. What follows is that each level of the overall structure of meaning is both somatic and significant. That is, we deal here with one process that is *both somatic and significant*, or, both mental and physical. As Bohm says:

> ...nothing exists in this process except as a two-way movement, a flow of energy, in which meaning is carried inward and outward between the aspects of soma and significance, as well as, between levels that are relatively subtle and those that are relatively manifest.'[12]

Matter, mind, and meaning

When discussing mind in terms of the activity of meaning, it became clear that mind has a somatic, or, 'material' side from which it is inseparable. Could it be that matter has in a similar way an inseparable 'mental' aspect?

Insofar as matter is considered to be a self-organizing activity of information, it can be said to have a kind of 'mental' aspect. That is, the enfolded information content of the super-wave function can be viewed as significance which is somatically actualized in the form of the explicate order of activity of particle-like manifestations.

If we suppose, as suggested earlier, that the super-wave function is the somatic unfoldment of a more subtle level of significance, and so on, we come to a process similar to that which takes place in the case of mind. That is, we come to a process involving a series of levels of active meaning, where each level organizes the next more manifest one. In other words, we come to the signa-somatic aspect of the activity of meaning in the context of matter.

As Bohm suggests, it is also possible to show that the soma-significant aspect of meaning is part of the activity of matter. However, if the quantum theory were to account for the many-level activity of meaning, and for the soma-significant aspect of this activity, it would need a fundamental extension. As it is now, it covers only the signa-somatic aspect of the two-level activity of meaning[13]. With regard to that, Bohm's position is that it is only a temporary state of affairs, and that further research can quite likely transcend the present form of the quantum theory.

But even the two-level activity of meaning that is accounted for by Bohm's causal interpretation of quantum theory, displays a close similarity of form to the activity of meaning as it is discussed in the context of the mind. We may therefore ask, whether we deal here with two kinds of activities, or with one and the same activity. Bohm's contention seems to be that both in the context of mind and in the context of matter we deal with basically the same overall process or activity of meaning.

Meaning as being

We were concerned with the relationship of matter and mind, and we arrived at meaning. What has this relationship to do with meaning? If we inquire, as Bohm has done, into what matter is, and what mind is, we shall arrive at meaning. In this way, instead of two distinct *substances* we have one overall *activity* that displays both material and mental aspects. The question of the relationship of mind and matter becomes therefore the more general question of the overall structure of meaning.

This structure, as we noted, is basically similar for matter and mind. Do we then, when asking about the overall structure of meaning, still ask about the relationship of mind and matter? Or, do we ask about something else? When we give up the assumption that matter and mind are fundamentally different, are they still in need of being related? The structure of meaning has been discussed in terms of the signa-somatic and soma-significant activity. Significance (i.e., the mental) was said to give form to the activity of soma (i.e., the physical). But by no means can it be narrowed down to saying that mind informs matter. Significance, or meaning in general, is not confined to mind, but as was pointed out, it is objectively present and active in matter as well.

In the present context, the relationship that Descartes attempted to formulate, and which he called the relationship of mind and matter, resembles in some respects the interaction of two levels of meaning. However, as Bohm proposes, the overall structure of meaning involves an indefinite, or perhaps infinite, number of levels. Furthermore, it applies both to matter and mind. Therefore, when discussing the overall structure of meaning, in some sense we include the traditional question of the relationship of mind and matter. But the structure of meaning comprises not *one* relationship, but a *whole series*, or, a whole order of relationships.

In this sense we can say that the question of the overall structure of meaning is far more general than the question of the relationship of matter and mind. However, to say that meaning applies both to matter and mind implies something more as well. It implies that meaning is intrinsic to the whole universe. What follows is that the signa-somatic and soma-significant activity, in terms of which mind has been discussed, could be seen as part of a much broader universal activity of meaning. This leads us to deny Descartes' division of the whole of existence into two separate categories, or modes of being. Instead, we can say that meaning encompasses both modes of existence, or as Bohm says, that meaning *is* being.

The nature of meaning

Since the statement that meaning is being may appear some-what puzzling, it may help to bring in Aristotle's concept of the formal and final causation that is in some sense similar to what Bohm understands as meaning.

Aristotle's claim was that to know things, was to know their four basic principles or causes. The causes were considered to be the proper subject of knowledge in the sense that to know them was to know how things come into being, how they act, transform, and pass away. In this sense the causes were under-stood as intelligible principles inseparable from what things are, constituting, as it were, the very mode of existence of things. He distinguished the following causes: (i) the material cause — as a kind of substratum in which the three other causes operate, (ii) the efficient cause — as an external source of motion[14], (iii) the formal (or, the formative) cause — as an immanent principle which makes things what they are, and (iv) the final cause — as an aim or 'telos' towards which any process of motion is directed.

Although these causes were said to constitute distinguish-able factors of each mode of being, actually they were not always different. In general, the formal cause of a thing was simultaneously its final cause. That is, the aim of the full reali-zation of forms, was at the same time the immanent principle of motion directed towards this realization.

In Aristotle's view, this immanent principle of motion con-cerned all nature. In fact, 'nature' at the time of Aristotle meant an intrinsic principle of motion operating within things[15]. He saw this motion as directed towards the full actualization of forms, that is, as brought about by the formative cause. The formative cause was therefore considered to be an intrinsic principle that made matter to actualize its potentialities. Then, he saw this universal movement of actualization as ultimately ordered by the 'unmoved mover' acting as 'telos' of the whole of nature. In this way, the formative activity was seen as guided by the 'unmoved mover' whose role was to organize this activity into an integrated whole of the cosmos.

As Bohm points out, something akin to the efficient and the material causes is still recognized by modern science, whereas the formal and the final causes are more or less put aside as not relevant to scientific needs[16].

One may suppose that the situation is due to the philosophical tradition originated by Descartes. Descartes banished the intrinsic principle of motion from nature, reducing in this way the concept of motion to displacements caused externally. He also needed an 'unmoved mover'. However, Descartes' 'unmoved mover' was no longer the immanent 'telos' that integrated things into the cosmos, but rather, it served as a mechanical assumption that was necessary to explain the origin of movement in the universe. Once moved, the universe was governed in its further movement by laws[17].

Formative activity directed towards some aim was therefore generally reserved for the 'thinking substance'. Perhaps this concept began gradually to function as a presupposition in science. Any attempt to explain a material process in terms of a self-organizing or teleological activity, keeping in mind Descartes' limitation of these to the 'thinking substance', would be equivalent to providing matter with consciousness. But the separation of matter and consciousness was believed by Descartes to be an essential part of 'certain' knowledge.

We may suppose that this tendency of avoiding teleological explanations in science is for the most part a habit whose origin has been forgotten. Moreover, as we mentioned earlier, Descartes' criterion of certainty does not make much sense. Therefore we are free to look at the issue anew, without any need to presuppose that teleological activity is confined to human behaviour.

Coming back to meaning as the activity in which somatic forms are created, sustained, and dissolved, that is, as the activity of making the forms 'what they are', we may say that meaning *is* being, in the same way in which Aristotle's formal and final cause of things *is* their being.

We should note that Aristotle's concept of formative (and teleological) causation provides only a limited analogy to meaning in that it leaves out the soma-significant activity. Aristotle's 'unmoved mover' can be said to be something like the second and ultimate level of meaning that informs the first one which comprises the whole universe. In other words, he assumes that the 'information content' of the 'unmoved mover' organizes the activity of the whole universe. However, if we take into account that the self-organizing activity of meaning consists of the signa-somatic *and* the soma-significant aspects, we do not need to assume that there is something like an ultimate level of meaning.

The soma-significant aspect points to the possibility of unlimited extension of the overall structure of meaning. That is, it is part of the nature of this meaning structure to be able to go into the meaning of meaning. But to go into the meaning of meaning is, in other words, to create new levels of meaning. This implies that the overall structure of meaning is never complete or fixed in its content, but rather, it is in a constant movement of creation and transformation. The self-organizing activity of meaning is therefore inseparable from the creative movement of going into the meaning of meaning, which is to say, it is inseparable from what was called intelligence.

Notes and References
1. Bohm, D., *Wholeness and the Implicate Order*, ARK Paperback, 1984: pp.196-207.
2. Bohm, D., *Unfolding Meaning*, ed. D. Factor, ARK Paperback, 1987: p.17.
3. Bohm, D., & Peat, F.D., *Science, Order and Creativity*, Bantam, 1987: p.90.
4. Taking into account that this new kind of 'informing' activity of the wave does not fall off with the distance, we get in this way a simple explanation of the wave-particle duality.
5. This, as Bohm points out, explains a non-local correlation of particles that could be apart from each other, but nevertheless capable of being affected by the information content of their common wave function whose effect does not fall off with the distance.
6. '...in the sense that not only is the actual activity of the whole field enfolded in it, but also all its potentialities.' Hiley, B.J., & Peat, F.D., *Quantum Implications: Essays in honour of David Bohm*, Routledge & Kegan Paul, London, 1987: p.43.
7. *ibid*: pp.43-4.
8. By 'structures' we understand here not only explicate objects, but also forms of their activity (i.e. movement and interaction).
9. See Bohm. D., this volume.
10. The constituent terms of these two names referring to the activity of meaning are: 'soma' as 'the physical', and 'significance' as 'the mental'.
11. For example, perception of the significance of a set of ideas,

perception in art and science concerning subtle orders and relationships, perception of the significance of life in general, etc.

12. Bohm, D., *Unfolding Meaning*, ed. D. Factor, ARK Paperback, 1987: p.78.

13. As it is shown in Bohm's causal interpretation of the quantum field theory.

14. The word 'motion' refers here not only to displacements of bodies, but also to all kinds of qualitative and quantitative changes (like becoming, modes of behaviour, transformations, disintegrations, etc.)

15. 'The word "nature" is etymologically derived from the word for "living thing". The Greek word φυσις, which we find reflected in *physics* and *physical*, has reference to the life of plants. Its Latin equivalent stems from *nasci*, "to be born". This has several forms: *na(c)tivitas*, "birth", and *na(c)tura*, "vitality", "vital operation", etc. This would imply that nature is conceived of as an intrinsic principle; that is, it refers to those basic operations which spring from the essence of an object, being developed in, from, and by the object rather than imposed on it from the outside. In other words, "nature" has always been considered as an existing principle of development from within. In short, "nature" is an intrinsic principle of operation within things.' L.A. Foley, *Cosmology, Philosophical and Scientific*, The Bruce Publishing Company, 1962: p.63.

16. However, recent developments in science are beginning to recognize the formative and teleological factors. For example, R. Sheldrake's hypothesis of formative causation in biology and beyond (see R. Sheldrake, *The Presence of the Past*, Collins, 1988), and Prigogine's theory of dissipative structures, applicable in a quite general range of domains (see I. Prigogine and I. Stengers, *Order out of Chaos*, Flamingo, 1985).

17. It is interesting that as long as nature was equivalent to an innate principle of motion (which was assumed to be ordered), there was no idea of 'natural laws'. As far as we know, Aristotle's concept of law was applicable only to the behaviour of people. Moreover, laws were said 'to be derived from "nature herself and the truth". The law that most conforms to "nature" is the best law.' (Lloyd G.E.R., *Aristotle: the growth and structure of his thought*, Cambridge University Press, 1968: p.34.) In other words, laws had to 'obey' nature. Since from the time of Descartes nature began to mean a disjointed collection of objects pushing each other from the out-

side, it was necessary to introduce the idea of laws which governed this multiplicity of movement, whereby providing it with some order. The laws began to function as a kind of 'outside' authority to be obeyed by the world of objects. In this context it is particularly interesting that the word '*αρχή*' which Aristotle used for what we translate as 'cause' or 'principle', means also 'seat of authority'. We may thus suppose that for Aristotle the causes that were inseparable from what things are, were at the same time their immanent 'law', or, their immanent 'authority'. That is, to *be* a thing and to follow 'laws' had an indentical meaning for him. Therefore there was no need for any 'external' law, or for any additional authority to keep things on the right track.

Bohm, Plato and the Dark Age of Cave Mechanics

PAAVO PYLKKÄNEN

Bohm's 1952 papers on quantum mechanics were for me a revelation. I have always felt since that people who have not grasped the ideas of those papers (and unfortunately they remain the majority) are handicapped in any discussion of the meaning of quantum mechanics. — J.S. Bell, 1987.[1]

In discussing Plato's famous myth of the cave[2], the philosopher W.T. Jones tells us that the prisoners in the cave might develop a crude empirical science which could predict the movements of the shadows of the objects carried by people passing the cave. Although the prisoners would have no knowledge of the world outside and of the objects whose shadows they saw, by observing the changing shadows on the wall, they might nevertheless recognize some regularities in their motions. Imagine, for example, that the cave is situated by the road favoured by sculptors commuting between Athens and one of its suburbs. So, on working days, statistically equally many people carrying their sculpture might pass the cave in both directions, and thus the prisoners could predict how many shadows, in average, would pass the wall during a day in each direction, even though they could not say with certainty what the single next shadow would do.

In other words, the cave dwellers could develop a primitive notion of *statistical causality*. But there are severe physical constraints to prevent them from getting more information about the individual shadows so as to be able to predict their behaviour better. After all, Plato tells us they are 'chained by the leg and also by the neck [and] the chains will not let them turn their heads'. Each prisoner trying to turn his head towards the mouth of the cave would get a severe epistemological lesson (epistemology, the theory of knowledge, deals with the problems involved in knowing). Indeed, his attempts to observe would be limited by the chains whose existence he is not aware of, and he might easily think that his inability to extend his vision was not caused by any real factor but was rather an inherent feature of reality.

Unless he became very theoretical about it, he probably would forget about what is behind his back. And if he became theoretical, and began to postulate unobservable entities which would be causing the shadows, he would run the risk of getting a lesson in consensus, for his positivist jailmates would most probably boo at him for 'such prisoners would recognize as *reality* nothing but the shadows' (positivism is a doctrine which wants to confine science to the observable and manipulable).

Modern quantum physicists, for instance Niels Bohr, have told us many fascinating things about the epistemological lessons they have learnt — but, on balance, they have had it easier than their chained-by-the-leg forerunners. On working days quantum physicists commute to their labs, set up their experiments, and observe the results appearing on a computer screen, for example. One by one, small points form an image on the screen — they represent points in which individual quanta have been registered in a measurement. The physicist cannot predict where the next individual point will appear. But, on the other hand, she or he does know that after a large enough number of quanta have registered, (i.e. after a large enough number of coffee-breaks), the TV screen will always show a regular pattern that was expected.

It is well-known that the attempt to gain information required for an accurate prediction of the behaviour of individual quantum particles has thus far failed, and it has been thought to be inherently impossible. In their experiments, quantum theorists are only able to observe 'shadows' or phenomena which do not seem to be caused by independently existing particles in any ordinary sense. Thus, most physicists have dropped the idea of there existing a well-defined quantum reality independently of the observation.

In the above respects, most of the accepted interpretations of quantum theory echo the crude science of Plato's prisoners. The vagueness of quantum reality is comparable to the vagueness of the reality of these prisoners. Quantum reality is sometimes called 'veiled' reality, and even here the analogy holds: for what prevented Plato's prisoners from seeing the shadows of people was '...a parapet,... like the screen at a puppet-show'. To sympathize with its historical predecessor, present quantum mechanics might thus be more aptly called *cave mechanics* (though some people prefer calling it wave mechanics — to put it simply, because quantum particles in certain situations act as if they were waves).

The real problem with cave mechanics — past and present — is not its statistical character, but rather its positivistic insistence that, in Plato's words, the 'prisoners [physicists] recognize as reality nothing but the shadows [results of experiment]'. In the context of the quantum theory this attitude leads to very strange paradoxes.

Since 1952 David Bohm has said that there is a way out of the cave, or that it at least makes sense to look for it. But to understand Bohm's escape plan we must first discuss quantum reality from the traditional, Niels Bohr's, point of view. That is, we must first be led to believe that we are in a cave before it makes sense to try to get out of it. In the course of the discussion we will discover features that are relevant to the theme of this book — for example, how the concept of *meaning* becomes central to the understanding of the quantum theory even in Bohr's view. In the second section we point to the problems of Bohr's interpretation and proceed to discuss David Bohm's alternative interpretation in terms of active information. Has Bohm found a way out of the cave?

In the third section, we will consider the relation between matter and consciousness in the light of the quantum theory. In particular, we discuss whether the subtle level of information in Bohm's theory is a relevant concept when trying to understand this relation.

Modern cognitive science with its assumptions that consciousness is a property of any suitably organized or 'programmed' system — be it a brain or a computer — *presupposes* the nineteenth-century Newtonian view of the universe as a mechanistic *machine*. The quantum theory, however, implies that the universe is a holistic, ultimately non-mechanistic *process*, in which active information and meaning play a key role. How would we characterize the brain and consciousness in the context of this new world-view?

1. A note on the ontological and epistemological problems of quantum theory

The questions about what exists and what is the essential nature of that which exists are called *ontological* questions in philosophical language. We already referred to epistemology, the theory of knowledge, which is concerned with questions like *what* and *how* can we know about that which exists. In the context of the quantum theory the ontological question asks what kind of entities exist at the quantum level of accuracy and the epistemological one asks what and how can we know about them.

The quantum theory was originated in 1900 by the German physicist Max Planck. According to the theory, emission and absorption of radiant energy are not continuous but take place in small, finite and indivisible amounts or *quanta*. When we try to observe matter at its finest level, such quanta play an important role, as we will see. But let us first consider the question of observation in more general terms.

When we want to know precisely where, say, an electron is, we have to use a very high frequency radiation to observe it. But high frequency means a lot of energy, and as a consequence of such a position measurement we, as it were, give the electron such an energetic blow that we have no way of knowing where it is going any more. And conversely, in order to observe where and how fast the electron is going, i.e. its momentum, we have to use very low frequency radiation so as not to upset it. But the frequency of the radiation has to do with its ability to carry precise information about the position of the electron. Thus, low frequency radiation with its relatively long wave-length cannot tell us exactly where the electron is.

So in this way we discover that with present techniques, position and momentum measurements are mutually exclusive. This is in strong contrast with our everyday experience in which we can observe objects without disturbing them, and we can simultaneously measure where they are and where they are going. In fact, if we got to know the position of a classical particle and the forces that influence it at a certain moment, we could, in principle, tell any of its future and past states by using the equations of classical physics to calculate this. This would amount to complete determinism. But one should note here that even for some classical systems it is today thought to be practically impossible to get information required for accurate causal prediction.

But quantum theory is more problematic. It is thought that it is *in principle* impossible to get simultaneously information about position and momentum. Of course we may suppose that this is due to the disturbance mentioned above, and that a quantum particle *does* have position and momentum simultaneously before our measurement, even if, due to the experimental limitations, we cannot measure them simultaneously.

That is, in ontological terms, we might suppose that electrons and the like *are* tiny particles which *have* objective properties such as position and momentum, independently of whether we observe them or not. If we make this assumption, we could hold onto our usual realism, even if the simultaneous existence of the properties is not directly backed up by experiment. For example, it is thought that Werner Heisenberg, one of the founders of modern quantum mechanics, at first did interpret the difficulty in the above way[3].

But Niels Bohr had a different view. He felt that the very experimental arrangement that was required to measure, say, position was such that it was *meaningless* to use the word 'momentum' in that context. In order to get exact experimental data about a given property of a particle, a specific experimental context is required. But it is peculiar to quantum mechanics, as seen by Bohr, that in an experimental context designed to measure one property (e.g., momentum), there will be another, 'complementary' property, (position), that has no meaning in that context.

Bohr said that the new character of the quantum mechanical measurement process

> forces us to adopt a new mode of description designated as *complementary* in the sense that any given application of classical concepts precludes the simultaneous use of other classical concepts which in a different connection are equally necessary for the elucidation of the phenomena.[4]

The concept of complementarity was used as the key explanatory notion in Bohr's famous Como lecture of 1927, which marked the first appearance of a consistent interpretation of the quantum theory. Thus Bohr, as well as later Heisenberg, concluded that it is meaningless to talk about particles as if they existed independently of measurement and had objective properties such as position and momentum. That is, Bohr claimed it was meaningless to ask questions about the particle before the measurement or between the measurements. Referring to our inability to gain simultaneously all the information needed for a classical description, Bohr said in 1929:

> Obviously these facts not only set a limit to the *extent* of the information obtainable by measurements, but they also set a limit to the *meaning* which may attribute to such information. We meet here in a new light the old truth that in our description of nature the purpose is not to disclose the real essence of the phenomena but only to track down, so far as it is possible, relations between the manifold aspects of our experience.[5]

Bohr's note reveals his positivistic attitude that we can only deal with our experience, and not with any essential reality beyond appearances.

For Bohr, a measurement not merely disturbed the particle, but during the measurement the particle could not be even *thought of* as being separate from the measuring apparatus. Such wholeness is very central to Bohr's position, and it has to do with the fact that according to quantum theory, all interaction between systems is in the form of *indivisible* quanta.

As Bohm (1980) tells us, in quantum theory

> movement is in general *discontinuous*, in the sense that action is constituted of indivisible quanta (implying also that an electron, for example, can go from one state to another, without passing through any states in between).... if all actions are in the form of discrete quanta, the interactions between different entities (e.g. electrons) constitute a single structure of indivisible links, so that the entire universe has to be thought of as an unbroken whole.[6]

Bohm notes that this single interconnected structure does not show up in the everyday level because the quanta are very small. But in a quantum measurement the situation is different, as he pointed out in 1951:

> ...the quanta connecting object and environment constitute irreducible links that belong, at all times, as much to one part as to the other. Since the behaviour of each part depends as much on these quanta as on its 'own' properties, it is clear that no part of the system can be thought of as separate.[7]

It is because of the above that '...at the quantum level of accuracy, an object does not have any "intrinsic" properties (for instance, wave or particle) belonging to itself alone; instead, it shares all its properties mutually and indivisibly with the system with which it interacts.'[8] For example, a position measurement would constitute

> a fundamental change in what could be classically called the 'intrinsic' nature of the electron, a change that is not further analyzable in terms of hypothetical component parts of the electron and its environment. This is the meaning of the statement that at the quantum level of accuracy, the universe is an indivisible whole, which cannot correctly be regarded as made up of its parts.[9]

If a classical experiment revealed to us the presence of an irreducible link between two objects, we would postulate a third object, the link, and give our usual type of explanation in terms of three parts, instead of two. But as Bohm notes, 'in quantum theory, quanta do not constitute separate objects, but are only a way of talking about indivisible transitions of the objects already in existence.'[10] Moreover, the fact that quanta are unpredictable and uncontrollable would, in any case, make them useless as a third object, because we could not ascribe definite observed effects to them.

According to Bohm and Hiley (1987), the essence of Bohr's approach can be put thus: the form of the experimental conditions and the content (meaning) of the experimental results are a single *whole phenomenon*, which cannot be further analyzed, because of the indivisibility of the quantum of action.[11] This unanalyzability means that for the experimental results to have any clear meaning, we must specify the experimental conditions. Bohr wrote: 'The unambiguous account of proper quantum phenomena must, in principle, include a description of all relevant features of the experimental arrangement'.[12]

The fact that a quantum measurement is a single whole implies that there is no *actual* distinction between the measuring apparatus and the quantum mechanical particle: these cannot be thought of as separate entities in interaction, because they are indivisibly connected by the quantum of action. And yet there is the problem of how to reconcile the difference between quantum and classical phenomena. Clearly atomic objects show behaviour that is very different from the behaviour of our everyday, large-scale objects. How did Bohr resolve this? In 1949 he said that

The essentially new feature in the analysis of quantum phenomena is ... the introduction of a fundamental distinction between the measuring apparatus and the objects under investigation.[13] ... The very fact that quantum regularities exclude analysis on classical lines necessitates, ... in the account of experience, a logical distinction between measuring instruments and atomic objects, which in principle prevents comprehensive deterministic description.[14]

But how can the above distinction be reconciled with the notion that observing apparatus and what is observed constitute a single unanalyzable phenomenon? Bohm and Hiley write:

> ...it should be clear that Bohr's distinction between these two, being only a *logical* one does not imply a real division or 'cut' between them. ... To put between the apparatus and the observed system even a purely conceptual disjunction or 'cut', implying that they can at least be *thought about* correctly as disjoint entities in interaction would violate the laws of their quantum mechanical connection, and this precisely in a domain in which these laws must expressly not be approximated by their classical limit.[15]

Bohm and Hiley note that Bohr introduced the distinction '...because he regarded it as necessary in the accounting for the functioning of the measuring instrument in purely classical terms'.[16] But ultimately this function, too, must be considered quantum mechanically, because of the indivisibility of the quantum of action.

Thus Bohr was on the one hand emphasizing the unanalyzable wholeness of the atomic object and the measuring apparatus, and on the other hand he wanted to account for the functioning of the latter in purely classical terms. Why was he doing this? He writes (1949):

> ...it is decisive to recognize that, *however far the phenomena transcend the scope of classical physical explanation, the account of all evidence must be expressed in classical terms*. The argument is simply that by the word 'experiment' we refer to a situation where we can tell others what we have done and what we have learned and that therefore, the account of the experimental arrangement and of the results of the observations must be expressed in unambiguous language with suitable application of the terminology of classical physics.[17]

Thus, the classical level plays a key role in Bohr's interpretation of the quantum theory. What, then, is the relation between the classical and quantum theory?

To show how these theories could be consistently related, Bohr presented the so-called correspondence principle. David Bohm describes it in his 1951 textbook *Quantum Theory*:

> This principle states that the laws of quantum physics must be so chosen that in the classical limit, where many quanta are involved, the quantum laws lead to the classical equations as an average. The problem of satisfying the correspondence principle is by no means trivial. In fact, the requirement of satisfying the correspondence principle, combined with indivisibility, the wave-particle duality, and incomplete determinism, will be seen to define the quantum theory in an almost unique manner.[18]

Intuitively, one might then suppose it is possible to *deduce* from the quantum theory our everyday classical concepts as limiting cases of quantum concepts, by using Bohr's correspondence principle — just as one deduces Newtonian mechanics as a limiting case of special relativity. This, however, is *not* a correct assumption, as Bohm points out in the final pages of his 1951 book.

The point is that quantum theory in the Bohrian form *presupposes* the correctness of classical concepts. Without an appeal to a classical level, quantum theory in the Bohrian form would have *no meaning*. In 1951, while still representing Bohr's point of view, Bohm continued this line of thought as follows:

> ...a description at the quantum level (i.e., in terms of the wave function alone) does not, in general, adequately represent the ... physical properties that the electron is capable of manifesting when it interacts with suitable measuring devices. In order to ... interpret ... the wave function, we must therefore *at the outset* postulate a classical level in terms of which the definite results of a measurement can be realized. Thus, *the correspondence principle is simply a consistency condition* which requires that when the quantum theory plus its classical interpretation is carried out to the limit of high quantum numbers, the simple classical theory will be obtained.[19]

The details of the above may seem difficult for those not familiar with quantum mechanics, but the important point here is to illustrate how we, in the traditional interpretation of the quantum theory, do not have a notion of an independent quantum reality.

If the principle is only a consistency condition, then it *cannot* be seen as a 'bridge' from an independently existing quantum world to the classical world. Bohm writes: 'As we go from small scale to large scale level, new (classical) properties then appear which cannot be deduced from the quantum description... alone, but which must nevertheless be consistent with this quantum description.'[20] Thus, the correspondence principle merely shows how the features of the quantum phenomena can be *consistent* with the features of the classical world; it does not deduce the latter from the former as our common sense might expect.

What is then the nature of this quantum world? Niels Bohr tended to avoid this question. Perhaps due to a positivist influence he thought that the task of physics is not to find out how nature is but to decide what we can *say* about nature. But thinking along lines similar to Heisenberg, David Bohm characterized the quantum world in 1951: '...the quantum properties of matter are to be associated with incompletely defined *potentialities*, which can be more definitely realized only in interaction with a classically describable system (a special case of which is a measuring apparatus).'[21]

Bohm concluded his 1951 discussion of the Bohrian view as follows:

> ...quantum theory has actually evolved in such a way that it implies the need for a new concept of the relation between large-scale and small-scale properties of a given system...:
> 1. Quantum theory presupposes a classical level and the correctness of classical concepts in describing this level.
> 2. The classically definite aspects of large-scale systems cannot be deduced from the quantum-mechanical relationships of assumed small-scale elements. Instead, classical definiteness and quantum potentialities complement each other in providing a complete description of the system as a whole.[22]

The reference to *complementarity* shows clearly how Bohm was still thinking along the same lines as Bohr.

In a later paper 'Soma-significance', Bohm (1987) relates the above question about the relation of quantum and classical theory to the concept of *meaning*. According to him, in order to understand Bohr's revolutionary viewpoint

> ...first we have to say that while the quantum theory contradicts the previously existent classical theory, it does not

explain this theory's basic concepts as...a simplification of itself, but it has to presuppose the classical concepts at the same time as it has to contradict them. The paradox is resolved in Bohr's point of view by saying that the quantum theory introduces no new basic concepts at all. Rather what it does is to require that concepts such as position and momentum, which are in principle unambiguous in classical physics, must become *ambiguous* in quantum mechanics. But ambiguity is just a lack of well-defined meaning. So Bohr, at least tacitly, brings in the notion of meaning as crucial to the understanding of the content of the theory.[23]

The above point about the ambiguity of classical concepts in the quantum theory is fundamentally important philosophically. For Bohm takes it to imply that no 'bottom level' of unambiguous reality is possible. Now this has serious implications to our concept of meaning in general, as he notes:

There is an inherent ambiguity in any concrete meaning. ...how the meanings arise and what they signify depends ... on what a given situation means to us, and this may vary according to our interests. But if there were a 'bottom level' of reality, these meanings would be exactly what they were, and anybody who looked correctly could find them. They would be a reality that was just simply there, independent of what it meant to us.[23]

But, as shown above, the quantum theory implies that matter *cannot* be seen as a bottom level of reality, onto which all phenomena, including the mind can be reduced:

...for Bohr the concepts (describing processes at the quantum level) are ambiguous, and the meaning of the concepts depends on the whole context of the experimental arrangement. The meaning of the result depends on the large-scale behaviour which was supposed to be explained by the particles themselves. So in some sense you do not have a 'bottom level' but rather you find that, to a certain extent, the meaning of these particles has the same sort of ambiguity that we find in mental phenomena when we are looking at meaning.[24]

Bohm emphasizes that this implication of the quantum theory that no 'bottom level' of unambiguous reality is possible, is not commonly realized. For example, physics is currently searching for a fundamental field, and people may easily assume this to be an unambiguous bottom level. But Bohm's point is that, according to the quantum theory, even this level would be ambiguous: the meaning of matter is *context-dependent*.

The above quote also illustrates the kind of circularity that is involved in the still commonly held assumption among scientists and philosophers, that it is in principle possible to reduce all the ambiguous phenomena of various fields of study to an unambiguous bottom level in physics. For example, the mind is thought to reduce to the brain, which in turn reduces to quantum mechanics. It is believed that no matter how ambiguous the phenomena of consciousness may appear to us, we can think that they ultimately *are* unambiguous if we conceive them at the safe rock-bottom level of physics. But if quantum mechanics shows that the meaning of the quantum particles is ambiguous in a similar way as our mental phenomena, then the reduction of mind to matter, in qualitative terms, returns to where it started from — it goes from ambiguity to ambiguity.

Bohm also points out that Bohr does not make clear *why* matter should have this context-dependence, but just says that matter gives rise to it. Bohm's own work in physics has gone more towards explaining why matter does have context-dependence. In this way he has carried further the line of thought Bohr began.

Having finished his 1951 textbook from Bohr's point of view, Bohm began to feel uneasy about the quantum theory. In fact, in the following year he was to publish an alternative interpretation of the theory, which is radically different from Bohr's interpretation, and provides a totally different way of thinking about quantum reality and our relation to it.

In 1987 Bohm characterized the orthodox quantum theory as

> a very truncated, limited, abstracted set of formulae which gives certain limited results having to do with only one moment of an experiment. But out of this truncated view, physicists are trying to explain everything, you see; the whole thing simply has no meaning at all. Think about it: modern physics can't even talk about the actual world![25]

2. Beyond cave mechanics: Bohm's new interpretation in terms of active information

As someone once aptly remarked, 'I do not know whether quantum mechanics is a beautiful building or a prison with very high walls.' With the appearance of an alternative approach at least a ray of light has appeared through those very high walls. — B. Hiley & D. Peat, 1987.[26]

Bohm felt and still feels that Bohr's view was consistent, unlike many of the other interpretations, such as von Neumann's. But he was also dissatisfied with Bohr's interpretation and was to present a serious alternative. Why? Bohm himself answers:

> What I felt to be especially unsatisfactory was the fact that the quantum theory had no place in it for an adequate notion of an independent actuality — i.e. of an actual movement or activity by which one physical state could pass over into another. My main difficulty was not that the wave-function was interpreted only in terms of probabilities, so that the theory was not deterministic; rather, it was that it could only be discussed in terms of the results of an experiment or an observation, which has to be treated as a set of *phenomena* that are ultimately not further analyzable or explainable at all. So, the theory could not go beyond the phenomena or appearances.[27]

So here we find that Bohm was not uneasy about the indeterminism of the quantum theory. Instead, he was dissatisfied because the 'theory could not go beyond appearances'. He was searching for a more realist notion of an independent actuality. But why was he doing this, if present experiments did not show such an independent reality?

Firstly, he felt that the theory of relativity, which was considered to be as fundamental as quantum theory, demanded a space-time process (in terms of fields) which constituted an independent actuality. And, as Bohm points out, the 'anti-realism' of Bohr's quantum theory becomes truly problematic, when relativity is extended to include cosmology:

> It seems impossible even to contemplate the universe as a whole through a view which can discuss only in terms of discrete or distinct sets of phenomena, for in a cosmological view the observing instruments, and indeed the physicists who construct and operate them, have to be regarded at least in principle as parts of the totality. There does not seem to be much sense in saying that all these are nothing more than organized sets of appearances. To whom or to what would they appear, and of what would they be the appearances?
>
> I felt particularly dissatisfied with the self-contradictory attitude of accepting the independent existence of the cosmos while one was doing relativity and, at the same time, deny-

ing it while one was doing the quantum theory, even though
both theories were regarded as fundamental. I did not see how
an adequate way to deal with this could be developed on the
basis of Niels Bohr's point of view. So I began to ask myself
whether another approach might not be possible.[28]

This new approach is the one Bohm developed in 1952.[29] It
is also the basis of his work related to active information and
meaning which is one of the central topics in this volume.

What is the nature of quantum reality in Bohm's new
interpretation? How does he avoid the difficulties of Bohr's
point of view? In order to answer these questions, I will discuss a recent paper by Bohm, entitled 'An ontological foundation for the quantum theory'.[30]

As you may remember, the new concepts of Bohm's interpretation can be summed up '...in terms of the notion that the
wave-function determines a quantum potential representing
active information, which operates to give form to the motion
of particles that, however, move under their own energy.'[30]
Bohm emphasizes that there is a further new point, and as
you will see, it is highly relevant to our present discussion:

> ...the quantum theory itself implies the independent existence
> of a large-scale manifest reality (i.e., one that is tangible and
> publicly accessible) in which the new quantum features can
> be neglected. This is contrasted with the subtle (i.e., intan-
> gible) quantum world of the wave-function. This subtle quan-
> tum world is then shown to be capable of revealing itself in
> the manifest world, especially in experiments that are sensi-
> tive to a quantum level of accuracy.[30]

In starting his article, Bohm again draws attention to the way
the '...quantum theory...is assumed to give nothing but
statistical predictions about the results of measurements.
Indeed, without the statistics of measurements, the quantum
theory would, in this view, be just a piece of pure mathematics,
with no physical significance.'[30] He points out that the above
situation gives a fundamental role to epistemology — for it is
only through its prediction of the statistics of measurement
that ordinary quantum theory gains physical significance. It
has no terms which refer to objects in an independent reality.
There's practically no ontology whereas epistemology is fundamental in the sense, that '...it is not even possible to express
the theory without an essential reference to our knowledge

of the world and to our means of obtaining it (e.g., through experimental observations and measurements).'[31]

What Bohm wants to do is to present a consistent ontological interpretation to the quantum theory. He feels that

> an ontological basis for the theory has certain important advantages, in that it helps to make the meaning of the theory more clear and easier to grasp, and to suggest interesting and significant new concepts with regard to the nature of the independent reality that is implied by the quantum theory.[31]

In his article Bohm discusses the relation between the quantum world and its classical 'limit' in terms of the concepts *manifest* and *subtle*. What is crucial here is that whereas in 1951 Bohm was defending the view that the classical world *cannot* be thought of as consisting of an independently existing quantum world, he has since 1952 been trying to do just the opposite: to show that such an independent quantum world *is possible*, provided we postulate the quantum potential.

Bohm points out that a detailed analysis[32] shows that the quantum potential is unimportant under typical conditions that generally prevail in the ordinary macroscopic domain of experiences:

> The crucial point here is . . . that in the large-scale limit, the wave-function generally no longer affects the motion of the particles in a significant way. The system of particles therefore follows a (Newtonian) law of motion, which refers only to the particle properties themselves.[33]

In Bohm's interpretation, it *is* possible to conceive of the classical world as deducible from an independent quantum reality, because in the large-scale limit (with a high number of molecules) the new quantum mechanical effects are negligible.

Thus, by postulating that the wave-function determines the quantum potential with its active information, Bohm is, in principle, able to represent the physical properties of an electron. Compare this with Bohr's type of view in which a description in terms of the wave-function does not adequately '. . .represent the definiteness of physical properties that the electron is capable of manifesting when it interacts with suitable measuring devices.'[18]

Moreover, in Bohm's present view there is no need to postulate the classical level in order to interpret the wave-function, which can be contrasted with Bohr's type of view that 'in order to obtain a means of interpreting the wave-function, we must therefore *at the outset* postulate a classical level in terms of which the definite results of a measurement can be realized.'[18]

Thus, in Bohm's causal interpretation, we *can* look at our everyday world as a large-scale limit of an independent quantum world. In the large-scale limit

> all the new properties implied by the quantum theory, including active information, non-locality, the dependence of the forces between the particles on the over-all quantum state, can now be left out of account. The large-scale limit of the 'quantum world' is thus essentially a kind of classical 'world on its own'. To use Bohr's own mode of description, this is just the ordinary public world of common sense, 'refined where necessary, to an expression in terms of the laws of classical mechanics'.[33]

From a philosophical point of view Bohm's view has a tremendous advantage, especially when compared to Bohr's epistemological view, which is in conceptual contradiction with the theory of relativity. But in order to have the above view of reality, Bohm's interpretation gives key importance not only to the manifest world of particles described above but also to the subtle, intangible world of the wave-function:

> Clearly the wave-function, which is of the nature of information, cannot be directly 'touched' by the senses. Rather it is inferred from the *phenomena* that can be observed in the manifest world, which arise in our act of touching and seeing, (as extended with our scientific instruments).[33]

Is Bohm bringing into physics something totally unobservable and abstract? Is not information such an abstract concept that it cannot possibly be considered as a basic concept in ontology? Is not information more like a *property* of the manifest world that *we* attribute to it, rather than something real? Here Bohm points to the significant feature of his interpretation, namely that the information he sees to underlie quantum reality is *active* and not *abstract*:

> The subtle world is not, however, permanently confined to inferences drawn about a domain of a purely abstract information. Rather, because it operates as *active* information, it

is able to reveal itself in the manifest world. A quantum mechanical measurement is a particular case of a process in which this takes place.[34]

As an example, Bohm then discusses the so-called Stern-Gerlach experiment and emphasizes that he can treat the measurement process as a single whole, without any break or 'cut' between classical and quantum mechanical levels:

> In principle, it is thus possible in detail to follow the process by which the subtle quantum level is gradually able to manifest itself. This is in contrast to what happens in conventionally accepted interpretations (e.g., those of Bohr and von Neumann) which begin by assuming a basic distinction between the classical level and what may be called a 'quantum reality' that might underlie it, with no possibility of following the connection in detail. In the causal interpretation, however, there is only one reality.[35]

We can speak of this reality by making a new kind of distinction between a 'subtle world' of the wave-function and the 'manifest world' of the classical limit. But what is crucially important here is that '...this distinction is not arbitrarily imposed from outside, (e.g., by assumption) but that it has been demonstrated to *follow from the overall theory itself*'.[35] The quantum theory is a way of describing nature, and in a fascinating way Bohm points out that the very formalism of quantum theory contains implicitly a distinction between the subtle and the manifest level.

Remember how Bohm was describing quantum and classical theory from Bohr's point of view in 1951 by saying that 'the classically definite aspects of large-scale systems cannot be deduced from the quantum-mechanical relationships of assumed small-scale elements.'[22] In contrast to this Bohm is now saying that '...the quantum theory itself implies the independent existence of a large-scale manifest reality (i.e., one that is tangible and publicly accessible) in which the new quantum features can be neglected'.[30]

3. Beyond cave psychology: the subtle world of the mind
The fact that the subtle quantum effects are negligible in the classical limit does not imply that our everyday world is totally devoid of any subtle features. On the contrary, the fact that the subtle level reveals itself in the behaviour of quantum par-

ticles makes it very plausible that some different kind of subtlety should reveal itself in the activity of more complex material systems, such as human bodies. Inspired by quantum mechanics, Bohm makes an interesting analogy to the activity of human beings:

> For a human being, the body is what is manifest or tangible. But human beings do not generally interact by mechanical forces, i.e., by pushing and pulling on each other. In general, each person is guided by information (rather as the electron is, but of course in a much more complex way). . . . the energy comes from the body, but the form given to this energy comes from information existing at a more subtle level (in this case, in the brain and nervous system). Evidently, we could never understand the behaviour of human beings without reference to this more subtle level.[36]

Bohm thinks that this more subtle level of consciousness goes beyond the manifest matter in the brain and cannot be reduced to it.

In this respect there is a crucial difference between Bohm and most researchers in cognitive science and the philosophy of mind. For most cognitive scientists are reductive materialists of some sort or another: most believe that mental states are properties of any suitably organized material system in which the mental states can have the right *functional relations* to other mental states and the environment (functionalism); others believe that the mind simply *is* the brain (identity theory/reductive materialism); still others believe that what people normally think of as their mind is largely an illusion and that by *eliminating* this illusion we arrive at a mind that is the brain (eliminative materialism); there are some that believe that mind and body are distinct substances which interact (dualism; most notably Eccles).[37]

So except for dualism, all these views in cognitive science make the assumption that the mind really *is* a material process. They think that we can, in principle, give a causal explanation for mental processes in terms of neurophysiological processes; and that the neurophysiological processes can ultimately be given an explanation in terms of atomic processes. And as quantum mechanics is at present the most fundamental theory of matter known to us, and as all these cognitive scientists think of themselves as materialists, they, at least implicitly, assume that mental processes can be given an explanation in terms of quantum mechanics.

I do not think any of the cognitive scientists believe that an explanation in terms of quantum mechanics or even in terms of detailed neurophysiology would actually *explain* much. Margaret Boden, who is a functionalist and a materialist, writes:

> Explanation of behaviour must include reference to...internal models, and to the general structure of the information processing going on within the system, whether organism or computer. ... A causal account, although in a sense fully *complete*, cannot be fully *adequate*, for it cannot exhibit structural features. In spite of behaviour which we most naturally explain in terms of 'the mind controlling the body', we need not abandon hope for a purely physicalist neurophysiology accounting for behaviour at the causal level.[38]

So Boden tells us here that a causal account is not fully adequate, although she emphasizes that a purely physicalist neurophysiology *can* account for behaviour at the causal level. She holds that ontologically speaking, the human mind *is* a suitably organized brain process. Thus, she thinks that we need not refer to any subtle level when we are explaining the causal workings of the brain. In so far as the brain is following the laws of classical mechanics, we can, of course, give a causal explanation to any brain process, at least in principle. But Bohm and Peat (1987) write:

> Neurobiologists have little to do with the theories of quantum mechanics. However, it has been found that, in certain ways, the nervous system can respond to individual quanta of energy. This opens the possibility that the current reliance of the neurosciences on everyday notions of space, time and causality may prove to be inadequate, and eventually notions from quantum theory may have to be brought into this field.[39]

Thus, insofar as quantum notions will be brought into the neurosciences, all materialist cognitive scientists will have to start thinking about just the questions on quantum reality we discussed earlier. They have to do this, if they want to have a clear philosophical understanding of the material level by which they think it is possible to give a complete account of the mind 'causally and mechanically'.

But even if we assume that we *can* explain all mentally significant neurophysiological processes with classical mechanics only, a cognitive scientist who takes mind to be physical in any philosophical sense cannot neglect quantum mechanics. For it is on the basis of quantum mechanics that we presently have to answer the question about the nature of matter.

The quantum theory poses difficulties to the whole tendency of science to reduce 'higher' levels to lower ones. We have already seen that in Bohr's view it makes no sense to think of reducing the classical world of, say, brains to the quantum mechanical level of atoms. For as you remember, we must postulate the classical level at the outset, and it is only in the context of experimental *phenomena*, which includes the classically describable measuring apparatus that we can talk about quantum properties. Thus, we do not have an independent bottom level of quantum reality in Bohr's view — or at least we cannot say anything about it.

There are other interpretations of quantum theory, which lead to even more striking views about quantum reality. Nobel laureate Eugene Wigner thinks that it is only after the results of a quantum experiment have registered in the *consciousness* of the observer that we can speak of the particle as having a specific state. This view takes the psychologist trying to reduce mind to matter into a truly circular adventure, as described lucidly by Harold Morowitz in his article 'Rediscovering the Mind'. He combines three views that are represented by recognized experts in their fields:

First, the human mind, including consciousness and reflective thought, can be explained by activities of the central nervous system ... Second, biological phenomena at all levels can be totally understood in terms of atomic physics ... Third and last, atomic physics, which is now understood most fully by means of quantum mechanics, must be formulated with the mind as a primitive component of the system.

We have thus, in separate steps, gone round an epistemological circle — from the mind, back to the mind. The results of this chain of reasoning will probably lend more aid and comfort to Eastern mystics than to neurophysiologists and molecular biologists; nevertheless, the closed loop follows from a straightforward combination of the explanatory processes of recognized experts in the three separate sciences. Since individuals seldom work with more than one of these paradigms, the general problem has received little attention.[40]

Wigner thought that quantum mechanics must be formulated with the mind as a primitive component of the system, for he had reasons to believe that the mind of the observer is able to change the state of the quantum mechanical system — in this sense the mind is a primitive component. According to Wigner, most physical scientists believe that it is 'not possible to formulate the laws of quantum mechanics in a fully consistent way without reference to the consciousness.'[40] Wigner also notes how remarkable it is that the scientific study of the world led to the content of consciousness as an ultimate reality.

It is ironical that here we have Wigner saying that most physicists believe that the content of consciousness is the ultimate reality, whereas almost all cognitive scientists believe that the ultimate reality is 'matter'. It seems that no academic field accepts the responsibility of discussing the nature of being, but instead, the question is passed around — a supreme form of academic bureaucracy!

I think it is only after understanding the above type of problems with the quantum mechanical concept of matter that one can fully appreciate the alternative interpretation David Bohm is proposing. For his view, unlike that of Bohr, provides us with a notion of quantum reality beyond the appearances; and unlike Wigner, he does not need to assume that human consciousness plays a fundamental role in quantum processes.

Thus, Bohm is able to provide more reality than Bohr, without getting into the strange Wignerian situation. At the same time we have seen that in Bohm's interpretation, too, we have to make some radical assumptions. For as shown in this volume, he invites us to consider that something analogous to information plays an objective role even at the quantum level.

How does Bohm then view reduction? Could we not think that, having established a notion of an independent quantum reality, we can reduce everything, including the human consciousness to it? Bohm answers in dialogue with the philosopher Renée Weber:

> **Bohm:** In the view I'm presenting nothing is being reduced. Pure idealism would reduce matter to an aspect of mind. Hegel was an example of that. Pure materialism attempts to reduce mind to an aspect of matter, and of course that's what we see in a great deal of modern science. My view does not attempt

to reduce one to the other any more than one would reduce form to content.

Weber: Spinoza says for every aspect of matter there is a concomitant aspect of consciousness, and vice versa. Do you accept that?

Bohm: They're interwoven. They're correlative categories of reality, always woven together just as form and content are woven together. Every content is a form and every form is at a same time a content. Another way of saying that is that everything material is mental and mental is also material, but there are many more infinitely subtle levels of matter than we are aware of.[41]

How can we understand quantum reality and consciousness in the light of the above? I think Bohm's crucial point in this regard is that there are subtle levels of matter. Matter cannot be thought of as consisting of basic manifest elements only: there is no one bottom level to reality. Instead, in order to understand and explain being, we need to make a distinction between manifest and subtle levels of matter. And note that by the word 'matter' Bohm refers simultaneously to something mental, while 'mental' also refers to something material. It is like when looking at a Van Gogh painting, we can refer to the form of the painting without implying that the form is actually separate from the whole content of the painting.

So in order to discuss quantum reality, Bohm refers to the subtle level of the active information described by the quantum potential. We can then ask: what is the nature of this information? Bohm makes clear that it is not an ordinary physical property like energy or charge: '. . . information is a very condensed form of meaning that has to be unfolded.'[42] It is thus a more subtle physical property. But it has to be able to show its effects in the manifest world of quantum particles.

But how can something subtle and not physical in the ordinary sense interact with the crude, manifest matter of quantum particles? If electrons were crude and material objects it is clear that they could not be in contact with the subtle level of matter. Thus, Bohm's view implies that, say, an electron must have a subtle internal structure, and in his article in this volume he argues that this idea is very plausible. In that sense the 'manifest' level is not crude — the electrons have, according to Bohm, a subtle internal structure.

Thus, the manifest level is not ultimately crude in its nature.

Why does Bohm then make the distinction between the subtle and the manifest? Again, this distinction is a logical one and does not correspond to any actual division in the objective world. It is a distinction that we make in order to speak of the reality. Thus, Bohm is not claiming that there actually exist separate levels in reality, as might be easily misunderstood. He suggests that we make the distinctions in thought.

Therefore, when we make a distinction between two levels, such as the particle and its active information, or the brain and consciousness, it is implicit that these levels have something in common which enable us to speak of their relationship to each other. We say that the manifest electron has a subtle internal structure, in order to understand how it can be guided by the subtle information described by the quantum potential.

In a similar way we can make a distinction between the brain and consciousness. The brain is more manifest, and we can think of it as consisting of the manifest quantum particles. The quantum theory presently implies that for most behaviourally important processes in the brain, the subtle effects of quantum mechanical active information are not important. It follows that the brain can be thought to consist of manifest matter, which follows the laws of classical mechanics. But then there is the more subtle level of consciousness which we experience directly, and which Descartes with great insight characterized as that which has no extension in space.

The problem of how the subtle level of consciousness and the manifest level of the brain are related is presently a mystery. Nobody has given a theory about it that would be comparable in accuracy to the way David Bohm can characterize the relation between the subtle level of information and the manifest particles at the quantum level. But at the same time Sheldrake, for example, has produced a hypothesis in terms of morphic fields which is applicable to the brain and conceptually consistent with Bohm's theory.

To conclude my article, let me give you an idea of how Bohm's thinking in physics could be used as a way of approaching the much vaster problem of brain and consciousness. First of all, let us assume that Descartes was right in characterizing mind as that which has no *extension* in space. But was he right in saying that matter is that which does have extension in space? As Arleta Griffor pointed out in the previous article, if this division is made absolute, then there is no way to understand the relation between mind and matter, without appealing to a supernatural agent.

Bohm's view agrees with Descartes in that mind has no extension in three-dimensional space. But there's a disagreement in the sense that for Bohm mind can be thought of as a more subtle material process. But is there any material process which has no extension in three-dimensional space? Bohm's model of quantum mechanics suggests that there is. For *active information* can be thought of as a subtle material process, and at the same time it has no extension in three-dimensional space. Bohm notes:

> One reason people didn't think that we could ever get a physical interpretation of quantum theory was the problem of multi-dimensional space. They said 'What does a multi-dimensional space mean physically?' But if we view it as a field of information, it becomes clearer since we know that information is organized in any number of dimensions. Therefore there is no reason why the information field around the electron cannot be said to be in multi-dimensional space.[43]

Thus, the quantum theory implies that matter cannot be exhaustively defined as that which has extension in three-dimensional space, as Descartes thought. In other words, it implies that what is essential to matter is a more subtle aspect, which is more like information. We could think that the same holds for human consciousness. To begin with, we could think of consciousness as information in multi-dimensional space, which would be related to the manifest brain *analogously* to the way the information field is related to the electron. Of course, human consciousness can be thought of as a much more subtle material process than the quantum mechanical information.

Bohm indeed suggests that human consciousness extends to very subtle levels of being which may not even be located in the body, in the sense that the brain and the body may be affected, as Sheldrake is suggesting, by fields which are not local. This prompts Renée Weber to ask Bohm:

> **Weber:** Are you proposing something like a *meaning field*?
> **Bohm:** Yes, that's exactly it. You could say (and Sheldrake seems to agree with this) that the morphogenetic field is a field of active meaning — meaning in the signa-somatic and soma-significant sense.[44]

The point is that we all have a direct sense of a subtle consciousness, and that this consciousness is immediately related to the brain and the body which is a more manifest system. Faced with a comparable subtlety in quantum phenomena, Bohm showed that it was reasonable to postulate a field of information. Thus we are lead to ask, can we not begin to understand and explain consciousness by suggesting that it is a field of information?

It is in this context that Sheldrake's hypothesis of morphic fields becomes extremely interesting. For Sheldrake suggests that all biological organisms, of which the brain is a special case, are in general associated with fields of information.

I will not discuss here in more detail how consciousness could be understood in terms of morphic fields, but refer the reader to Sheldrake's recent book *The Presence of the Past* (1988).[45] But our study in this article has shown that fields of information are relevant when we try to understand the nature of matter quantum mechanically. And if fields of information are essential to matter in general, there is no reason why they could not be essential to human consciousness and the brain, which, after all, is the most subtle material process known to us presently.

Notes and references

1. Bell, J.S. (1987), 'Beables for quantum field theory', in *Quantum Implications: Essays in honour of David Bohm*, ed. by Hiley, B.J. and Peat, F.D., p. 227, London, Routledge. Bell is referring to Bohm, D. (1952), *Phys. Rev. 85*, p. 166; p. 180.

2. In his metaphor of the cave, Plato asked us to '(i)magine the condition of men living in a sort of cavernous chamber underground, with an entrance open to the light and a long passage all down to the cave. Here they have been from childhood, chained by the leg and also by the neck, so that they cannot move and can see only what is in front of them, because the chains will not let them turn their heads. At some distance higher up is the light of a fire burning behind them; and between the prisoners and the fire is a track with a parapet built along it, like the screen at a puppet-show...

Now behind this parapet imagine persons carrying various artificial objects, ...which project above the parapet... Prisoners so confined would have seen nothing of themselves or of one another, except the shadows thrown by the fire-light on the wall of the Cave facing them, would they?...And if they could talk to one another, would they not suppose that their words referred only to those passing shadows which they saw?' Plato, *Republic*, quoted in Jones, W.T. (1969), *A History of Western Philosophy. The Classical Mind*, second edition, pp. 135-6, San Diego, Harcourt Brace Jovanovich.

3. Stannard, R. and Coley, N.G. (1981), 'Introduction to quantum theory' in *Modern Physics and Problems of Knowledge*, p. 99. Milton Keynes, Open University Press.

4. Bohr, N. (1961), *Atomic Theory and the Description of Nature*, Cambridge University Press. Quoted in Coley & Stannard (1981), p. 114. (ref. 3).

5. Ibid., p. 18.

6. Bohm, D. (1980), *Wholeness and the Implicate Order*, p. 175, London, Routledge.

7. Bohm, D. (1951), *Quantum Theory*, p. 166. New Jersey, Prentice Hall. Republished by Dover, 1989.

8. Ibid., p. 161.

9. Ibid., p. 162.

10. Ibid., p. 166.

11. Bohm, D. and Hiley, B. (1987), 'Sequence of interpretations of the Quantum Theory', p. 1. Preprint.

12. Bohr, N. (1963): 'Quantum physics and philosophy', in *Essays 1958-62 on Atomic Physics and Human Knowledge*, p. 4, New York, Wiley. Quoted in Ibid., p. 2.

13. Ibid., p. 3.

14. Ibid., p. 6.

15. 'Sequence of interpretations of the Quantum Theory', p. 4.

16. Ibid., p. 5.

17. Bohr, N. (1949), 'Discussion with Einstein on epistemological problems in modern physics', contribution to *Albert Einstein: Philosopher-Scientist*, p. 209, Illinois, The Library of Living Philosophers Vol. 7. Quoted in Coley & Stannard (1981), p. 114.

18. *Quantum Theory*, p. 31.

19. Ibid., p. 626, latter italics mine.

20. Ibid., p. 626.

21. Ibid., p. 625.

22. Ibid. pp. 627-8.

23. Bohm, D. (1987), *Unfolding Meaning*, ed. by Factor, D., p. 84, 2nd edition, London, ARK paperbacks.

24. Ibid., p. 85.

25. Bohm, D. (1987), in discussion with Sheldrake, R., *A New Science of Life*, 2nd edition, p. 248, London, Paladin.

26. Hiley, B. and Peat, D. (1987), 'General Introduction: The development of David Bohm's ideas from the plasma to the implicate order', in *Quantum Implications*, p. 18.

27. Bohm, D. (1987), 'Hidden variables and the implicate order', in *Quantum Implications*, p. 33.

28. Ibid., p. 34.

29. Bohm, D. (1952), *Phys, Rev.*, *85*, p. 166; p. 180.

30. Bohm, D. (1987), 'An ontological foundation for the quantum theory', in *Symposium on the Foundations of Modern Physics 1987. The Copenhagen Interpretation 60 years after the Como Lecture*. Joensuu, Finland 6-8 August 1987., ed. by Lahti, P. & Mittelstaedt, P., p. 83, Singapore, World Scientific.

31. Ibid., p. 84.

32. Bohm, D. and Hiley, B. (1987), *Physics Report 144*, p. 323.

33. 'An ontological foundation for the quantum theory', p. 97.

34. Ibid., p. 98.

35. Ibid., p. 99, italics mine.

36. Ibid., p. 100.

37. Churchland, P.M. (1984), *Matter and Consciousness*, chapter 2, Cambridge, Mass., The MIT Press.

38. Boden, M.A. (1981), *Minds and Mechanisms*, p. 68, Brighton, Harvester Press.

39. Bohm, D. and Peat, D. (1987), *Science, Order and Creativity*, p. 71, New York, Bantam Books.

40. Morowitz, H.J. (1981), 'Rediscovering the Mind', in *The Mind's I*, ed. by Hofstaedter, D. and Dennett, D., p. 39, First appeared in *Psychology Today*, August 1980.

41. In Weber, R. (1986), *Dialogues with Scientists and Sages*, p. 151, London, Routledge.

42. Weber, R. (1987), 'Meaning as being in the implicate order philosophy of David Bohm: a conversation', in *Quantum Implications*, p. 442.

43. *Dialogues with Scientists and Sages*, p. 111.

44. *Quantum Implications*, p. 444.

45. Sheldrake, R. (1988), *The Presence of the Past*, London, Collins.

The Mystery of Mathematics

KARL GEORG WIKMAN

Introduction: What is mathematics?
Mathematics — its essence, inner world and correspondence with reality — raises some of the deepest and most fundamental questions about the nature of human mental functioning and ultimately about reality itself. Concepts such as meaning and creativity are inseparably associated with mathematics and the very process of doing it.

It is generally agreed that mathematics is the most advanced example of structured human reasoning. Some of its particular features contribute to this picture: a mathematical proof justifies the truth of a statement or a theorem. An explicit proof gives everybody the possibility to inspect and critically examine the validity of the reasoning behind a statement. It is also peculiar to mathematics that it does not have to refer to anything in particular. This leaves much less room for subjective interpretation, which leads to various disagreements in other sciences.

The demand for correct reasoning is thus particularly pronounced in mathematics. This is due to the fact that just one unnoticed false statement could ruin all of mathematics. This is so because from such a false statement it would, in principle, be possible to arrive at *any* conclusion; that is, it would be possible to prove any false theorem true. Finally, as was shown by Kurt Gödel in 1932, mathematics is capable of revealing its own inherent limitations.

One of the most distinguished mathematicians of this century, Thomas Hardy, once said:

> ...there is another reality, which I call mathematical reality; and there is no ... agreement about the nature of mathemat-

ical reality among either mathematicians or philosophers. Some hold it is mental and that we in some sense have constructed it, others that it is outside and independent of us. A man who could give a convincing account of mathematical reality would have solved very many of the most difficult problems of metaphysics. If he could include physical reality in this account, he would have solved them all.[1]

These riddles crystallize into three main issues, as follows: (a) Great mathematicians throughout the last centuries have been able to arrive at deep mathematical truths by a sudden flash of insight or intuitions. In many cases they themselves have not been able to give a proof for their new theorems and results themselves; in other cases this proof has not been found by others within their lifetime; and finally, some theorems have never been proved. But even these can be so useful and basic that they are used in further developments of mathematics. By common standards of judgement, it seems rather mysterious that a science celebrated for its strict and logical step by step reasoning should take such giant leaps in the process of finding new mathematical truths.

(b) Another philosophical question of great concern is why mathematics is so free from contradictions. In fact, it must be free from contradictions in order to work at all. The problem became acute after Kurt Gödel in the early thirties once and for all demonstrated that mathematicians had to live with the fact that it is impossible to prove that mathematics is both complete and free from contradictions. Yet, not a single inner contradiction has ever been found.

(c) Finally, the deepest problem is why mathematics can so accurately describe and predict physical phenomena.

I will connect the above questions with Bohm's thinking[2,3] at relevant points. In the last section I will look at the problems in a cosmic context and raise the question whether mathematics could be seen as the way the universe refers to itself. And here again we will find a link to Bohm's thinking, for although the concept of self-reference is only occasionally mentioned by him, it is nonetheless implicit in his philosophy to a high degree.

Creativity in mathematics
Mathematics is often characterized in three ways: as a philosophy, a science and an art. When mathematics is seen as an art, the creative aspect of doing mathematics is emphasized.

Let us start our investigation of the role of creativity in mathematics by looking at what some eminent mathematicians say about their personal experience.

Henri Poincare, one of the greatest mathematicians of the last century, has given a famous account of the creative process. Poincare was particularly interested in the process leading up to the perception of a novel mathematical truth or a theorem. In his writings, he stresses that this process involves two different stages: the preparatory phase and the insight itself. The first part is a period of hard conscious effort, while the second involves an effortless flash of insight.

He further contrasts mathematics with a game of chess, pointing out that mathematical creation

> ... does not consist of making new combinations with entities that are already known. That can be done by anyone, and the combinations that could be so formed would be infinite in number, and the greater part of them would be absolutely devoid of interest. Discovery consists precisely in not constructing useless combinations, but in constructing those that are useful, which are an infinitely small minority. Mathematical discovery is discernment, selection.[4]

Mathematical reasoning has beauty and elegance:

> The hallmark of these orderings of mathematical entities is the harmonious arrangement of their elements, so that the mind can, without effort, take in the whole without neglecting the details. This harmony is ... an assistance to the mind which it supports and guides. The quality of the relationship between mathematical entities is seen to guide the mind towards an apprehension of the mathematical significance of the combination as a whole: by setting before our eyes a well-ordered whole, it gives us the presentiment of a mathematical law.[4]

Poincare is saying that what is characteristic of a non-trivial mathematical law is a quality of beauty 'holding it together' and this is what guides our minds in conceiving it. A non-trivial mathematical law epitomizes some important mathematical quality. The mental processes at work during such mathematical insights are of a subtle and unconscious nature. Poincare refers to a special 'sensitivity', particularly evolved in the gifted mathematician. He underlines the non-mechanistic nature of this process many times:

> ... the rules which must guide this choice (of mathematically important combinations) are extremely subtle, and it is prac-

tically impossible to state them in precise language. They must be felt rather than formulated. Under these conditions, how can we imagine a sieve capable of applying them mechanically?[4]

The sieve he mentions has to do with his suggestion that there is a 'filter' at a subconscious level which only lets the meaningful mathematical combinations pass through. He emphasizes that this filter is not of an intellectual character by stressing the emotional nature of the experience.

Let us move on to Thomas Hardy, who is recognized as the leading mathematician of his time. Hardy saw mathematics primarily as an art. Like Poincare, he contrasts mathematics to the game of chess; a particular chess problem can be seen as an exercise in pure mathematics. In spite of this, Hardy regards chess problems as unimportant, whereas mathematics at its best has a great value:

> The seriousness of a mathematical theorem lies not in its practical consequences, which are usually negligible, but in the significance of the mathematical ideas which it connects ... we may say that a mathematical idea is significant if it can be connected, in a natural and illuminating way, with a large complex of other mathematical ideas. Thus a serious mathematical theorem — a theorem which connects significant ideas, is likely to lead to important advances in mathematics itself and even in other sciences. No chess problem has ever affected the general scientific thought: Pythagoras, Newton, Einstein have in their time changed its whole direction.[5]

If we give *significance* a primary status, as Bohm does in his current thinking, the difference between a chess problem and an important mathematical theorem becomes much more clear. Significance or meaning is always related to a context. In general, the more limited the context, the more insignificant its related meaning. Even if a problem in chess can bring about solutions which are ingenious and intricate, the framework is of a much more restricted nature than that of mathematics.

Going back to the creative and sudden nature of mathematical insight, Poincare is not alone in emphasizing it. Many eminent mathematicians have seen mathematical truths in a flash. Karl Gauss, whose mastery of mathematics no one would question, had for years been trying to solve a certain problem about whole numbers, when he saw the solution:

> Like a sudden flash of lightning, the riddle happened to be solved. I myself cannot say what was the conducting thread which connected what I previously knew with what made my success possible.[6]

From the common mechanistic point of view, the working of the subconscious in such cases of sudden insight has been explained by comparing it to an automata, capable of producing an immense number of combinations of, say, mathematical symbols or entities. The conscious part of the brain is then said to be able to select those relations which are true or meaningful in a given context. The above examples, however, indicate that this is not how mathematical insight works. Firstly, the potential number of combinations would be almost infinite. Secondly, in many cases the mathematical insight involves the discovery of new basic principles. If we assume that the subconscious actually operates in such a combinatorial way, somewhere along the way to conscious experience there must be the recognition, or rather the selection of these principles. This would be almost analogous to maintaining that in the formulation of a philosophical insight, the subconscious mind reshuffles an enormous number of words, and then from all of those mostly completely meaningless sentences, the relevant one is filtered out.

The elusive nature of such mathematical insight is also seen from the fact that the result of the insight is in many cases not proved until long after its conception. Some of Riemann's theorems are still unproven after 75 years of an immense amount of work. Some of the theorems were proven after many years but even this required volumes of complex mathematical reasoning. It is very hard to see how a mechanical process of trial and error could give rise to results so hard to prove.

However, this ability to 'perceive' mathematical truths is not restricted to gifted mathematicians. In history there have been many cases of 'autistic savants' with remarkable abilities to perform lengthy calculations without any aid. Autistic savants are mentally retarded people who are exceptionally talented in some narrow field. Recently this rare set of symptoms has received world-wide attention due to the film *Rain Man* and D.A. Treffert's book *Extraordinary People*. Particularly interesting are the talents of two American brothers, both mentally retarded, but outdoing the computer in naming and finding prime numbers. This is particularly striking as they had great difficulties in performing normal additions, were almost incapable of making subtractions and were totally unable to divide. In spite of this, they were able to tell within minutes whether a certain number, from 10 to 20 digits long, was a prime number.

Calculating prodigies might not be a very convincing example if considered in isolation, for their success could in principle be explained by the 'combinatorial model' mentioned above. But the ability of the autistic savants can be seen as a particular instance of a general human capacity to gain direct mathematical insights. This capacity could metaphorically be called the sixth sense. Just as we are able to perceive meaningful sounds, music, visual images etc. via our normal senses, it seems we can also perceive meaningful mathematical structures via our sixth sense. And because our physical theories are expressed in the form of mathematics, our sixth sense also perceives the structure of physical reality. A particularly well-known and puzzling example of a person with such a sixth sense was S. Ramanujan.[7]

He was born about a hundred years ago in India in a poor family, and had only a high school education. Being isolated from contemporary mathematics and uneducated in standard mathematics, he nevertheless left behind a wealth of four thousand mathematical formulas, when he died at the age of 32.

Now, a hundred years later, many of the formulas remain unproven in spite of huge efforts. A mathematician, Jonathan Borwein, who is part of a team investigating Ramanujan's work, said:

> He seems to have been functioning in a way unlike anybody else we know of. . . He had such feeling for things that they just flowed out of his brain. Perhaps he did not see them in a way that is translatable.

It was the English mathematician Hardy who realized the genius of Ramanujan. When he first saw a sample of Ramanujan's formulas, he was amazed. He could prove some of them only with difficulty, using the current full machinery of mathematics, and some others defeated him completely:

> I have never seen anything in the least like them before. A single look at them is enough to show that they could only be written down by a mathematician of the highest class. They must be true, because, if they were not true, no one would have the imagination to invent them.

Ramanujan's way of working illustrates clearly his direct insight into mathematical truths. He wrote down his results directly in his notebook, feeling no need to prove that they were true. He often used to write down mathematical results immediately after waking up. Even if he had had a standard education in mathematics, his accomplishment would be extraordinary. He gave results which have taken one hundred years for European mathematicians to achieve, and in his last year, he produced more mathematical results than an excellent mathematician does during his whole life. When we consider that he had no familiarity with most of the mathematics of his day, his achievement appears to be a total mystery.

But if we look at such a genius in the light of Bohm's soma-significance, it is not a total mystery. According to Bohm, a new mathematical insight occurs at a very subtle level of thinking, where the significance of the mathematical law or result is seen. The insight then unfolds to a more explicit intellectual level. This unfolding is a signa-somatic process,[8] in which a more subtle level of meaning acts to order the more explicit level of separate elements. Poincare, too, pointed out that once the mathematical law is felt as a whole, the pieces will fall into their natural places.

Bohm's view implies that once such a law has been made explicit in a mathematical language, it will hold the potential of activating new processes in the mind, going even beyond the mathematical 'depth' from which it was unfolded in the first place. In this way Bohm's concept of soma-significance provides a framework in which we can at least begin to discuss the otherwise mysterious process of mathematical insight.

There is an important difference between mathematical creation and creation in art, such as painting or music. A very innovative idea in mathematics has to be consistent with a potential infinity of relations with other theorems and entities. In music, for example, there is no such compelling dependence on other styles or pieces of music. Mathematics is extremely sensitive to false statements or premises. One unrecognized falsehood would be enough to ruin a large part or even the whole of mathematics. Why? Because one would be able to deduce from such a false premise, for instance, that one equals zero.

This circumstance is in sharp contrast to a game with a definite set of rules. In bridge, the game would not be ruined if a player cheated occasionally. It would only be more complicated, but not meaningless.

Regarding the inner consistency of mathematics, let us make two points: Firstly, no inconsistency has been found within mathematics, and secondly, in spite of tremendous effort all attempts to prove that mathematics is consistent have failed. Kurt Gödel managed to prove in 1932 that any formal mathematical system, which is subtle enough to embrace at least ordinary arithmetic, even if it is actually free from contradictions, has the inherent limitation that its consistency could never be proved within the system.

The master mystery: mathematics and the physical world
Let us now consider the relationship between the inner and the outer reality, namely between mathematics and the physical reality.

Mathematics can be described as an introvert science, where the mind is quite free to inquire into analogies and structures of a symbolic nature. On the one hand, mathematical thinking is not very constrained by 'objective facts', as its symbols do not have to refer to anything particular. On the other hand, it is a form of disciplined thinking with more logical restrictions than other kinds of rational thinking.

How strong is the relationship between our inner symbolic world and the external world? The answer is that the explanatory power of mathematics in the natural sciences, particularly in physics, is not only overwhelmingly strong, but is often considered to be the only way to get at the essence of physical laws. In fact, speaking about 'understanding' in the natural sciences, in most cases refers to just what is explainable or predictable by mathematics. Seen from a historical perspective, the main significance of mathematics has thus been its power of application to our outer world of events and structures. But it is a deep and unsolved philosophical problem why mathematics is so efficient in dealing with the physical world.

Eugene Wigner once gave a lecture called 'The Unreasonable Effectiveness of Mathematics in the Natural Sciences'.[11] Let us consider two points he raised in his lecture.

Firstly, mathematical concepts are turning up in entirely unexpected connections. As an example he gave the Gaussian distribution curve, which is used in statistics to describe distributions of various parameters of a population, such as height, IQ, etc. In the formula for this curve we find pi, known from geometry as the ratio between the circumference and the diameter of the circle. Why does this constant show up in the context of distributions? He also notes that these mathematical concepts give a close and accurate description of the phenomena studied. This is a mystery, especially as we choose a small set of the facts which we use for testing the theories.

Secondly, as we do not know why mathematics is so useful in describing phenomena, we cannot decide if a certain mathematically-formulated theory is the only one fitting the facts or could others fit as well:

> We are in a position to that of a man who was provided with a bunch of keys and who, having to open several doors in succession, always hit on the right key on the first or second trial. He became sceptical concerning the uniqueness of the coordination between keys and doors.

What have the other physicists been saying about this issue? Einstein, too, wondered how it was possible that mathematics, a product of human thought that is independent of experience, fits so excellently the objects of physical reality?

> Can human reasoning, without experience, discover by pure thinking properties of real things? As far as the propositions of mathematics refer to reality they are not certain, and as far as they are certain they do not refer to reality.[12]

Hertz, who found a practical application for Maxwell's abstract formulas of electromagnetism in radio waves, once said:

> One cannot escape the feeling that these mathematical formulas have an independent existence of their own, that they are wiser than even their discoverers, that we get more out of them than was originally put into them.[13]

These thinkers thus raise the following three problems:
(a) Why is there a relation at all between our world of mathematical 'fantasy' and our external world?
(b) Not only do the mathematical formalisms incorporate the known physical facts consistently, but the consistency stretches much further in the sense that purely formal elaboration of the formalism, when given a physical interpretation, can successfully predict new physical facts.
(c) We seem to have a sixth sense in hitting upon a functioning mathematical theory, even when only a small set of phys-

ical facts are known and when we can only make guesses about the phenomena.

In order to more fully appreciate the subtlety of these problems let us briefly look at the main attempts to explain them, and why these attempts have failed. The most 'obvious' explanation is that mathematics originates from our observations of nature. If all of mathematics has its roots in regularities in the physical world of our everyday experience, part of the problem would be solved. The situation is, however, rather to the contrary: basic mathematical concepts, with no conceivable connection with the empirical world, play a fundamental role in the mathematics used in dealing with physical reality. Let us look at some examples.

One of the most essential concepts in mathematics is that of infinity. If the notion of infinity was taken away not much would remain of mathematics. At the same time infinity does not have any counterparts in our everyday world of experience. Infinity not only means something infinitely large but also something infinitely small, the infinitesimal. This concept was absolutely necessary for the theory of calculus, developed by Newton and Leibniz.

There are various kinds of infinities in mathematics. The simplest kind is called denumerable infinity, best illustrated by the sequence: 1, 2, 3, ... but it is another type of infinity which is of crucial importance to mathematical physics, namely *noncountable* infinities. To this category belongs the set of real numbers.

The correspondence between points on the line and real numbers is one of the first and most basic applications of mathematics to our external world. This correspondence is far from trivial. It is actually a postulate, introduced by Descartes without rigorous mathematical justification, saying that there is a real number corresponding to each distance on a line. The non-intuitive character of this concept of infinity is illustrated by the fact that it was only about 2000 years after the period of classical Greek mathematics that it was developed.

The success of mathematics in fields of application very remote from everyday experience is another powerful argument against the suggestion that the explanatory power of mathematics derives from an extrapolation based on observation of regularities in nature. One example is the theory of relativity which describes phenomena dealing with scales and velocities of magnitudes which in principle cannot be perceived in the external world.

There is also the example of the quantum theory, originally applied to the physics of atoms, displaying such counterintuitive features as non-locality and indivisible wholeness. The mathematical formalisms underlying these features involve such non-empirical concepts as complex and imaginary numbers and analysis.

Let us finally see how tenable the thesis of 'objectively originated mathematics' is in the realm it takes as basic. This is the world of everyday phenomena, following the laws of classical mechanics and thermodynamics. Let us start with the most common of the everyday phenomena: the weather. In spite of an arsenal of the most powerful computers available, and thousands of sensors for reading temperature, humidity, wind, convection and the like, it is possible to forecast the weather only a few days ahead. Still the physical laws ruling the weather all belong to classical physics, to 'simple' cause and effect physics. The question to be answered is: why have we not developed earlier a powerful mathematical formalism in order to predict weather?

The answer is that simple and cause-effect systems with only a small number of elements can give rise to random behaviour. This is a very recent discovery, made with the help of computers. It has generated a whole new field called chaos theory.[14]

The theory of Newtonian mechanics, applying to our human scale phenomena, has even in simple systems, such as the pendulum and that of a dripping tap, been shown to exhibit this non-reducible randomness. From a mathematical point of view, the mathematics needed to demonstrate this is very simple: an iteration of a second degree function and access to a PC is all that is needed.

Chaos theory has the following bearing on our discussion: Why should the same mathematics which originated from observed regularities in nature, such as Newton's mechanics, be able to deal with and reveal the opposite to regularity, i.e., randomness? It is even worse: not only does this mathematics faithfully describe the onset of chaos, i.e., the twilight zone between regularity and chaos, but it can also reveal totally unexpected regularities *within* chaos.

To cope with this situation, we would also need access to

an in-built ability to deal with chaotic and random phenomena. However, it is known from psychological experiments that we are very bad at creating even a small random series of numbers. Furthermore, why did we not disclose such order in chaos much earlier, without the help of advanced computers?

The above examples of quantum, relativity and chaos theory show that mathematics cannot originate from observations of everyday phenomena. By the failure to give mathematics an empirical foundation, are we then led to say that there is an *irreducible element of subjectivity in mathematics*?

At attempt to explain the success of mathematics which answers the above question in the positive derives originally from Kant who said that we see in nature only what our minds allow us to see. Eddington took up the argument and went further. As a simple metaphor, he suggests that our mental set-up functions as a filter. We can only perceive such phenomena which can pass our sensory and intellectual filters.[15]

In this view, the regularities we find in nature are determined by the nature of these filters and so is mathematics. The close parallel between mathematics and the real world would then derive from the fact that both are determined by our filters.

The main weakness of this argument is the passive role of the filter. A filter implies a permanent reduction of the available information. The question arises: Why is it that the filtered information cannot only describe but also predict the regularities in nature? It seems that what is unaccessible or filtered away is not relevant to the process of describing and predicting. But what is the status of that which is filtered away? Obviously, this information is also about an independent reality. But why should reality be so divided into two 'streams running parallel', one having no observable consequences in the phenomenal world? We are left with yet another problem.

Finally, we are going to consider the Platonic point of view. In a simplified way this view can be expressed as: Mathematical truths are independent of man. Mathematics 'exists' in an independent realm, which mathematicians discover and explore in the same way as other scientists explore their fields (jokingly: 'pi is in the sky'). In order to allow for a relation between this world of mathematical truths and our physical world, the modification is nowadays made that the physical universe expresses itself in the language of mathematics.

Within the philosophy of mathematics, this school of thought

has been questioned since the creation of non-Euclidean geometries and has become even more vulnerable to criticism since
the introduction of non-standard analysis. Both these criticisms
attack the idea of the absoluteness of mathematical truths. Also,
I point again to Wigner's observations about the ease by which
we are able to find mathematical theories which apply to the
world of physics. This, when combined with the Platonic idea
that mathematics pre-exists, implies that the total number of
mathematical structures in the physical universe is quite small.
For why would we otherwise be so successful in hitting upon
appropriate mathematical structures, or in Wigner's words,
finding the right key? Furthermore, the Platonic view also
implies that we have already discovered most of mathematics,
or that we have most of the keys in our hands. There is, however, no sign of this. Mathematical innovation is increasing
rather than decreasing.

Yet another observation weakens the Platonic argument. If
mathematical truths are absolute and reality expresses itself
in these truths, why should there be alternative mathematical
languages for the same phenomena? This non-uniqueness of
mathematical formalisms for describing physical processes is
true for two main physical theories: classical mechanics and
the quantum theory. Both can be formulated in more than one
way: classical mechanics by the principle of least action, and
the quantum theory by Feynman's path integrals, and even
by Heisenberg's matrix formulation. Thus, on the whole, the
Platonic view seems an implausible explanation for the success of mathematics in describing the physical world.

There is yet another curious feature about the relation of
mathematics and nature. For the unexplained success of
mathematics in the physical sciences does not fit in with the
common view about how science progresses. In a simple form,
this progress is usually seen as a feedback process involving
three steps: formulation of a tentative theory, experimental testing, and modification of the theory, which involves elimina-
tion of discrepancies between the theory and experimental
data. This suggests that science progresses by trial and error,
mainly step by step by making better and better adjustments
to the body of experimental facts.

But the above view does not explain how manipulations of
a mathematical formalism predict completely new and quan-
titatively new phenomena. For example, it cannot explain

Dirac's prediction of the existence of the anti-electron or the positron from the mathematical consequences of a theory.

In summary of this section, we have looked at the attempts to explain the 'unreasonable effectiveness' of mathematics in the empirical world. The first explanation, namely that the fundamental basis of mathematics originates from perception of regularities in natural events and structures, was seen to be inadequate firstly because mathematics used to explain physical phenomena contains basic concepts which have no connection with the world of sensory perception. And secondly, mathematical formalisms are very successful in describing and predicting phenomena which we cannot possibly have had any direct experience of, like those in the sphere of relativity and quantum theory.

The second explanation, the modified Platonic view, says that mathematics exists independently of us and that the physical universe expresses itself through mathematics. There are two serious problems with this view: firstly, why do we so quickly find the right mathematical 'keys' for unlocking physical problems; and secondly, why are there alternative mathematical 'keys' (formalisms) fitting the same 'lock'? In addition to these difficulties, history shows that there does not exist *the* mathematical formalism, i.e., we have both Euclidean and non-Euclidean geometries, real and hyperreal numbers, and so on.

The most natural alternative is to say that mathematics has an irreducible and important subjective aspect, or that it is to a large extent created by us. How then can something that is to a large extent created by us in our inner mental sphere harmonize so well with the outer world? Why should the objective orders of reality correspond to mentally invented orders in our rational thinking? In the last section, let us make a tentative attempt to explain and understand this mystery better.

A self-referential universe
A possibility that suggests itself is that both the physical world and the mathematics in our consciousness are aspects of one larger system — let us call it the universe. For if we cannot explain the correlation between two things as having been caused by their interaction, the obvious possibility is that their common features are either due to their having a common origin, or is merely chance. Just as it would be absurd to think

that chance can explain mathematical creativity, I believe that the relation between mathematics and the physical world is not a mere accident. In the rest of this paper I will thus consider the possibility that mathematics and the physical reality are related because they are both aspects of one underlying system, the universe.

The latter suggestion has very curious implications. From the point of view of the universe, the fact that human consciousness discovers mathematics and relates it to the physical world means that the universe itself forms an image or display about the structure of a part of itself, the physical world. For human consciousness is part of the universe, and the universe does everything that human consciousness does. Thus, through the human activity of mathematical imagination, the universe displays its own physical nature to itself.

From the point of view of the whole universe, mathematics would then be a very fundamental instance of *self-reference*. A system which can be said to refer to itself must in some sense be capable of reflecting some information or meaning *to* itself *about* itself. And when we look at the human mind as part of the universe and note that mathematics refers to the physical world which is also part of the universe, then we have a kind of self-reference.

Mathematics is not a picture of the physical world — it is not a copy of it. But what is essential is that we find the same ratios in mathematical formulae as we find in the regularities of the physical world. This similarity of ratios suggests that mathematics is an *analogy* of the physical world. Thus, the deeper way in which the universe makes a display about itself to itself is not through a representative picture, but rather through an analogy. Mathematics has the ability to capture the essential relationships that hold between measurable quantities in the physical world. We can think of this either as a human capacity, or we can think of it as a capacity that the universe has, depending on how we want to look at the issue.

If we look at human consciousness and the physical world as two separate entities, then the ability of mathematics to describe reality is left a mystery. But if we look at these two as aspects of one undivided system, then we can explain the match between them by saying that the universe refers to itself through mathematics in the human mind. And what is essential in this process of universal self-reference is the *analogous* relationship between mathematics and reality. And moreover, this self-reference is not a passive relation between mathematics and nature but rather a dynamic process which has consequences to the system as a whole. And this indeed is what happens as we transform the environment with our science and technology guided by mathematics.

In the framework of Bohm's 'meaning view' it is indeed possible to consider the above kind of self-reference:

> The problem of conceiving of a universe that can refer consistently to itself has long been a difficult one. . . . However, we can see that if there is a generalized kind of meaning, intrinsic to the universe, including our bodies and minds, then the way is opened for understanding the whole as self-referential through its 'meaning for itself'.[17]

Another eminent physicist, John A. Wheeler, has for several years been working on fundamental questions of relativity and quantum theory. In his work he was first led to give up the concept of an isolated observer and instead introduced man as a participator of the universe. He has said that when inquiring into the origins of the universe we cannot escape asking whether a basic principle in cosmogony is self-reference. In his paper 'Is physics legislated by cosmogony?' he thus suggests that ' . . . the universe as a self-excited system was brought into being by "self-reference". The universe gives birth to communicating participators. Communicating participators give meaning to the universe'.[18]

In the light of these brief considerations, it seems at least possible that mathematics is an essential part of the meaning the universe has for itself. Man establishes a meaningful relationship between himself and reality through mathematics. This relationship then takes the form of a dynamic dialogue which, indeed, can be seen as a significant aspect of a constantly creative dialogue which the universe has with itself.

Notes and references

1. Brown S., Fauvel J. and Finnegan R., 1981, *Conceptions of Inquiry*, The Open University Press, 32-35.
2. Bohm D., 1985, *Unfolding Meaning*, Routledge, Chapters 1-2.
3. Bohm D. and Peat D., 1987 *Science, Order, and Creativity*, Bantam.
4. *Conceptions of Inquiry*, pp. 12-21.

5. *Conceptions of Inquiry*, pp. 32-35.

6. Hadamard, 1949, *The Psychology of Invention in the Mathematical Field*, Princeton University Press, p. 13.

7. Newman J., 1956, *The World of Mathematics vol. 1*, Simon and Schuster, chapter 13.

8. See Bohm, *Unfolding Meaning*, chapter 2.

9. Kline M., 1980, *Mathematics*, Oxford Univ. Press, chapter 6.

10. Tymoczko T., 1985, *New Directions in the Philosophy of Mathematics*, Birkhauser, pp. 300-309.

11. *Conceptions of Inquiry*, pp. 65-71.

12. *Conceptions of Inquiry*, pp. 62-65.

13. *Mathematics*, p. 338. Editors note: Hertz' way of thinking is strikingly similar with Karl Popper's notion of objective knowledge and especially with the way in which Popper characterizes scientific theories in the last paragraphs of his *Unended Quest*.

14. Gleick J., 1988, *Chaos*, Viking Press, see especially introduction and chapter 1.

15. Eddington A., 1958, *The Philosophy of Natural Sciences*, Ann Arbor, chapter 3.

16. *Unfolding Meaning*, chapter 2.

17. *Unfolding Meaning*, p. 92.

18. Wheeler J., 1982, 'Physics Legislated in Cosmogony' in *The Encyclopedia of Ignorance*, Pergamon Press, pp. 20-45.

Deconstruction, Soma-significance and the Implicate Order:

Or, Can David Bohm and Jacques Derrida Have a Dialogue?

SRINIVAS ARAVAMUDAN

Academic discourse, in this century, has developed towards an increased formalization of its own principles and a corresponding self-referentiality. The rise of scientific discourse has exercised a powerful pull towards deterministic modes of thinking about the world and about our sense of ourselves. Whether it is the complex formulae of theoretical physics, or the genetic codes of biology, the increase in abstract knowledge has had far-reaching effects on all the academic disciplines, and their increased differentiation and establishment of territories of specialized knowledge. It might seem that this tendency is less marked in the humanities and social sciences when compared to the explosion of knowledge in the natural sciences, but in fact, the immense expanse of knowledge in these fields — which we might call the humanities — have raised issues more similar to those facing the philosophy of natural sciences than we might initially suppose. The appeal of what has broadly been termed 'formalist' or 'structuralist' approaches in the humanities has often been branded a scientific impulse, if not a scientific take-over, and the impulse to be 'scientific' alternatively repels and attracts the humanities, and especially those disciplines which like to see themselves in that ambiguous realm called 'social science'.

The history of the creation of 'social science' from the bellelettristic tradition of the humanities in the West can be traced back to one distinct and important 'origin' — the revolutionary developments of modern linguistics this century, beginning with the insights of Ferdinand de Saussure, who saw language as a *system* of relational differences with no positive terms.[1] The rise of a new methodology of analysis, using the various powerful tools of linguistics, was seen as creating 'scientific' methodologies for the analysis of language and this analysis was soon extended to an analysis of culture through the discipline of anthropology. This development elevated linguistics to a social science (whereas, until then, it had been philology), and this advance brought with it a host of technical, methodological and ultimately philosophical issues regarding the criticism of literature and language and their proprietary relationship towards meaning. Progress in linguistics and semantics promised the hope of a science of language and of all signs — a science of 'sémiologie', as the pioneer of linguistic structuralism Ferdinand de Saussure envisaged it. Structuralism brought with it a range of rigorous thought from Claude Lévi-Strauss's contributions towards an objective methodology in his books *Structural Anthropology* and *The Savage Mind* to Northrop Frye's taxonomical analysis of literature in his *Anatomy of Criticism*. Disciplines such as semiotics rose entirely due to the possibilities promised by structuralism for a science of signs, others such as sociology and psychology benefited greatly from the debates surrounding these new methods.

Yet, the insights of structuralism were exhausted by the early 1970s and humanistic scholars began looking to a new wave of philosophical and historical thinking that later came to be characterized as 'post-structuralist'. These new developments took the form of repudiating many or most of the founding premises of structuralism, and going beyond or against the limitations of a philosophy of 'humanism'. Structuralism's use of formal principles of analysis could not do more than produce sophisticated attempts of classification, binary distinction and delineation of an ordered field of analysis. Many leading structuralists themselves began to have profound doubts about the efficacy of structuralism's philosophical assumptions. 'Post-structuralism', a retrospective term for a host of anti-formalist thought arising from the work of Paris-based philosophers Michel Foucault, Jean-Francois Lyotard, Gilles Deleuze, Julia Kristeva, Jean Baudrillard, Pierre Bourdieu and Jacques Derrida, began as a response to what has increasingly been perceived as the failure of structuralism.

If we look closely at the work of Jacques Derrida as an example, we might begin to see some of the assumptions of what many have called the post-structuralist project.[2] Derrida is engaged in a radical critique of Western philosophy, which takes the form of a 'deconstruction' of what Derrida calls 'the metaphysics of presence'. Western philosophy and its modes of inquiry all the way since Plato, according to Derrida, systematically hides its dependence on language and metaphor in order to communicate a hidden agenda of 'metaphysical' and ideological positions. While it would be impossible to produce an exhaustive list of all the positions that traditional Western philosophy has advanced, we could briefly consider the 15 sets of oppositions listed below:

Man	Woman
Speech	Writing
Presence	Absence
Reason	Imagination
Work	Play
Origin	Derivation
Author	Reader
Host	Parasite
Central	Peripheral
Meaning	Language
Soul	Body
Inside	Outside
Essence	Structure
Truth	Rhetoric
Philosophy	Literature

Crudely speaking, it has been deconstruction's task to demonstrate that Western philosophy has systematically attempted to characterize the ideas in the second column as inferior to, or derivative from, and secondary to, the first column. Deconstruction attacks this hierarchy from within, by showing that the works of the Western philosophical tradition systematically downplay and disregard the second column; by closely reading the texts of philosophy, deconstruction reverses these hierarchies to show that the dominance of the first column would be impossible without the priority and the anteriority of the second column. Of course, deconstruction does not stop at the mere reversal of a binary opposition, but aims towards a *general displacement of the system*, the very establishment of a system of binary oppositions that created this situation. In that sense, structuralism as the theory of binary opposition *par excellence*, is fundamentally flawed for perpetrating the oppositionality of binaries — however, it should also be recognized that structuralism, in attempting to spatialize and systematize knowledge, already contains the implicit recognition of the lack of a center, or the 'absence' and relationality which are fundamentally aligned with the second column. Deconstruction dismantles the authoritarianism of binary oppositions for the heteregeneous multiplicity, polyvalence and 'free-play' of the linguistic sign.

Derrida's critique of philosophy and language hence has a profound impact on our attitude towards meaning. Philosophy (and human behaviour) has consistently devalued writing in deference to speech. Writing was always regarded as secondary and derivative, while speech was seen as living, because of the illusion of self-presence. Philosophy then transferred much of its impatience with the problematic aspects of language to the iniquities of writing. The features of 'writing' became a scapegoat for the problems of 'speech'. Derrida convincingly argues that language itself is inevitably subject to 'différance' — a term which indicates both the concept of relational difference (in space) and temporal deferral (in language's postponement of reaching and achieving a metaphysical presence).

Structuralism, which attempted to impose a description of language as a system of spatial difference, fails to acknowledge 'différance' because it is dependent on the synchronic at the expense of the diachronic, and continues to privilege speech. Derrida argues that the creativity of language is possible precisely due to a spacing and a timing that depends upon an absence, without which a linguistic sign would not be either possible or necessary. The sign works precisely because it is invested with the traces of all other related signs: this is a fundamental insight that goes all the way back to Ferdinand de Saussure. The word 'dog' semantically means dog only because it is distinguished from, and in relation to, 'cat', 'puppy', 'bone', 'kennel', and so on; language is a system of *relational* differences, and this holds as much for phonology as for semantics: the sound 'd-o-g' is distinguishable because the phoneme [d] is differentiated from the phoneme [t]; it is the *trace* and the *absence* of all other phonemes of the English language that makes, or constitutes, the *presence* of the phoneme [d]. Hence presence/absence is not an existential dichotomy but a hyphenated simultaneity which is a condition of all language. The simple question of relationality on the level of the phoneme and the level of semantics will also hold true at a more complicated level: for instance, in terms of the relationality and the contextuality of historical work, and for that matter, any interdisciplinary work.

Speech, with its illusory offer of self-presence, instant correction and modification, has normally been hierarchized over writing which is always regarded as supplementary and derivative. Careful observation should show us, says Derrida, that 'writing' in the *general* sense — or, the existence of the linguistic sign itself (and not merely the existence of a technical system of phonetic or ideogrammatic transcription) — has to precede the very possibility of speech. A linguistic system of differences, and the internal separation of the sign — what Saussure called 'signifiant' and 'signifié' (signifier and signified) — is indeed what makes all language possible. Therefore, 'writing', in the philosophical sense, is based on absence, and the possibility of speech exists only on this foundation. By this logic, 'writing' precedes, and is anterior to speech. Derrida sees himself as performing a 'grammatology' — a writing about writing. Derrida's aim, by reversing the hierarchy, is to displace it altogether, and in so doing release the until-now unidirectional energy spent by language through its constant search for a metaphysical presence.

Furthermore, it is Derrida's thesis that social structures and material institutions are similarly predicated on this general law of absence, while also deeply involved in a 'metaphysics of presence'. Derrida's claim that 'Il n'y a pas de hors-texte' (there is nothing outside the text) questions the neat separation between philosophy and the world, language and reality, meaning and matter.[3] His acknowledgement of 'intertextuality' functions in a similar way to what David Bohm recognizes in physics as 'quantum interconnectedness' — the trace-like relationality of seemingly disparate phenomena. Deconstruction's 'aims', I wish to argue, are remarkably similar to the repercussions of David Bohm's theory of the 'implicate order'.

Philosophy abandons the quest for ultimate meaning, but instead allows the free play afforded by language to bring fresh insights to inquiry. Consciousness itself, or the experience of a self present to itself, an essence, is an *effect* of the process of 'logocentrism' — the monolithic concern with logos, the metaphysics of presence, since classical times. The subject — the thinking and speaking 'I' — is constituted by and through language, which takes place by and through absence, not presence. It is in allowing free rein to 'play' and the multiple dissemination of meaning that the self can both be liberated and dissolved from the tyranny of presence — as Bohm himself suggests, play ('ludere') is the most creative and energetic aspect of consciousness. Deconstruction, which has often been branded frivolous, unserious, nihilistic and anarchistic, has been misunderstood precisely because it sees the potential for play as inevitably embedded in language. What deconstruction sees in terms of 'language', Bohm sees in terms of 'thought', and while many might dismiss the creativity of free play as anarchistic or iconoclastic irreverence, both Bohm and Derrida would rather describe it in terms of 'seriousness' recognizing that it too is a game, except with rules and assumptions that are not readily exposed. Both Bohm and Derrida pay great attention to the conditions of possibility, the presuppositions and assumptions that govern the production of meaning. Both thinkers have this decided tendency towards playful/ serious discourse concerning language and etymology. Bohm's creative play with the 'rheomode' in his book *Wholeness and the Implicate Order* is an interesting and stimulating thought-experiment leaving much room for further exploration. Derrida consistently and persistently exploits multiple and divergent etymologies to disrupt the stable and unified meaning that metaphysical discourse attempts: in his essay, 'La pharmacie de Platon', on Plato's *Phaedrus*, Derrida shows how writing is described as a *pharmakon*, which means both a remedy, and a poison. (In the *Phaedrus*, Socrates claims that writing was created for mankind as a remedy against amnesia, but that it has become a dangerous drug that should be decried.) Derrida deconstructs the argument by showing that the Greek philosophical tradition is rife with contradiction and ambivalence regarding this double etymology of remedy and poison. The *pharmakon* constitutes the two differential opposites of remedy and poison, but is itself the medium of their dissociation. Much of Derrida's project is a painstakingly close reading of Western philosophy as a writing which wants to suppress its status as 'writing'.

Deconstruction therefore concentrates on the 'aporia' — the Greek word for an insoluble conceptual and logical gap, an impasse — in a significant philosophical, theoretical or humanistic text. The intense reading involved in unravelling these conceptual paradoxes often reveals that moments of greatest insight are inseparable from those of profound blindness; the double bind is that not only do the most powerful philosophical texts strongly suppress their inescapable contradictions, but they continue to draw attention to themselves precisely for this reason.[4]

David Bohm demonstrates this problem in a totally different context of theoretical physics, by the striking visual analogy of the implicate order as demonstrated by an ink-and-glycerine experiment. A double cylinder of glycerine has a drop of dye on the surface of the glycerine. When the cylinders are rotated in a controlled way in opposite directions (so as to prevent diffusion), the ink disappears into the glycerine; when the moves are exactly reversed, the ink reappears in the original position. Bohm uses this analogy to explain the idea of an implicate order underlying physical phenomena, complicating the example to suggest that if two drops of ink were dissolved at different points, such that one 'unfolds' just as the other is 'enfolded', then the model might explain some of the unintelligible features of non-locality in quantum mechanics.[5] This seems very suggestive of the blindness/ insight dichotomy recognized by deconstruction, as every insight is founded upon a *necessary* blindness, every 'explicate' order is necessarily related to the 'absence' of an 'implicate' order. Quantum interconnectedness corresponds to the 'intertextual trace' proposed by Jacques Derrida.

Observable phenomena, according to Bohm, are 'manifest', or displays of an 'explicate' order; whereas unresolvable problems of contiguity and contingency are due to the result of the explicate order enfolding itself into an implicate one, which again remanifests itself at another point in a space-time continuum. Bohm recognizes that both components are relationally productive — in a sense it is a *différance* that Bohm means, when he proposes this kind of model of the implicate order. The repercussions of this theory demonstrates that no privileged vantage-point exists from which we can observe, record and explicate all knowledge. In fact, we might go the extra mile in suggesting that the ink-and-glycerine experiment itself is subject to an inescapable *différance*; it is almost as if aggressive explication is met with and balanced by a counter-mode of implication which is inherent to the process of that explication, a duality of blindness and insight. An explicate order, a moment of metaphysical certainty, analogous to the illusion of determinate and stable meaning and presence, is *generated* by an implicate order, which is a recognition of the absent trace at that very moment of explicitness, a recognition of indeterminacy precisely at the moment which seems most promising in terms of metaphysical meaning. All this reveals that presence and absence are mutually determinate and necessary parts of the same process, which we might alternatively term 'language', 'thought', or 'signification'.

Deconstructing an argument is not so much an exercise in refutation, but a recognition of the rhetorical inescapabilities and limitations of the argument's thesis. When a text attempts to suppress dialogue and achieve a certain closure, a presence, a last word, or an ultimate insight which ends all others, it is engaged in 'logocentrism', a term Derrida coins from the history of Western philosophy's constant teleological hankering after the complete presence of 'logos', from the time of Plato. 'Logos' is roughly equivalent with the 'manifest' or 'explicate' order at a given moment; while language obviously oscillates between the 'explicate' and the 'implicate', from the logocentric imperative of the desire to make a statement that would end all statements, to the disseminatory impulse, the urge to broadcast meaning and endlessly differentiate itself from other statements and hence facilitate endless play. While deconstruction, in its response to structuralism, takes place in a totally different disciplinary context, it is indeed closely comparable to Bohm's desire to examine the foundational assumptions and presuppositions of thought — especially in Bohm's great sensitivity, during the process of group dialogue, to the way linguistic predeterminations govern our apprehension of consciousness.

If we could put this idea a little differently, the connection being made here between Derrida and Bohm is novel, precisely due to the possibility of free play and linguistic creativity. I say this not to flatter myself, but rather to argue that any use of language is creative, in the sense that Derrida and Bohm have taught us that all meaning is context-bound, but that contexts happen to be infinite.[6] Even if we assume that this connection between Bohm and Derrida has been made hundreds of times by others, it would not mean exactly the same to you, the reader, at this precise moment. As a reader, you might resist this connection, or wish to read it against the grain. These possibilities vary even if you reread exactly the same physical text — the same words, the same typefaces — because the set of significations you would derive from it would differ, from radically different to ever so slightly different. No text, canonical or otherwise, can be completely read. There is no final interpretation. On the other hand, all novelty is always already ('toujours déjà') because it is prefigured in the *différance* which precedes all communication.

The idea of the hermeneutic whole, which with its hierarchical relationship is greater than the sum of its parts, remains a pervasive feature of certain modes of philosophy, such as phenomenology. In terms of Saussurean structuralism, the hierarchy of the universal is revealed as a distinction between 'langue', the ideal language-system, and 'parole', the actual utterance. (Noam Chomsky's linguistics distinguishes between the ideality of linguistic 'competence' — a native speaker's passive awareness of the rules of her language — and the flawed pragmatics of actual and active linguistic 'performance'. However, the holographic model pioneered by Bohm's conception of wholeness proposes that the part contains the whole: the simple linguistic unit, the trace, implies the relationality of the entirety of all the features of language. This conception of language-as-a-system in Saussure has been modified by Derrida to a notion of language as a heterogeneous field. Structuralism's desire to posit an ideal language is an untenable ultimate reduction, just as is the constant search in physics for the ideal particle, law or theory. The 'part' and the 'whole' in both Derrida and Bohm, implicate and explicate each other, without recourse to a hierarchy of the whole over the part.

It has to be said in Saussure's defence that he was aware of the problems inherent in dividing the 'signifiant' (signifier) from the 'signifié' (signified). He proceeded nevertheless on the assumption that linguistic abstraction is necessary, in the notes taken down as his famous *Cours de la linguistique generale*:

> Language can be compared with a sheet of paper: thought is the front and the sound the back; one cannot cut the front without cutting the back at the same time; likewise in language, one can neither divide sound from thought nor thought from sound; the division could be accomplished only abstractedly, and the result would be either pure psychology or pure phonology. (p. 113)

It is inherent in the nature of abstract knowledge (a concept Bohm relates to the French word 'savoir')[7] to appropriate an aggressive truth value or immanence. The abstract representational and modelling process of 'savoir' emphasizes the diagrammatic mode as indication of a persistent immanence, a true meaning behind the diagrammatic sign — usually exposed and expressed as a law, a rule, a structure or a formula: on the lines that '$E = mc^2$' is the ultimate meaning of the universe. The logocentric drive towards ultimate truth is destructive. Derrida points out that the very 'structuralist consciousness is a catastrophic consciousness, simultaneously destroyed and destructive, *destructuring*, as is all consciousness, or at least the moment of decadence, which is the period prior to all movement of consciousness' (*Writing and Difference*, p.6).

In contrast, Bohm uses the French term 'connaître' to suggest a personal knowledge which is strongly aware of its contextual significance and self-reflexivity, and presents itself as a process rather than gospel truth, welcoming 'fuzziness' as complexity and clarity rather than uncertainty. Bohm and Derrida seem engaged in a similar anti-formalism, which is relevant to its contextual mode of 'theory' as nothing more elaborate than a way of looking at the world, and stripping our perspectives of its assumptions, actively encouraging divergence and heterogeneity. A contextualist response does not seek to grasp at meta-rules, extrapolate formulas and delineate hierarchies. Instead, the concern is to liberate meaning horizontally and laterally, freeing it from the crystallization of a vertical structure of meta-rules and hierarchies.

The methodological moves that can be identified in Bohm or Derrida cannot be canonized as laws, fundaments, axioms or precepts. A stable description is relevant only at the given point of observation in a highly relativized space-time which is non-axiological, unlike axiological descriptions which are based on a world-perspective that has to posit a fundamental 'belief' or an unquestionable foundation. The aim to establish identity and sameness is also an attempt to suppress alterity and difference. It is not the aim of this essay to reduce Bohm and Derrida to simulacra of each other's thought — rather, this should be seen as an attempt to both 'bridge the divide' as well as 'burn the bridges' between the two thinkers' radical projects. Bohm's theories of the implicate order and soma-significance are located in a completely different theoretical context from Derrida's. The attempt is not so much to 'reconcile' the two but to provoke and stimulate a dialogue between them by creating a basis for discussion, and this dialogue is necessarily a dialogue of difference. Lifting both of them out of their specific contexts is both escaping the significance of their thought even as it is attempting to forge new connections between the two heterogeneous fields of work we choose to designate by the convenient reduction of two proper names — 'Bohm' and 'Derrida'.

The paradox of this essay is that of all interdisciplinary work. We are trying to bridge conceptual gaps by the import/export of ideas. Involved in this is decontextualization, and one could be subject to attack by both 'Derrideans' and 'Bohmians'. However, the aim of interdisciplinarity should not just be a polite 'exchange of ideas', but rather a deep questioning of the very constituting of the individual disciplines themselves.[8] A loose body of work of such nature in the humanities goes by the name of 'theory', because it cannot be pinned down to the limited territory of any one subject. Bohm very much enters this discourse by *implication* rather than his directly addressing 'issues' that purportedly affect literature and philosophy of language in a singular fashion.

Derrida would recognize that lifting language out of one context and placing it in another is its most inescapable linguistic feature.[9] In resituating Bohm and Derrida next to each other, there is both irony and meaning — because both men have not physically met, have little or no knowledge of each other's work, and are engaged in radically different projects — yet it is their 'absence' to each other which creates the possibility of this attempt to show a certain 'similarity' of their approaches, a similarity which also underscores tremendous differences, and can never approach 'identity'. The nature of their work has the peculiar consequence of profoundly affecting disciplines which they are not consciously or unconsciously engaging in. What better example of implicate order, quantum interconnectedness or intertextuality?

As Bohm points out in *Wholeness and the Implicate Order*, 'what prevents theoretical insights from going beyond existing limitations and changing to meet new facts is just the belief that theories give true knowledge to reality' (p.6). Bohm's insistence that fragmentary approaches cannot be met by an 'integration of thought' — like the Hegelian dialectic, a cancellation and a transcendental unification — is met by Derrida's concerns about the similar integration and transcendental unifi-

cation prescribed by the logocentric and metaphysical impo-
sition. While the ultimate results of the mythical and originary
differentiation (the fragmentation caused by 'measurement'
which Bohm identifies at the beginning of the Western tradition) can be seen most vividly in the advances of science and
technology, the culture of fragmentation produced by measurement does not need denial but reinvestigation. Is the fragment a debased notion because of the priority given to
organicism, or could it reveal, within itself, a holographic
potential? In an important sense, we could perhaps discover
that within the analysis of the fragment lie the necessary conditions of the generation of the mythical unity that attempts
to subsume difference.

The explicatory approach to literature could be a particularly
significant heuristic example. Taxonomies and classifications
are the oldest ways to read literature, but we can see that these
tools were designed to limit literature, and precisely *not* read
it. Starting from Aristotle, theories of rhetoric and theories of
genre limited and 'fixed' literature's multiple and disruptive
meanings. A deconstructive approach would tend to shy away
from this vertical stratification of literature. Taxonomies deceit-
fully promise the unfoldment of an ultimate meaning, while
in fact they entirely avoid close and careful attention to textual
reading. Instead, deconstruction would point to the multiplicity
of liberating or centrifugal devices, such as the enfoldment per-
formed by Derridean 'dissemination' or Bohm's implicate
order, rather than the unfoldment of logocentrism or centripe-
tality of a metaphysical unicity.

Linguistic heterogeneity, or 'heteroglossia', as described by
Russian literary critic Mikhail Bakhtin, shows us that language
is always the force of the 'other'. The words, the language we
use, are always another's, in fact, that of many others. Language consists of multiple voices, it consists of a rampant dialo-
gism always far in excess of any attempt to frame a monological
discourse. Plurivocity and dialogization are the runaway centrifugal forces which cannot be reined in by a centripetal order.
The importance Bohm gives to a dialogue without specific purpose has much in common with Bakhtin's approach. Bakhtin
actively analyzes society in terms of the centrifugal and heterogeneous, in terms of the 'dialogization' of previously fixed
modes, through the creativity of cross-generic literary modes,
such as the novel, or certain subversive features of social insti-

tutions, such as the carnival.

Dialogue participates in a hybridization of voices, cultures and stable genres, and this 'heteroglossia' of multiple voices can result in a radical transformation of the individual and social realities. While Bohm's theory of dialogue is not as literarily based as Bakhtin, it seems clear that Bohm constantly encourages hybridization, laughter and play — for instance, his notion that dialogue involves 'entertainment' implies both the hybrid and carnival aspects that Bakhtin speaks about.

All this leads us to the correspondences implied by the fascinating theory of soma-significance. A post-structuralist would see Bohm's work as a blinding insight that deconstructs the age-old distinction between matter and mind in Western philosophy and renders irrelevant the regressive tussles which idealist and materialist positions have enacted over centuries. Furthermore, Bohm debunks the anthropocentric perspective of all speculative thinking which assumes 'psyche' and 'soma' to be essences, leading to the hierarchies which often took the form of soul over body, mind over matter, or animate over inanimate. Bohm shows that matter and meaning are relational definitions which can only be contextually defined. The concept of *différance* in Derrida's work similarly de-essentializes the body-soul dichotomy, but translates all relationality to a realm of both spatial and temporal materiality.[10]

The triangulation Bohm creates between matter, energy and meaning can be applied to several areas of humanistic discourse. As meaning is the key which collapses the artificial separation between physical and mental worlds, we can reconfigure the heterogeneous field in terms of meaning, or *différance*. While we can speak exclusively of a certain meaning at a given moment, we cannot ignore the other, which has only been momentarily backgrounded. A very simple example would be the thesis that 'all language is about a topic', often described as 'the matter' at hand — that which is being discussed. However, if we closely examine the crystallization we treat as a topic, we realize that the topic itself consists of a tissue of complicated relationships (call it energy) which we take for granted at that moment. A topic such as 'Hiroshima' is obviously embedded in a welter of complicated relationships ranging through historical, scientific, social and political meanings linking matter and consciousness. On the other hand, all these meanings lead to other topics (matter), which in turn extend (or intend) towards other meanings.

A purely technical example in language would be the disassociation between 'word' and 'meaning', which reappears in much more sophisticated ways as the desire to separate the phonetic (acoustic) or graphemic aspect of the sign from the semantic — the separation between signifier and signified. However, upon attempting this division, we find that we need a secondary level or metalanguage in order to talk about semantics; but its effects are no different from those of language itself. We are caught in our inability to escape using the very process we seek to examine objectively. We confront this problem in the mathematical logic of formal semantics — or better still, in the conventional example of a dictionary, which describes one word only by the aid of other words, which in turn point infinitely in permutations and combinations to themselves. To say that 'everything is language' does not mean we are therefore lost, but rather it means that explicated orders of meaning crystallize as language-thought, a material process. Meaning can then be seen as the creative surplus or excess, of which further language (for instance, this very sentence) is a consequence. Therefore, just as there is meaning in language-matter, there is also language-matter in meaning. There is no privileged relationship of inside to outside — we have to discard the conventional notion that the meaning is always the essence, which lies at 'the heart of the matter'. Matter also lies at the heart of meaning; context and content are interchangeable; language creates meaning just as meaning creates language.

The increasing subtlety of trying to explicate the implicate leads, in fact, to a greater and greater field of the implicate, the intertextual, and the trace. One should perhaps avoid the notion of extratextuality because it implies, in conventional terms, that language is describing something outside itself, and therefore language is secondary, useless and limited. Rather, language is involved in a process of simultaneous domestication and alienation with respect to meaning. Language is not the poisonous antidote or the divine remedy that the Greeks juxtaposed; it is rather the medium, the element that we manipulate and are manipulated by, in turn. We could see the textual and the stated language as the explicate, and the silence between and amongst language(s) as the implicate. The two are mutually correlated, as there would be no silence without sound.

Bohm points out that ultimate reduction is both unnecessary and impossible. To search for ultimate meaning would be 'the attempt to reduce one level of subtlety in any structure completely to another' — perhaps exemplified in physics by the futile search for a unified field theory, or a theory of everything; or in literature and philosophy, the search for the final word on the significance of a given text. If the world is seen as 'one vast web of soma-significant and signa-somatic activity', as Bohm says, we can no longer think in terms of archaic notions such as the presence and absence of spirits — animate and inanimate. If we need to talk of the aspect of 'intention', it can be seen as the relative function, or change of flow of 'energy'. The matter-energy-meaning triangle proposed by Bohm has tremendous potential application, especially as it is not hierarchized (unlike the Hegelian dialectic). All three are interdependent and reproductive, and mutually constitutive in Bohm's theory.

In linguistics, 'matter' could be physical language, the phonemes and graphemes that indicate the materiality of the sign; 'energy' is then the potentially infinite structure of semantic differences, and 'meaning' is then *différance*, the articulation of a contextual signification that mediates between matter and energy, which itself involves a spatialization and a temporalization, as well as a movement of the trace. A relevant alternative in literature/philosophy would have the 'matter' as the corpus of established literary and philosophical works (e.g., Shakespeare, Plato, Marx, Freud). 'Energy' would reveal itself in the functioning of their peculiar and particular language, (i.e., the language of psychoanalysis, the language of Marxism and so on) and 'meaning' would again be the constant change and interaction between the two as a result of *différance*.

Of course, the scenario is much more complicated, because language itself is changed by meaning — as our reading of Marxist or Freudian vocabulary is subject to historical changes. For instance, we cannot ignore engaging with the way Lenin read Marx, irrespective of whether we agree or disagree with his interpretation. So much so, it could be argued that the very text we refer to as 'Marx' is itself metamorphosing, diverging and disseminating. (A critic who wished to count claimed that there were 56 different kinds of Marxism.) Can we ever read the original Marx? Scholars would have it that we should go to the German text and not a translation; then the emphasis shifts again to issues revealed in the manuscripts which are not highlighted in the printed text. Biographers would try to reveal the incidents in his personal life as the ultimate meaning behind his manuscripts; historians of philosophy would look to Hegel and Marx's debt to his work. The task of ferreting out immanences would continue unceasingly if we were obsessed with getting it right about Marx. On the other hand, a recognition that Marx could mean infinitely would put to rest a search for the ultimate meaning of Marx; rather we would engage with Marxist issues necessarily, without having to resort to a fixed position or stand which will always be right about Marx.

Another instance of an application of Bohm's vocabulary — in terms of Marxist theory — might see 'matter' as capital and the instruments of production, 'energy' as economic (re)production and the possibility afforded by the social and historical forces and 'meaning' as the particularly constituted social hierarchies and representations in a certain society, which again has to be 'read' as *différance*. Hence the meaning of Marxism in the Soviet Union would be very different from the one in China, because the social *différance* in either case would have to be non-identical. Again, Marxism would mean a totally different thing to a feminist discourse, where crucial relationships may not be determined through socio-economics alone, but more significantly through the exercise of patriarchal and psychosexual power alongside an economic power which is exercised over women rather than the traditional Marxist conception of the proletariat.

I would hesitate to call these various possibilities 'applications' because that would imply a certain relationship between theory and practice and award a certain status to theory which we would do better to avoid. In one sense, applications cannot be avoided, because meaning has implications, which soon tends to concrete into a topic, a matter, an 'ism'. The freshness of 'Bohmian theory' is its dynamism, in that it tends to move on to a new theory once a fresh insight has been formulated, often leaving slower readers, like us, to pick up the loose ends.

Bohm could be seen as recognizing the fundamental insight of the much-maligned Derridean paradox, that there is nothing outside the text, which we mentioned earlier. As Bohm states in *Unfolding Meaning*, 'the field of meaning can refer to itself, and of course, it also presupposes the context of the universe to which it refers' (p.92). His suggestion that we understand 'the whole as self-referential through its 'meaning for itself' while neatly avoiding the problems of metadiscourse, nevertheless generates a certain slippage — would this 'meaning for itself' also reveal an excess which reveals that the whole is only a part?

Bohm's encounter with the humanities reveals firstly, that while the attractions of a deterministic social science may be tempting, it will remain an unachievable goal. While it is conceded that determinism for methodological, experimental and heuristic goals will not go away, just as the necessity for technology will remain, it should be clear that determinism can exist alongside only an equally strong indeterminacy, like explicate and implicate orders. All the same, there is no longer a distinction between a universal and local level — rather all situations are 'general' in the sense that they are productive and excessive of themselves — but this type of 'generality' implies a firmly-rooted explicit locality and an indefinite and unavoidable non-locality. A locality cannot exist except in relation to a non-locality and vice versa, and it is at this paradoxical level that we can make judgements in a post-Newtonian/post-structuralist moment of affairs. Meanwhile, Bohm should easily convince us that the populist characterization of all the natural sciences as totally deterministic and unconcerned with epistemological and theoretical issues is uncharitable.

David Bohm belongs to a minority of inter-disciplinary scientists, but there are doubtless other thinkers like him who bridge the largely irrelevant boundaries of academic taxonomies, even as they disrupt and problematize the stability and unicity of their own specialized field, rendering it heterogeneous and multiple. If fields are still dominated by disciplinary purists, we must realize that it is largely due to the urge for endless explication and abstract knowledge. We need to remind ourselves of its destructive effects, which Bohm suggests is a result of our desire for familiar notions of universal order. Bohm warns us that the process of knowledge contains 'presuppositions which largely control the general operation of the mind, without our being conscious of their existence' p.12. We should realize that Derrida and Bohm unmask the ideology governing metaphysics and epistemology, and they expose the workings of this ideology through a predominantly creative interpretation of language. Exposing the devices of epistemological control should lead us towards the horizon of an alternative and radical politics that makes us constantly and freshly aware about the traps of knowing, in as many different possible ways. This is what 'theory' is all about. In that respect, Bohm's and Derrida's insights are invaluable.

Notes

1. For an excellent and lucid introduction to Saussure, see Jonathan Culler, *Ferdinand de Saussure* (London, Fontana; New York, Penguin), 1976.
2. It is important to note that Derrida himself nowhere uses the term 'post-structuralist'.
3. See Jacques Derrida, *Of Grammatology*, p.158.
4. Paul de Man's *Blindness and Insight: Essays in the Rhetoric of Contemporary Criticism* (New York, Oxford University Press), 1971 is a very important text of deconstruction and American literary criticism.
5. Here the only other solution is to propose a supraluminal exchange of information or 'action at a distance' between particles.
6. See Jonathan Culler, *On Deconstruction*, (Ithaca, N.Y., Cornell University Press), 1982, p.123.

Note also Bohm in *Unfolding Meaning*, p.99: 'Every finite form is somewhat ambiguous because it depends on its context. This context goes on beyond all limits, and that is why creativity is possible.'
7. See 'Insight, Knowledge, Science and Human Values', in *Education and Values*, ed. Douglas Sloan (New York, Columbia Teachers College Press), 1980.
8. Such a questioning should involve both a historical and materialist analysis of the interests and ideologies that delineated disciplines, and an understanding of the epistemological presuppositions involved in the notion of an autonomous and self-sufficient theoretical paradigm, proposed by Thomas Kuhn and radically critiqued by Paul Feyerabend.
9. See Derrida's critique of the speech-act theory of J.L. Austin in his essays, 'Signature Event Context', *Glyph* 1 (1977), 172-97.
10. It is important to note that deconstruction has been severely attacked for being too idealistic, textual and non-materialist by Marxist critics; on the other hand, Conservatives have seen it as nihilistic, and politically subversive — in other words,

institutionally threatening. These criticisms from two extremes show that the destabilization of the soma/psyche opposition is one of the rich resources of deconstruction.

Works Cited

Bakhtin, M.M., *The Dialogic Imagination: Four Essays*, Ed. Michael Holquist, Trans. Caryl Emerson and Michael Holquist, Austin, University of Texas Press, 1981.

Bohm, David, 'Insight, Knowledge, Science and Human Values', in *Education and Values*, Ed. Douglas Sloan, Columbia University, New York, Teachers College Press, 1980.

Unfolding Meaning: A Weekend of Dialogue with David Bohm, Ed. Donald Factor, London, Routledge and Kegan Paul, 1987.

Wholeness and the Implicate Order, London, Routledge and Kegan Paul, 1980.

Chomsky, Noam. *Cartesian Linguistics: A Chapter in the History of Rationalist Thought*, New York, Harper, 1966.

Language and Mind, New York, Harcourt, 1968.

Culler, Jonathan, *Ferdinand de Saussure*, London, Fontana, 1976.

On Deconstruction, London, Routledge and Kegan Paul, 1984.

Structuralist Poetics: Structuralism, Linguistics and the Study of Literature, Ithaca, NY, Cornell University Press, 1975.

Deleuze, Felix and Guattari Gilles, *Anti-Oedipus: Capitalism and Schizophrenia*, Tr. Robert Hurley, Mark Seem and Helen R. Lane, Minneapolis, MN, University of Minnesota Press, 1983.

Derrida, Jacques, *La Dissémination*, Paris, Seuil, 1972.

Of Grammatology, Trans. Gayatri Chakravorty Spivak, Baltimore, MD: Johns Hopkins University Press, 1977.

'Signature Event Context', *Glyph* 1 (1977): 172-97.

'The White Mythology: Metaphor in the Text of Philosophy', *New Literary History* 6.1 (1974): 7-74.

Writing and Difference, Trans. Alan Bass, London, Routledge and Kegan Paul, 1977.

Frye, Northrop., *Anatomy of Criticism*, London, Weidenfield and Nicholson, 1961.

Lévi-Strauss, Claude, *The Savage Mind*, London, Weidenfield and Nicholson, 1966.

Saussure, Ferdinand de, *Course in General Linguistics*, Tr. Wade Baskin, New York, Philosophical Library, 1959.

A Soma-significant Cosmology: the First Surge

FRANCIS FRODE STEEN

'God is creating the world and all things in an ever-present Now'.

— Meister Eckhart

Introduction
This piece forms part of the philosophical travelogue *The Timeless River*, and is a poetic adaptation of Bohm's notion of soma-significance to the issue of cosmic evolution. For Bohm's three major realms of being — the explicate order, the implicate order, and a source or ground beyond both — I have borrowed Meister Eckhart's terms of 'world', 'God', and 'Godhead' ('the fountainhead').

The protagonist has reached the source of the Tiber on mount Fumaiolo in central Italy, and as he is setting out to follow the river southwards, he has a dialogue with himself on the nature of the finite and the infinite, structure and freedom. The tone is playfully assertive, in the spirit that 'thought with totality as its content has to be considered as an art form, like poetry, whose function is primarily to give rise to a new perception, and to action that is implicit in this perception, rather than to communicate reflective knowledge of "how everything is".'[1]

Around midday I walk down the slopes of the Fumaiolo, along the road, putting out my thumb now and then, but really enjoying the walk and letting cars pass. It's sunny, with a refreshing breeze.

Where is freedom? I pass a field of rye already brown and overdue for harvest; before me a partridge suddenly startles and flies off the road. Not the senseless freedom of irresponsibility, but the explosive freedom of complete attention. The fountainhead of all being. Here, Now, Always, untouched by words. Where all categories and opposites unite.

It's a feast day and the tiny village square is jam-packed with shouting children, parked buses, the old men chatting over their walking-sticks, women leaning out of flowered windows, laughing, hooting, the cars lining the roads, sweating. There's no bus anyway, so sooner or later I'll have to hope for a lift; yet it's such a delightful day, I only want to walk.

Where is freedom? In this moment, I say: in the utter absence of persistence, pattern, and structure, there is primordial and ultimate freedom.

— *Who says this moment is devoid of structure?*
— I say this moment is devoid of God, devoid of all attributes the mind can concoct.
— *No, look: new-born lambs are frisking in meadows filled with fragile alpine flowers: celebrate this beauty where freedom fuses with necessity, where things resplendently proclaim their being!*
— Do you deny the moment? You do! You deny the fountainhead!
— *Let me ask you, when were you born?*
— I was never born. My existence has no duration, no beginning and no end. I am.

Splendid sunlit ledges lie like level lids across the old volcano — *Fumaiolo* meaning 'chimney'. Ice and rain beat it now, the flaky shale crumbles, slips into the gorge, washes seawards or windborne blows away. Stone signifies the whole of nature: the fire that forms it, the water that breaks it; the air that scatters it, the earth that holds it. And in this meaning lies its being: it *is* its relations, there is nothing else. But yes; behind or within it all is beauty: the scurrying clouds daring its cutting edge, the sheer grey faces. Why do we marvel so, that something so simple should be so beautiful? That in the plodding faithfulness of rock beauty should deign to live? As were we closer to life's source than it, more privy to life's secret? Yet surely not; its majesty proclaims 'I am': strong, delicate, firm, crumbling, resplendent, untiring, ancient, ever new: more thrives than I that spend, Sir, life upon Thy cause.

In the fountainhead of God there is no becoming. God erupts, God proposes division — between here and there, now and then, light and darkness. Playfully like Him I speak with myself as another:

— *You say there is no persistence, yet I'm still talking to you!*

— You recreate me in the image of your memory: you are God's henchman!

— *There, I told you! This moment is shot through with the memory of God!*

— This moment is freedom.

The valley here is for a large part *brulla,* or devoid of vegetation; just the bare shingly rock and eroding gravel. Dramatic, raw, brutal. Deep in the gorge is the splendid bridge of the motorway; over the *vale* the sky is all blue. All new is this moment, all fresh and unpredictable, streaked with a fathomless beauty.

God proposes, meanings catch and enshrine themselves as worlds, as *tempo brutto* coasting forth behind me over Monte Fumaiolo, black and threatening rain, only to vanish without a trace back into the generative nothingness. There is no history, no scribes.

— *How then do you explain the persistence of form?*

— There is no continuity, nothing to persist or to persist in. Time is a series of timeless moments.

— *So God proposes, a flash of insight enshrines itself as structure?*

— A universe, a river, a woman.

— *Then obliterates this manifestation in the next moment, spends it, utterly destroys it?*

— Soaks it into Himself again, like morning dew.

— *Then we agree?*

— Stop this pretence: I am you.

A few drops; I get worried. Just when I really *depend* on a lift, there's hardly a car — people signal as they pass: there's no space, we're turning off. It's too far to walk; I don't know what I'll do. But then suddenly as I look up, the clouds have dissolved and passed onto the *vale;* above the sky is yet again an interpenetrating starwards depth of blue.

    I pass a house:

'Buon' giorno! Si far una bella camminata, eh?'

'Si, si.'

Why is God creating the world? Playfully, maybe, in freedom. Or, God is creating the visible world so that He can gain cognizance of His own being? Blasphemous! Heretical!

— *Structure feeds back into the proposal, matter back into meaning, enriching it, modifying it or transforming it:*

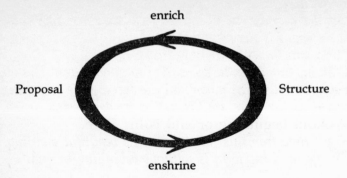

enrich

Proposal   Structure

enshrine

—Hey, where'd that circle come from?
—*It's not a circle, it's a spiral.*
—It's a helix?
—*It's a whorl, it's a vortex. As you say, there is no real persistence. God creates all things in an ever-present Now.*
—Thanks. Thanks for coming around.

Suddenly the valley appears beneath — a bus passes, incredibly stops; I run after. 'Where shall we let him off?' For 500 lire they take me down the mountain, maple and pine in the rills; then go off in the other direction.

Parallel to the autostrada is a disused road hugging the hillside, washed out by seasonal rains, invaded by clinging acacias, cracked and challenged by its new inhabitants, the dancing god celebrated deafeningly by inexorable unlocalized cicadas in rolling waves of syncopated fugatoes:

—**Ananda natamaduvar tillay**—*blissfully he dances in the temple of the forest.*
—His form is without beginning or end.
—*He and the universe are one, and he is born as the universe comes into being. The heavens are his stage.*
—Without beginning or end is his form.
—*As waves grace the boundless sea, so the world of form adorns the infinite: free of sorrow, without defeat.*
—His form is without beginning or end.
—*Insight bursts into form as his third eye opens. With ashes — matter purified by the flames of his attention — he smears his forehead, arms, and chest.*

— Without beginning or end is his form.

— *He is the Lord of destruction and creation. See: all things rise in him like the crescent moon, and look: the river of life springs afresh even from his fiery knotted hair!*

— His form is without beginning or end.

— *With his tiny drum he keeps the rhythmic patterns of the universe. Hear the bells! The moon and the sun are his ornaments, and as bright as the stars are his feet as he dances his cosmic dance.*

— Without beginning or end is his form.

— *Right here from his heart does this beautiful swirling universe emerge, and his form is without beginning or end.*

And I realize why God thus bursts into a full-fledged Now, playfully pretending an outline of form and a hardness of substance, joyously exploding into a semblance of time and space, the river still tiny there at the bottom of the valley, the ecstatic and unprecedentedly unrepeatable song of the merry starling, these slender stems throbbing with a beauteous promise: sick of omnipotence He hides Himself in pretended limitations; tired of the feasible God sets Himself an impossible task: to reveal, by means of what is finite and limited, the infinity of His own being. Doomed to failure He pushes on, recklessly proposing combinations and creations ever new to explicate the inexplicable, playfully labouring to construct a vessel fit to hold the non-existent — playfully, with great aplomb and artistry, for this is the only possible attitude to His impossible task. And we, slight mortals pearling on His giant forehead, rejoice in His necklace of sculls and sing His praises (let all praises be His!) as each instant He scraps His work — an inevitable failure — and burst afresh like spring from sodden ground.

— *But God remembers!*

— God is dead. See: this moment is freshly forming now, like transient whirls in the timeless river, like flowers sprung even this instant from the terrible and gracious seed of God's death.

— *Ah! You admit it — you acknowledge a past: a lingering on, a rebirth. Consider: thirteen billion years ago the emptiness rippled into form, exploded into light. There was a before and after. You cannot deny it.*

— I deny nothing. I see your words as lucid crystals present in my mind right now. I deny nothing.

— *You deny the light that burst forth and comprehended the darkness. You deny the love of the first instant: the daring restraint. You deny your own being.*

— Listen! That bird! Listen intently!

— *You deny the unfathomable fact of cosmic history, that the void burst into light. A cubic centimetre of empty space burst into being. One cubic centimetre harboured all that is. You deny that this happened thirteen billion years ago, that the light whirled into leptons, mesons and baryons. Not now. You're not facing up to the necessity of history.*

— I see no such necessity. Look: this moment the world is freely being born afresh; the emptiness is rippling into form, bursting into a hardness of substance, whirling into cascades of leptons, throngs of mesons and baryons, the asphalt shimmering along silver-leaved ashes glittering in the sunlight, exploding into light and darkness in the shade of the rustling leaves, free of sorrow, without defeat. I see no such necessity of history. Each instant in an instance of transcendence.

— *That's it! That's what I mean: this birth is a rebirth, this surge is a resurgence. This moment's newness has been beaten into form by history, tempered by time. There is a persistent pattern. Otherwise your words have no meaning*

— Yes. We said that. This moment is itself a seed that falls into the ground, a whirl dissolving back into the timeless river, enriching the proposal. We already said that. God remembers.

In David Bohm's causal interpretation of the quantum theory, the probability field — containing information about the environment — acts as a quantum potential to direct the particle. This accounts for the so-called wave-particle duality of matter, but at the cost of postulating a non-local effect: the potential is determined not by the intensity of the field but simply by its form. It's like saying that the particle is affected by what the field says rather than by how loud it says it. As shown by the Einstein-Podolsky-Rosen experiment, this means that widely separated particles can influence each other instantaneously.

— *But you're also saying that the very actualization of these particles takes place this moment?*

— Yes. Just as the activity of the particles is guided by the quantum potential, so is their very existence — their creation, maintenance, and annihilation — every moment non-locally organized by the super-quantum potential of the wave-function of the universe.

— *Outrageous. And this super-field remembers?*

— That's the idea of the Implicate Order. Every moment the world is projected from an unmanifest wholeness, as a wave is thrown up by the sea. And every moment like the wave it again subsides, influencing the next manifestation.

This is a new notion of time: not a deterministic chain of causes and effects but an unceasing bursting forth and curling back, in such a way each daring and creative moment is enriched and tempered by the fate of the foregoing. A deeper and more subtle order projects the world-moment, which is fed back to it again to form a matrix of stability and change. There is a mitigated, open-ended causality of sorts, in which each local and particular manifestation non-locally affects the whole, determining the subsequent manifestation.

What does this mean? This is as much as if to say the universe perceives itself afresh each moment instantaneously, and this perception is the cause of its coherence.

— *That's a pretty staggering suggestion!*

— Look: this moment's attention brings the world into being, giving the emptiness form.

— *Then there are no restraints?*

— Ultimately, none. This world is a movement of freedom.

— *You're fooling yourself — you're denying your own being: you are a restraining factor on large parts of cosmic history, right from the creation!*

— How so?

— *Those initial whirls of light were hurled with just such strength apart as matched their mutual attraction, or else you could not live: the big bang would whump at once back into the void, or scatter matter far too thin into the dark. If gravity itself were stronger, planets would not form, or if weaker, last too short for us to walk upon them. I say, this present moment strongly puts a limit on the freedom of initial conditions and the basic laws: they could not have been otherwise and still engendered us to talk about them. Your very **being** presupposes this cosmology!*

— I presuppose nothing. Awareness tunes me to my inner being, the dancing god. That constant blossoming is a sustained insight generating the appearance of time.

—*Precisely! Your hidden form was vaguely present in the universe right from the start!*

—My form **is** the universe. This **is** the start: the wind in the trees. That simple. The wind in the trees. Do you see?

Just as roses flower into seeds of other roses different yet similar in kind, just as fishes sweep behind them eggs of fishes to repopulate the shallow waters they shall leave behind, just as clouds in heaven spill their rain upon the earth in order ceaselessly to form afresh new curling patterns on their turquoise loom, just so does this magnificent world-moment die and spend itself in order to rebirth anew, alike and different, out from the sacred shelter of the cosmic womb. Quickly it flickers, in and out of existence, its pattern sustained by the memory of previous moments, just as my words only signify in relation to those no longer heard, reverberating in your memory.

—*Yet this is not it!*

—No? Weren't you suggesting just such a cycle of meaning-being where God is creating the world and all things in an ever-present Now?

—*Whatever you say it is, it isn't; it's always something more and something different. Yet more subtle currents guide the eddies of the timeless river; reality overflows any description. In terms of the cycle of meaning-being, this is like saying that the process of enriching the proposal is unending: the structure reveals or takes on ever new and unforeseeable meanings in ever new contexts.*

—In a deep sense of course one cannot predicate the moment at all: all knowledge is of the past, of the no-longer-existent.

—*Conversely, the description always overflows reality, the proposal overshoots any particular structure. Thus, light bursts forth into being concealing itself in the form of particles, assembling in holarchies of cycles of meaning-being like petals around a flower:*

*Yet this flower was not quite the one in mind; each petal shows
an incongruity, a slight mismatch between structure and proposal;
even the central structure uniting all the others falls somewhat
short of its overarching purpose, like rosebuds too delicate to open,
like a hidden fragrance speaking of a beauty so inward and so entic-
ing even God — playfully coalescing into myriads of such
conundrum-flowers — knows in his heart of hearts to be impossible.*

Meaning enshrines as matter, realizing a certain proposal,
which in turn is born out of the wholeness of the previous
moment. Yet this is not it. Yet more subtle currents guide the
eddies of the timeless river. Deep within its quiet surge are
hidden whispers of a life not yet proposed, of pathways
secretly selected to make possible a distant vision.

The river of the moment swirls the present into patterns of
the past, confirming a future already implicit, quivering with
a profound unrealized intention. Intention is a sustained
insight into the vaguely possible, acting as the structure's *telos*
or goal: its final cause, guiding the present choices towards
future forms.

— *Welcome to the club! So you're admitting to the necessity of purpose, of a subtly guiding force?*
— I said awareness, not necessity. I said the world perceives
itself afresh each moment, and this includes not only what
already is and has been, but also that which is good and
unutterably beautiful, that which is possible and that which
is just about impossible.
— *A bursting within that guides the bursting forth into a world?
So that final causes — the intention to create a rich and varied
world — determined the selection of initial conditions and fundamental constants at the time of the big bang?*
— Awareness tunes all structures to their final causes, making them resonate not only with what was but also with what
can be: what the universe perceives as possible and thus
in some sense already is but not yet in its fullness, **già e
non ancora.**

This is the first surge: the big bang ripples on a sea of infinite
and subtle energy, enshrining final causes as necessary and
pregnant balances of initial asymmetries, guided by awareness
of its budding destiny to gyrate into simple hydrogen in
clustered galaxies. From the uncertain and potent depths of

this awareness — the heart of the flower, always at the edge of the possible, the harbinger of insight, turning final causes into reality — the first surge spends itself as matter clings like abandoned children into huddled masses in a cold and isotropic darkness.

Notes

1. Bohm, D., *Wholeness and the Implicate Order*, (London, Routledge and Kegan Paul) 1980, p.63.

PART FOUR

Living in The World

To Reconsider One's Life: An Exploration in Meaning

DAVID SCHRUM

Introduction

Life is lived according to meaning. How we respond to a situation, relationship, or idea will depend on what it means to us. Numberless meanings fill both the culture of society and the life of each one of us, shaping intentions, guiding actions, and evaluating results, but behind this unending array there lies one particular which is central and which everywhere reaches out to penetrate the rest — it is the sense of meaning to our life as a whole. Within it we find the essential challenge in the field of meaning: to discover in the entirety of our living, meaning that is deep and true.

To go into the question of true and deep meaning in life, I think that it is obvious our inquiry must go beyond an academic, intellectual approach. We must leave behind these idealized, verbal territories and face the actualities of our living. To find out what is involved in that — and to do it — is the only real inquiry: what is involved for each of us, is to reconsider his life.

Still, it is important in discussion to use words precisely and in a way that is jointly understood by both the reader and the writer. Therefore, I will begin quite academically, stating definitions and making vocabular distinctions. My intention is to build up a background of clear concepts and, in the development of these, to open out an inquiry into the subject of meaning.

The Meaning of 'Meaning'

What do we mean by 'meaning'? What do we mean by the meaning of a word or symbol, a gesture, activity, or situation? In the western movies that I watched as a child, when the

Indian chief raised his hand it meant, 'I come in peace'. In the schoolroom, the same action on my part signified a request to be recognized by the teacher. In still another instance, my hand held up might indicate no more than elevation of a cut finger to reduce bleeding. The whole background against which raising my hand took place defines its significance. This relativity of meaning, it seems, is quite generally the rule.

Consider the word 'camera'. In the context of an English sentence, it refers to a piece of photographic equipment; whereas against the background of a Latin text it becomes 'room' (as in 'in camera'). The frame of reference with which a Russian child meets the same word might indicate only 'some foreign word in an odd alphabet', while to a young Chinese, even the concept of alphabet could be absent. A primitive bushman would likely see no more than 'marks on paper'. Meaning again depends on context. But this is no longer just the more objective context of environment or external background. It now involves the whole pattern of thinking and content of knowledge brought by the reader.

In a similar way meaning in human relationship, the meanings of various ideas and beliefs, and meaning to life as a whole all derive from a context gradually, over the years, built within. This background, however, is much less obvious in its roots. Here we experience a territory the source of which is often shown only by implication, a field of tacit perspectiveness and motivations founded on principles veiled even from ourselves. In this arena there is continual movement as vantage points shift about and situations continue to evolve.

All this must challenge any sense of inherent meanings in our life — significances that are in indwelling, essential, and apart from reference to a further framework. It suggests, instead, that meaning can never arise in isolation but only from some content seen in relationship to a background referent. Following out of these observations, therefore, let us consider for exploration, and as a point of departure, a provisional definition for the word 'meaning': the meaning of a content is its significance with respect to its referent context.

Meaningfulness and Meaninglessness
Since meaning derives from content in relationship to the context in which it arises, then *meaningfulness* must come about when the particular content finds itself in *harmonious relation-*

ship to its context. The world is full of meaning when activity, intercourse, or understanding fits happily into our sense of life as a whole. Imagine Mary, who, in her own terms, would at first seem to have captured this plenitude in living:
John's everything I've dreamed of in a man; since I began to date him, life is rich in meaningfulness.

But when that vital accord falls into disorder, the sense of meaningfulness also collapses: *I used to feel such depth and beauty in my relationship with John until I found he was also seeing Jane, and now all that meaningfulness, like so much dust, has blown away...*

The waning of meaningfulness paves the way to a sense of meaninglessness. When what was felt and appreciated as harmonious has faded, its mere absence may of itself strike a discordant note. In meaninglessness things don't agreeably fit. The sense of order, grace, and beauty is gone. As meaningfulness implies harmony, *meaninglessness* analogously indicates a clash of content with its referent context in a *relationship of disharmony*.

Meaninglessness and No Meaning

The feeling of meaninglessness is an experience we all have likely had. Nothing we do seems relevant to our lives, and we consequently find ourselves lost for direction, confused in action, and generally dispirited — lacking both energy and motivation. Escape from these sensations through distractions or attempts to capture something meaningful is the usual response. But, while existence burdened with such uncomfortable qualities may create a sense of meaninglessness, such living, as our definitions imply, is not empty of all meaning.

If meaningfulness depends on harmonious relationship, while meaning requires only relationship — without restriction — then living in meaninglessness does not indicate no meaning, but, rather, none with harmony: it is rife with the more unfortunate sort. Boredom, uncertainty, anxiety, unhappiness — these are all meanings which inconveniently, yet obviously, exist in meaninglessness. Only if a situation involved complete lack of comprehension or structured relationship within the context under consideration, could it be said to hold no meaning.

This distinction between *meaninglessness* (lack of harmonious relationship) and *no meaning* (absence of clear relationship in general) should be helpful to both clarity in discussion and the avoidance of semantic traps. Essential psychological problems do not arise from no meaning — for example, languages, customs, and technical information, which, for lack of knowledge, we do not understand. Rather they come out of content lacking harmony with life, hence pervaded with meaninglessness.

Disharmony in Meaning

Content may fall into disharmony with a balanced, orderly context because that content is simply incorrect — in error with reference to a clear and structured situation. Some mistake, for example, has been made in balancing the books of a business, but the book-keeping system is sound and well-understood. Such difficulty can, in time, be resolved by working carefully with content. It is a temporary, technically correctable matter, dependent on bringing order to some particular. It is a *contingent disharmony*.

In contrast is failure to harmonize because the referent context is itself in disorder. This is the problem of the flat-Earth mathematician trying to map major cities of the Northern Hemisphere so as to appropriately represent distances between them. Local charting may be effectively achieved in good approximation, but attempts to similarly fit far-flung locations cannot succeed. Correct relationship between Moscow, Tokyo, and Bombay must leave New York in inherent contradiction; correlation of the latter with all the former can be bought only at the cost of destruction of the previous harmony. Working any content will necessarily fail: no matter how, within the flat-Earth context, it may often seem that global order might be just a step away, this hope must always ultimately prove to be in vain. Such conflict is an *essential disharmony*.

It is common for essential disharmonies to be taken as contingent and dealt with by revision of those particulars which seem problematic. The juggling which makes possible the hoped-for incorporation, however, must always cause the appearance of some new disorder. Development of this pattern of contradiction is symptomatic and may be taken as an indicator strongly suggesting a conflict which is essential.

In the psychological realm, fundamental disorder of context is particularly elusive. The ground from which we live seems neither fully rational, explicit, not easily accessible to consciousness: in a territory of submerged and convoluted contexts, it is difficult to come to grips with hidden contradiction. Furthermore, against the shifting background of changing circumstances, it is easy to lose the significance of content which never fits in a way which is more than partial, approximate, and temporary.

Take as an example the desire for companionship in which there will be a complete intimacy and a sense of total security. It is clear that, *within the context of a self that cannot face its shortcomings*, this must always heighten inner conflict. True closeness in relationship must give an honest reflection; this factual mirroring cannot but cause hurt, which destroys the hoped-for sense of being secure and brings about withdrawal; in withdrawing to a sufficient psychological distance to buffer hurt, what intimacy can there be?

From within such a context, it is not usually clear to us that we are in essential contradiction: in this case, that our fundamental thrust is to demand intimacy — but at a distance! Rather, it may seem that detail after detail goes wrong and that no situation ever comes out totally right. Such living is ripe soil for a deep sense of meaninglessness.

The particular value I see in the understanding so far developed is that it makes apparent the general nature of the problem of meaninglessness. It cannot be resolved and new harmony found through revision, replacement, or addition of some content or other — that much is clear. Just one thing is left to us then: it is to find out what is involved in coming face to face with the context in which these difficulties have come about.

False Meaning

The fundamental discord that we have been examining must, it seems to me, come out of *false meaning*, meaning which is essentially out of harmony with living as a whole. When false content enters a context — itself a collection of contents, along with the relationships that hold them together — that falsity must condition the other contents through its relationship to them and, thus, in some sense, invade the whole. This gives a pervasive quality to meaninglessness.

But it is not only in meaninglessness that false meaning runs amok; we find it as significantly in the pleasures, fulfilments, and apparent security which generate a sense of meaningful

living. Consider a boy in the Hitler Youth. His life is gorged
with emotionally-stirring meanings: a sense of belonging to
something greater — his unit, his country, and its superlative
culture; the psychological lift of pomp and pageantry; participation in a momentous historical movement; and living
embodiment — himself! — of the master race. False meanings
of this sort, glorious and/or comfortable, are ones with which
we are not keen to part.

But both the meaningful and the meaningless need tackling
if we are to come to grips with false meaning. Everything,
therefore, is in question; nothing may be taken for granted.
Falsity as likely exists in our habit and convenience as it does
in difficulty and discomfort; hence, effective enquiry may be
bound by neither. What is required is an unrestricted investigation of the whole: a reconsideration of the entirety of our
living.

To reconsider one's life — what is involved in doing this?
The submerged and entangled contents of our consciousness
do not conveniently expose themselves, and it is not at all obvious how we are to ferret them out. Deeply, it would seem,
we do not know what we are. *What we do*, however, would
seem to point us more to that actuality. I think that it is in our
actions that we will find best revealed our fundamental values
and intentions.

Meaning as Action

Meaning at root is action. Observation of ourselves makes this
apparent: meaning involves response — outward and visible,
or subtler, more inward; specific or general; unrestrained or
suppressed — in one way or another, in some sense we act.

As an operational definition of meaning, it would be no exag-
geration to state that 'the meaning of a content *is* its action'.
This in no way contradicts our conceptual definition (significance with respect to referent context); it just makes clear
that 'significance' reveals and manifests itself as action.
Granted, the action may not be specific, nor even outwardly
expressed, but still, at some level it must have an operational
basis in process or movement, and it does, therefore, act.

Action which is *suspended* (as in 'intention') and/or *generalized* (as in 'attitude') is common. In the woods at night, a sound
in the bushes may bring forth, simultaneously, a generalized
(non-specific) intention toward all of the following: flight, fight,

and freeze. A dream, an adventure film, or memory of a personal conflict may stimulate, say, a desire to lash out physically, verbally, or, possibly, only imaginarily — still, this is expressed in action through tiny muscular contractions and subvocalizations. Though we instantly suspend forceful release, vocal cords and skeletal muscles carry out in miniature what we intend, and, both physically and fancifully, with small movements, *we actually do it*.

By contrast, intellectualizations are meanings which play themselves out without significantly reproducing the physical (muscular and hormonal) state we would experience in fully acting them. In these more abstract representations, meaning finds operational expression in the play of symbols. This doesn't much stir the physiology but still may be considered an action — though now in a less tangible realm. Such conceptualization is useful when, say, buying a family burial plot or considering dental insurance, since to go prematurely through the emotions or discomforts of these imagined situations would be both impractical and inappropriate.

Investigations into meaning in life, however, seem to require more direct, physiological representations. Consider fear: abstract discussion fails to feel and follow it in ourselves and is unlikely to approach the actual, inner root, exposing it to investigation. In fundamental questioning of the human psyche, therefore, it may be not so much the intellectual meaning, but more the visceral, that are key.

In consequence, it would seem relevant to question the nature and efficacy of any enquiry into our life: do we sense the issues of our investigation deeply and immediately, or is our interest more an intellectual exploration which can be done at arm's length? Is our relationship to the enquiry one of concern with our way of living, or is it more on the level of stimulation by ideas? Have we, at root, an urge to actually meet these challenges, or are we satisfied with academic discussions? I think it is important, at some point, to examine the nature of our interest and find out how far it actually goes.

On the other hand, it would be unfortunate if these considerations were to drive us to the extreme of denying the intellect its value and its place, for the intellect brings rational order, and, as well, opens other doors. Still, if we do not touch anything other than intellectualization, then it would seem we are avoiding those issues in the field of meaning which are most relevant to our lives.

The True, the False, and the Convenient

At this point in our discussion of meaning, it is appropriate to briefly retract our steps, draw together various lines of thought, and fill in where further elaboration is necessary. The understanding so far developed is as follows: meaninglessness in the life of man would seem to grow out of a disharmony between the particulars of his living and the framework of the whole. The root of this disorder is context in internal contradiction — a pervasive cancer which cannot be locally remedied. False meaning is its underlying cause.

But it has also been made clear that meaningfulness set in contrast to meaninglessness does little to clarify the issue, since both may be equally false and destructive. Rather, the essence of our investigation lies in distinction between *false* meaning and meaning that is *deep and true*.

It would seem, however, that the deep and true cannot be directly defined or specified, for then we have already limited it to our preconceptions. Instead it must be a meaning not that we have fixed in habit, belief, or some other convenient meaningfulness but one in which we can grow, which is always open to the exploration of further possibilities and the discovery of significances not bounded in depth, scope, and subtlety. But if the true is, in itself, beyond our circumscription, at least the false may be delimited and when uncovered, dropped. This wiping away of the false, it would seem to me, is itself at least an essential element — if not the whole — of that meaning which is deep and true.

In contrast to the true, the field of false meaning may appropriately be descriptively explored. Take, for example, the Eastern view that at heart the wrong thought and action that embodies false meaning is *ignorance*. This perspective would, in fact, seem useful provided we acknowledge that there are both *accidental ignorance* and the *ignorance of convenience*.

At first it might not be clear that the latter is a genuine ignorance, for how could one be ignorant *at convenience* unless one were already cognizant? It could happen, however, that some particular content goes consistently unattended, not so much through direct evasion as through a more diffuse avoidance of the whole psychological territory in which that content is found. This may easily happen in realms where expectations or experience promise an unpleasantness that does little to stir enthusiasm for exploration. Reluctance of this sort can and, I suggest, does account for ignorance that is both genuine and — paradoxically — conveniently maintained!

Accidental ignorance is, as the name implies, ignorance of a circumstantial kind, deriving from some sort of chance oversight. The common upshot of this, we could reasonably expect, would be a contingent disharmony resolvable within its own context. Ignorance of convenience contrasts. Here, pursuit of the psychologically comfortable and avoidance of the unpleasant systematically leaves critical areas unexplored. It is this systematic quality which almost certainly assures a confused and unexamined context, and consequent essential disharmony. The deep root of inward falsity consists simply, then, in life conformed to the *psychologically convenient*.

To bring to an end false meaning in our life, I would once again suggest, is our essential challenge, though our convenience and our urge may be more to seek the true in searching out new values and directions to build on unexamined foundations. But effective examination, it is clear, is necessary and must include both the meaningful (convenient to hold) and the meaningless (convenient to avoid) in a way that runs contrary to our convenience. From this process new values and intentions will, of themselves, naturally arise.

In practice this investigation involves exploring our values and intentions through awareness of our actions — especially the more inward — and observing their operation. False meaning, when we care to look, is often revealed by values whose processes (what they do) do not correspond to what they say. Any means which in action contradicts its intended end may serve as an example: committed certainty in belief (When there is clear perception, is belief necessary; when there is not, is commitment appropriate?); implacable hatred of an oppressor (Will violence matched with violence end oppression or sustain it?); direct hypocrisy in any form.

It is important in all this to challenge the meanings we hold dearly, but not in an aggressive way that sets us at war with ourselves and leads to eventual paralysis. On the other hand, while we may hold these meanings with a certain care and affection, it is essential that we do not cling to them in a way that resists open enquiry; otherwise we are lost to habit, staleness, atrophy. Exploration, therefore, involves a necessary balance and grace.

To Reconsider One's Life

To reconsider one's life is, at heart, clearly a daily concern, not something to have done and be done with doing. We have seen that this actually comes about only by seeing what we are, revealed not so much through intellectualization as in our actions, through simple observation of what we do. All this becomes possible only when we are prepared to penetrate the whole process of our lives, including aspects which are unpleasant or inconvenient to examine.

But what will, in fact, actually cause us in this way to reconsider? What could move us to freely enter that psychological territory which seems to promise nothing more than various forms of disturbing experience? What would give us the energy to stay with the inwardly painful and ugly and to intimately penetrate to its root?

Possibly what will sustain our enquiry is an understanding of the tragedy of life lived from repressed pain and ugliness, for those 'hidden' contents must pervade our whole context to paralyse and drag us down. I suggest that this is the case and put forward investigation of this notion as a vehicle by which to explore it.

Intimacy with the tragic pattern of human life in general — the truth of life spoiled, withered, wasted — brings with it the energy and steadfastness of concern. To begin to see even the edge of all this is, it seems to me, to kindle that drive which will cause each of us to most fundamentally reconsider his life.

Ultimate Questioners: The Search for 'Omnivalent' Meaning

JOHN BRIGGS and FRANK McCLUSKEY

David Bohm has observed that human thought's proclivity for constructing the world in terms of absolutes creates endless conflicts around such issues as truth, religion, social relationships, personal identity, morality and aspirations. The conflict takes place both inside individuals and between them, and inside and between societies. Bohm argues that strife comes about because humans fail to recognize that some apparently absolute meaning which they hold dear actually exists in a larger context or web of meanings. One's absolute religious convictions have been shaped by the context of culture, culture has been shaped by history, history has been shaped by belief and so on. As these meanings inosculate and loop around each other, they fold in numerous contradictions and paradoxes. In other words, Bohm suggests, there is a fundamental ambivalence to our absolute meanings which goes unrecognized. He suggests that if people committed to their absolute ideas about truth, relationship, morality could touch that underlying, enfolded ambivalence in these ideas, conflict might be avoided, to be replaced by an ongoing dialogue. This would be possible, he proposes, because touching upon the fundamental ambivalence inherent in the meaning of any idea opens up creative possibilities which cannot exist while adherence to a rigid conception of meaning holds sway.

For centuries artists have grounded themselves in the ambivalence of meanings and have worked to reveal to us the nuances and uncertainties that infiltrate our apparently absolute perceptions and truths about life. Perhaps a better word for the type of ambivalence unearthed by art would be 'omnivalence'. Omnivalence is a mental state in which many meanings converge in so many ways that one feels the immensity of meaning without being able to pin down any absolute meaning specifically. It is one's experience of a Shakespeare play or a Picasso painting. Bohm has proposed that an experience of what we are calling here omnivalence might be a basis for dialogue, as well as for great works of art.

Below we report an informal experiment into one kind of omnivalent dialogue. The experiment grew out of our speculation concerning a similarity between art and philosophy. It was our feeling that the primary motivation of great philosophers has not been the one commonly ascribed. It has not been to devise grand schemes and propound absolute sets of conclusions and logics. On the contrary, it has been to produce an omnivalent state of mind.

Our experiment was also motivated by the unhappy observation that the activity of philosophy has become disconnected from human experience. Philosophy students 'study' philosophy, they don't do it. For most people, philosophy has become — while perhaps not altogether a meaningless subject — a subject of restricted meaning. The experiment involved devising and testing an approach we hoped would encourage people to explore meaning philosophically in something like the 'artistic' way we believe great philosophers have done. In short, we wanted to facilitate the creative aspect of philosophizing. So we started with ultimate questions.

Ultimate questions are philosophical questions which cut to the core of existence. They are basic, perennial questions like, 'What is happiness?', 'What is truth?', 'Is there life after death?''What is honesty?' How individuals have answered these questions determined much of their behavior. The approach which we developed to help people probe their answers and hence their behavior is a process with 10 stages. Though we have spelled out the stages as distinct steps, in practice when an individual engages in a solo or group dialogue, the movement is fluid and seamless.

Ultimate Questioning Stages
Stage 1: Initiating the Question
An ultimate question is about what is shared or universal in human experience; it is a question which is 'open' and contains no obvious assumptions; and it is a question of vital importance to the questioner. The first stage is to choose and frame an ultimate question which seems especially significant

to the questioner.

Stage 2: Let Answers Pop Up

In fact, the mind already has stored many answers to the questions chosen. What are they? In the thrust of daily life we don't let all our answers come to the surface. One answer bubbles up and we quickly apply it to the current situation. In Stage 2 *all* that store of answers is allowed to emerge and the answers are noted down.

Stage 3: The Five-Door Review

At this point ask, Where did all these answers to this question come from? While not everything about our thought processes is conditioned, much of it is. And our conditioning about ultimate questions has a profound effect on how we behave. Here the questioner starts to look at the conditioning that lies behind the answers noted in Stage 2. What is the source of the questioner's answers to this question: 1) religion, 2) formal education, 3) culture, 4) family, or 5) personal experience? These are the five doors through which our conditioning comes.

Stage 4: Matching and Tracing

Here the questioner goes deeper into the conditioning, deriving a family tree or genealogy of the answers (s)he has about the ultimate question. What are the circumstances and links which gave birth to these apparently absolute answers?

Stage 5: Patterns and Conflicts

The questioner now looks at his or her answers and notices which ones are in conflict. William James said: 'The greatest enemy of any one of our truths may be the rest of our truths'. We generally aren't aware of contradictions in our answers. The patterns of contradictions are a clue to the omnivalence that lies hidden in every ultimate question.

Stage 6: Walking in Different Moccasins

Here the questioner engages in a thought experiment. What if he or she were born in another culture or another time, had different conditioning? How would she or he answer the question then?

Stage 7: Bracketing

Now that the questioner has seen and felt how all answers to the ultimate question are conditioned, he or she sets answers aside, brackets them. Can he or she think about the question without these old ideas?

Stage 8: Questioning the Question

The questioner stands alone before the question. Stripped of preconceptions, he or she can now begin a dialogue with it. To do this, he or she questions the question. Why is this question important? How does this question affect who I am or what I do? Why do I individually ask this question and why do I as a representative of all human beings ask it? What is the point of this question? Why is it an 'ultimate' one?

Stage 9: Coming to Terms

The questioning of the question continues, but now more intimately. What do the terms of this question mean? What are they really asking for? What would an answer to this question (these terms) consist of?

Stage 10: Asking Afresh

The questioner, from this new perspective, now asks the ultimate question again. By this point the omnivalent 'answer' has probably begun to take shape.

Meditating on the Omnivalent Answer

In a sense ultimate questions can be defined as questions which have no final answer, yet in this moment the questioner sees that an ultimate omnivalent answer has formed. The questioner considers, How is this new answer different from the old ones?

The informal results of our informal experiment suggest that the ultimate questioning process facilitates contact with the omnivalence of the question and one's conditioned 'absolute' answers to it. The usual absolute, judgemental state of mind may in fact grow quite creative and subtle in the process as the following example illustrates.

From Absolutes to Omnivalence

'What is happiness?' This was the ultimate question that Marilyn Wellport (not her real name) chose to ask. It was a particularly powerful question for her the summer of 1983. Marilyn's father had just died, the first death she had experienced in her immediate and close-knit family. And there were other troubles. Her oldest daughter, a divorced 27-year-old woman, had been afflicted since childhood with learning disabilities which were now forcing Marilyn to the difficult decision of having to place her in a nursing home. At the same time Marilyn was told that her daughter's five-year-old child, the grandchild in Marilyn's custodial care since the age of six months, also had learning disabilities. Meanwhile, Marilyn had another daughter at home who was going through a difficult adoles-

cence. Recently Marilyn had also received confirmation that
her husband was stricken with a rare nerve disease; she was
herself suffering increasing back pain and psychological tension created by a religion course she was taking in which the
teacher was vehemently attacking the tenets of her Catholic
belief at the very time she was reaching out to religion for comfort. 'I guess there was a lot of focus for me on the idea of
happiness,' Marilyn wryly said to us later.

We weren't aware of this personal unrest when we asked
Marilyn if she would take our written description of the 10
ultimate question stages, choose any question she wished and
try out the process on her own. We were acquainted with Marilyn as an adult student of ours, someone interested in writing, obviously an intelligent and reflective person.

We asked Marilyn to keep a record for us of her process.
Two weeks later she brought back some notes she'd typed up
and we spent several hours interviewing her. During the inter-
view, Marilyn said about her choice of the question, 'What
is Happiness' (Stage 1) that she not only thought happiness
was the most important question on a list of sample questions
we have given her, when she looked at the other questions,
she felt 'happiness was all of them'. There was also one other
question she considered, however, but we'll come to that later.

After deciding on the right question, it took three days for
Marilyn to traverse the next nine stages and arrive at her
'answer', working about three hours a day.

Marilyn's (Stage 2) list of pop-up answers to the question
'What is happiness' was the following: 'family', 'loving',
'belonging', 'peace','solitude', 'quiet', 'fun', 'energy', 'smiles',
'doing things well'.

As she considered the doors of her conditioning (Stage 3),
one of the things that struck her was how many conditioning
sources she had for each of her ideas of happiness and how
all of her answers about happiness were shaped by personal
experience which confirmed the conditioning. In other words,
she saw (Stage 4) that once the pattern of absolute answers
had been established, it was increasingly reinforced. She wrote
us in a note: 'Originally I saw the answers "solitude", "peace"
and "quiet" as a result only of my religious training, remembering myself in time long past kneeling or just sitting in the
whispered, relaxed aftermath of the Saturday confessional.
Then, as I remembered this, I realized how later in life I had

sought to relive this feeling on pre-dawn beaches or often on an isolated patch of bare land with its only occupant a huge, hollowed tree. I had built my own "outside" churches in these places. Suddenly I recognized the personal involvement required, and I realized any answer involves personal experience.'

She noted that she spent considerable time remembering — as with the scenes in church and the later scenes on beaches and lonely places — the sources of her ideas of happiness in her own life. Her experience with her religion was particularly vivid because of the course she was taking and what she felt was the professor's attack on her religious 'answers'.

In Stage 5 Marilyn discovered a central pattern of conflicts in her absolute answers. Her idea of happiness as 'belonging' was opposed, she noticed, to the idea of happiness as 'solitude'. Similarly the answer 'energy' opposed the answers 'quiet' and 'peace'. She discovered in herself a sense of happiness as wanting and needing others, which was significantly opposed to happiness as being free from the demands of others, alone and at peace. At this point, 'I felt confused because I saw that they were conflicting. I realized that at times I am selfish. I want independence. At other times I want someone to lean on. I saw it makes me a more difficult person to live with. I never really saw that before. Maybe I'm not that easy to understand. After going through the questioning process, I found I had more compassion and understanding about how other people, especially my family, might be experiencing me.

'The other thing that surprised me here was my idea of "doing things well" as part of happiness. Education, religion, culture all demand you do well. If you don't do well, you're not liked. If you're not liked, you're not happy. It's a terrible equation'. Marilyn's new omnivalent 'answer' would emerge to daringly challenge this equation.

Though she wasn't aware of it at the time, Stage 6 marked a turning point in her thinking about her ultimate question. In this stage she took our suggestion of 'walking in different moccasins' literally and wondered what she would think about this question if she were an American Indian. Her first associations were that an Indian would find happiness in 'respect, independence, freedom, having things as they once were, good health. To have their own culture, to own a horse and land, to see all white men disappear from the face of the earth. Just to have things as they once were'. Then she thought further that the emphasis on happiness for the Indian would not be on 'doing things well' but on 'the most natural thing in the world, something we had even before we were born — just to have food, to be warm'.

A Native American might object that the ideas on Marilyn's list are not his ideas of happiness at all but the point of this stage of the process is not sociological verisimilitude; it is, rather, to step away from the tyranny of one's personal conditioning for a while and discover other ways of perceiving things. It's something like what a writer or actor does when he creates a character. The character is different from him but also comes from him.

After she had bracketed her old answers (Stage 7), Marilyn's new answer began to unfold as she was asked questions about the question (Stage 8 and 9). In asking 'Why is this question important?' she concluded. 'Happiness is important because we seek it'.

She explained: 'Is happiness our goal in life? Why? How would life differ if we didn't desire happiness all the time? Why are humans so concerned with it? Are animals? Does happiness as a goal separate us from other forms of life?' She remembered watching a TV special which 'showed this very tiny bird, in Africa. It likes to eat ostrich eggs. But this bird with its tiny beak can't peck through the shell. So this bird goes and gets stones, picks them up with its beak and keeps dropping them on the egg. I think it's the first bird known to use a tool. For hours it will go get stones. Sometimes other bird friends join. They keep dropping stones until the egg cracks. It's like Sysiphis. That bird has a certain amount of intelligence, does it also have feelings of happiness? When it gets that shell to crack after two hours, is that bird happy? Or is that one of the things that separates humans from animals. Do we *seek* happiness as a goal? Is that all mixed up with intellect? As our intellect got stronger through evolution, did this move us away from a natural state of happiness?'

This led her to further questions: 'Is happiness one thing or many things? Could I live harmoniously without the sensation of happiness as a goal? I realized what it all comes down to is indoctrination. We're happy because this is what we were told.'

If you took away goal-directed happiness, what would 'natural' (perhaps more animal-like) happiness be? What would it feel like? 'Contentment, being at peace with oneself and others, satisfaction, relating well, feeling comfortable in your spot, whatever it is.' At this point Marilyn's new answer blossomed. The key was her reflection on what she called the 'old' variety of happiness. 'When I think of my mother and father born just after the turn of the century, happiness to them was simple: a good meal on the table, a new pair of shoes. This was pure happiness. Now our happiness is so complicated; it's impossible. Their wants were simple and that made life simple and happiness easy. When your wants are complex, life is complex and happiness is difficult to attain.' The Indians didn't change for thousands of years. They didn't need a technology such as ours based on progress and achievement. In their unchanging, non-goal-driven self-sufficiency they were (she believed) happy.

She now saw inner happiness as 'a kind of acceptance of situations over which we have no control really. I mean I was born in this century, I'm white, female, have had four children, am a grandmother, a middle child'. Happiness, she reasoned, is not the same for everyone or from one moment to the next.

'Happiness isn't a goal. It's the state we're born in. Everything is born in it. It's there. All the things we strive for destroy this original state. Happiness is always there. We don't have to find it or seek it out. All we have to do is eliminate or at least subdue any interference to what it is.' Therefore, the pursuit of happiness, Marilyn decided, is unhappiness. Happiness is to abandon the pursuit of happiness. She was aware of the paradox. She couldn't make abandoning the pursuit of happiness a goal. 'But I realized I don't have to pursue. Happiness is where I am; it's what's available to me.'

This led to a profound realization about her own life and her quest for happiness. 'I spent my life doing many things, all the different jobs I worked at, my job as a mother, my work as a girl scout leader, PTA. I've been looking for the one thing that would make me happy. Since thinking about this question I don't feel a great need to do that any more. I don't feel that pressure. There are these different things. I do them. I can be happy with them. I don't have to always have the feeling of the goal.'

Her insights also led her to some discomfiting thoughts. 'It seems the more intellect society gets, the more unhappy we become. Children are smarter today than they ever were. They're also much more unhappy. More subtly, deeply unhappy. I can imagine a time when the mind will only be goal-orientated.' She feared a time when the mind would be so totally consumed with goals it could never pause to discover the fallacy of goal direction, so consumed with achieving happiness that it would never for an instant have it. She concluded that the pressures against seeing the fallacy of goal direction are enormous. 'If you took away the goal-directed pursuit of happiness, most of the major underpinnings of our society would collapse — acquisition, competition. That's why it's so hard.'

To illustrate her new understanding of happiness, Marilyn talked about how that previous summer she had 'run away from home. I left notes for everybody on what to do and then I left. I didn't even know where I was going'. She ended up on Cape Cod with her typewriter and a book. 'I knew I could stay there. I was happy.' But she realized she was happy with her family too. 'I knew for the happiness I could derive alone I would also be unhappy. You can't get away from unhappiness.' As she saw it now, if you understand that happiness contains unhappiness you can find inner happiness because you won't try to escape the one to get the other.

'I can do it better now since this questioning exercise. I never realized the wealth of happiness that I really had to draw on. I find it's there. Whenever I think it's not there, I try to remember all this. I remember the process. I know now I can find it again because I found it before. I have an added strength. It's strange too because I'm Catholic and I pray to get strength and this for me is like a kind of prayer. Because prayer is really hard work. You're working at something. You're talking to God. You're talking to something intangible. It's the same thing if you're talking to yourself — you're talking to something that's intangible. In a sense it's a religious experience. That helps me a lot because since coming to college I've been in many classes where we've exposed religion and many of the ideas I was taught growing up and I've been disturbed. It made me feel a little rocky. I thought everything was just so and now they're telling me it could be different. Maybe all that I felt in religion really isn't there. But in a sense doing something like this becomes a religious experience. It seems to enlarge. I don't feel as rocky. I see how everything is all tied in together. I can't explain that exactly. Maybe there's more than one way of praying. I have to think more about it.'

Reflecting on her experience with the process, she was surprised at her outcome. 'I didn't know it was working. At points I felt, "What am I doing this for?" Then right towards the end I began to see a real difference' One of her many insights looped her back to the beginning of her questioning process when she had difficulty choosing which of two ultimate questions to explore, What is happiness? or What is love?

'In the beginning I couldn't get away from the idea that love and happiness were synonymous, but after I went through the questioning I realized you could be happy without "being in love", I mean the kind of love you usually see portrayed in books and stories. I began to realize there's a deeper love, more subtle. Now I see love and happiness are the same, but I've changed my definition of happiness and I've changed my definition of what real love is. It's not what I thought it was. If you have that kind of feeling yourself — this kind of reaching in that you can do — you extend that to the people around you. If you can help all of them to reach into their own happiness, that can give more harmony. Then you're building upon your happiness with the people around you and that's where love can come in. Solitude is also part of it, part of reaching in. That fits somehow because to do this process you have to have solitude. And doing it I find I have a lot more compassion and patience for the people around me. I'm amazed when I think what I first thought about the question and how it evolved so I came to what happiness really is, which is just so simple.'

Marilyn's answer is tacit, couched in a language that has great meaning for her and which at times approaches the paradoxical suppleness of a poem. One minute she sees how 'love' is the opposite of happiness, the next she finds again that love and happiness are the same. She seems to have dialogued with her absolute judgements about happiness and love and revealed their larger context. Happiness is now a meaning pervaded for her by something which, as she puts it, involves 'more compassion'. Interestingly, this new meaning doesn't strip her of her old ones (solitude, for instance), but seems to set them dialoguing with each other. Marilyn's 'answer' seems a thing in movement, rather than an absolute idea.

Group Dialogues

Most of our informal ultimate questioning research was done with groups of 20 to 40 people. Here the individuals experience omnivalent answers that result from a communal dialogue. Group work was always surprising because some groups became intensely personal and emotional in the discussion of their ultimate question, while others remained more intellectual and abstract. There are all shades of group tone, impossible to predict. Here is one quick example of group effect.

A large group of 40 people was discussing the question, 'What is honesty?' In the dialogue, group members brought out many personal examples of conflicts over this issue. For instance, one man said a friend of his had recently given him a poem for a critique. The man didn't like the poem and didn't want to tell his friend. At the same time he wanted to be honest. The conflict was severe because he knew his friend took writing poetry very seriously. After about two hours the group came to a tacit and fairly complex understanding that honesty is an appropriate response to the moment, not an absolute or fixed set of responses defined as 'being honest'. The next week, the man reported that the group's insight about honesty had given him a clue which enabled him to honestly convey to his friend how he felt without becoming negative about the poem.

A History of Ultimate Questioners

Ultimate questioning reveals to the questioner that his or her deepest-felt ideas are not absolute, they exist in a larger context. Seeing this larger context opens up creative insight. Literary artists have developed a number of techniques to accomplish this same end.

In a literary metaphor two logically dissimilar things are said to be identical, as in Stephen Spender's lovely metaphor about sight: 'Eye, gazelle, drinker of the horizon's fluid line.' Here the eye is said to *be* a gazelle and then, in a metaphor within a metaphor, this gazelle is said to be drinking a fluid line which is the horizon. Obviously the eye is not logically a gazelle. It is an anatomical feature with describable properties. Gazelles are animals that live on the African veldt. These two ideas are normally filed in quite different parts of consciousness. But the poet brings them together. We might say that the mind, which at any given moment likes to have absolute certainty about what it's thinking, isn't used to this kind of treatment. The result of this collision of absolutes is a new kind of meaning, an omnivalent meaning of multiple and elusive connections. The effect is not unlike Marilyn's 'answer' to her ultimate question.

Irony is another powerful literary device for disassembling the seeming absoluteness of ideas. All irony is based on a perceived contradiction. In everyday irony (such as the contradiction involved in calling someone a 'computer whiz' just after he has fouled up a program), the contradiction is a dramatic way of making a specific point, conveying a particular, absolute idea (this person is actually a computer bungler). In the kind of irony that appears in literature, however, the point being made is difficult if not impossible to pin down, though the ironic statement by no means lacks clarity. Oedipus says at the beginning of Sophocles' play that he's going to find his father's murderer no matter who he is. As it turns out, the murderer he is looking for is himself. What's the essential 'idea' of this irony? Oedipus first sees the murderer as someone he is opposed to and then discovers the person he's opposed to is also himself. Critics have argued about the Oedipus irony for centuries and have developed and defended various contrary theories. The irony seems true in some deep way, but we can't agree on how to reduce this to a single absolute idea of what that truth is. The truth is an omnivalent meaning.

There is no doubt that literature raises ultimate questions — and that it answers them. But their answers are in the form of metaphor, irony, and what William Empson called 'ambiguity'. Literary answers are, therefore, perceptions into the fundamental uncertainties of ideas. Keats wrote that the artist could discover truth by exercising what he called 'negative capability, that is the ability to live in doubts and uncertainties.'

A literary metaphor like Spender's or the irony of *Oedipus* challenges our absolute conceptual assumptions about the world. In a similar way, artists like Cezanne or Picasso can create visual metaphors and irony through form and color, portraying a simple table or a bowl of fruit or a face in such a way that what we see in the painting challenges our visual absolutes. Composers like Bach or Stravinsky can challenge auditory absolutes by creating metaphors of sound. Metaphor, irony and the musical and visual counterparts are artists' ways of asking and answering ultimate questions.

Though it may come as a surprise, philosophers and artists have much in common in their approach to ultimate questions. When most people think about philosophy they think of ideas, systems, logics, conclusions, absolute statements. In short, they think of all those things we said are the antithesis of the omnivalent meaning that arises in artistic process and in the ultimate questioning process Marilyn explored. But the image of philosophy as an absolutist enterprise is a misconception. Philosophy is also an omnivalent enterprise. In brief, here are examples:

Rene Descartes has become for many people these days the *bête noire* of philosophy's bent toward absolutism and reductionism. But Descartes may be receiving a bad rap. In one of his most important works, he meditated on the ultimate question, 'Of what can we be absolutely certain?' To find an answer Descartes felt he needed to dismiss as false anything that contained the slightest cause for doubt. The more he thought, however, the more he realized what he had to rule out: Science, he reasoned, might be wrong so it would have to be dismissed. Everything learned as children must also be suspect — dismissed. The whole of religion was dismissed. Even the experience of Descartes at his writing desk was excised because of the slim chance that he was really in bed sleeping and dreaming or was insane and hallucinating. It was at this point Descartes saw that the only certainty is God. But this conclusion has to be taken against the background of his discovery, through logic, that nothing else is really certain. Since God contains all that is and, moreover, remains beyond anything which can be thought, Descartes' conclusion is (to say the least) a paradox: the only certainty in the universe is that which contains all uncertainty. Perhaps the conclusion wasn't really a conclusion at all but was a deeper sense — perhaps even a vivid clarity — about the omnivalence and uncertainty to be discovered in asking the question, 'Is there anything certain?' Unfortunately, the paradoxes which lead to this amazing vision are generally ignored and the usual history of philosophy leaves students with the arid Cartesian idea that only God is certain. That idea isn't Descartes' philosophy. His philosophy is the process of thinking that animates the idea, infusing it with omnivalence. In that sense Descartes' God is not a certain fact but a certain uncertainty that is happening to the thinker as he thinks about the question. Descartes dis-

covered omnivalence through the application of careful, logical thought. This is the philosopher's art.

In the *Republic* Plato condemns all drama where the author
speaks through the voices of many characters and thereby
hides his own true purpose. A work so perverse as that would
not be allowed into the ideal sate which is being proposed in
the *Republic*. But then there's the irony: the *Republic* is itself
a dramatic dialogue; its main character is Socrates. Plato, the
author, never speaks or reveals his actual intentions in the body
of the work. In effect, the *Republic* would not be allowed in
the Republic.

Plato also writes in his book that any work which contains
naughty stories of the Gods should be banned from the new
state because it would set a bad example for children. He then
proceeds to tell such stories and give examples. Throughout
this Platonic dialogue the irony of the poet is employed in a
way that has led more than one scholar to observe that the
book is as much art as it is philosophy. What is the purpose
of such irony? We might imagine Plato and Socrates desiring,
as so many humans have done, to build a just society (main
theme of the *Republic*). So they try to imagine a perfect state,
a Utopia. What do they discover? States, by their very nature,
make rules, prohibit some things, set up hierarchies and
values. The process of state building is naturally dogmatic and
tyrannical. So to make the State 'just', the kind of open, undog-
matic process engaged in by poets and artists would have to
be banned. By implication so would Plato and Socrates, the
Republic's creators. So the question remains. We want to build
a just society but can we do it without denying ourselves? But
here lurks another irony. Haven't Plato and Socrates created
a just and ordered society among themselves in the very act
of the dialogue? Plato's irony, his humour, his puns, allow
for openness and the free play of ideas. The movement of his
dialogue brings participants together in common understanding. What could be a better state than that?

Wittgenstein expressed omnivalence through a different technique. He wrote *Tractatus* in which he talked at length about
the self, the mystical, ethics and the absolute. Then in the last
section of the book he explained that these things he was talking about cannot be talked about. 'My propositions,' he wrote,
'serve as elucidations in the following way: anyone who understands me eventually recognizes them as nonsensical when

he has used them — as steps to climb up beyond them.'

Heidegger, on the other hand, wrote a Latin-like academic style in which ideas seem to be physically struggling to get free of language. At the same time, the philosopher repeatedly told his readers that the things of the world speak plainly in their own voice and that truth is something which is constantly being 'revealed'. His style often takes the reader through mind-bending rapids of philosophical logic and just when one reaches the point where the author seems ready to draw his conclusions, concepts seem to melt into each other. A story is told that one time Heidegger was lent a book by the Zen scholar D.T. Suzuki containing Zen koans, each only a sentence or two long. Heidegger returned the book after a time with the comment that the Zen approach was just the kind of thing he was trying to do.

Eastern philosophy, including Buddhism and Taoism, is often presented in cryptic, logically nonsensical stories and questions. 'You have heard the sound of two hands clapping, what is the sound of one hand', goes the famous Zen Buddhist koan. A small quote from the Taoist sage Chuang Tzu also illustrates this mode of philosophy.

> The ten thousand things [in other words, everything] and I are one. The one and what I have just said about it are two and the two and what I have just said about that are three. If we go on in this way even the cleverest mathematician can't tell where we'll end.

In contrast, Western philosophy is seen as logical and methodical, plodding from idea to idea to erect vast systems of complex interrelated absolute concepts. But from its beginning, much of Western philosophy has been riddled with paradox and blatant inconsistency, usually unrecognized. Such a procedure was in operation among the very earliest Western philosophers. Heraclitus offered a thought not wholly dissimilar to that just quoted from Chuang Tzu:

> The bones connected by joints, are at once a unitary whole and not a unitary whole. To be in agreement is to differ; the concordant is the discordant. From out of all the many particulars comes oneness, and from oneness comes all the many particulars.

Most Western philosophers make such extensive use of reasoned arguments and logic it is easy to imagine that if there are paradoxes, the philosophers did not intend them. It has been thought that Plato was simply contradicting himself and Descartes misunderstood his own method. However, does it really make sense to think that these minds, which are acknowledged to be among the greatest and most incisive the world has ever produced, were victims of simple logical errors which can be easily detected by first year philosophy students?

What is the point of these paradoxes that stretch from East to West, from Heraclitus to Plato and Descartes to Wittgenstein, down to the present? Perhaps the point is that while philosophers appear to have made claims and built systems, philosophy, like art, is really to do with discovering the limitations of absolute meanings.

Plato's irony, Descartes' sudden jump, the paradoxes of Chuang Tzu and Heraclitus, the metaphors of Melville, Shakespeare and Virginia Woolf are twists and turns that keep the dialogue going, though the words are frozen on a page. In his book *The Heart of Philosophy* Jacob Needleman points out that the most important thing about Socrates was his so-called 'socratic ignorance'. He did not know the answer and he knew he did not know. He wanted to inquire. His relentless inquiry into assumptions, Needleman asserts, creates an incredible state of mind, what we've called here a state of omnivalence.

Our ultimate questioning experiment suggests that this incredible state of mind is accessible not only to great artists and philosophers but to anyone. It is a state of mind which changes the very meaning of meaning; moves it from its imprisonment in absolute conclusions and perceptions into an open terrain where all kinds of new dialogue is possible. If David Bohm is right that our meaning affects matter, then living out our meanings in their larger context might have an incalculable effect on the world we live in.

Mind and its Wholeness

ARLETA GRIFFOR

In my previous paper in this volume it was said that mind can be understood as the many-level activity of meaning. This would imply that creative perception of ever new meanings should be natural for the human mind. Such a perception, as Bohm suggests, plays a crucial role in maintaining the overall harmony of human existence. On the other hand, we do not see much harmony in the life of individual human beings or in society, and even less in the international context. It is apparent that the global threat of annihilation and misuse of the planet cannot be taken as a display of cosmic harmony.

We may therefore ask, why perception of new, creative meanings does not take place. What is blocking it, or interfering with it to the extent that it seems impossible to see it as having any significant place whatsoever in the overall order of human life? We do not seem to be inclined to consider seriously even its possibility. In this paper we will inquire into these questions with the help of Bohm's 'meaning view'.

Absolute necessity, or the trap principle

The important point which Bohm makes is that the meanings which constitute the content of consciousness are limited[1]. There is obviously nothing wrong with that to the extent that these meanings are not confused, and correctly inform our activity within a range of domains where they are relevant. This is actually what takes place in some areas of our technical, practical, and functional activity.

However, the limitation of meanings becomes very serious, if not destructive in its consequences, when we are not aware of it. What takes place in such cases is that meanings which may be relevant within certain limits, become confused when applied beyond these limits.

In the first place we are concerned here with general assumptions and presuppositions which constitute, as it were, a formative level of our activity. What is special about confused meanings at such a fundamental level is that once they are adopted, the whole of our activity becomes a kind of self-sustaining trap designed to defend them.

One form of such a trap is to hold rigidly to one's world-view. That is, to regard it, tacitly or explicitly, as a necessary truth about 'how things really are'. What takes place in such a case is that an absolute necessity is attributed to the meanings that are limited. In this way they appear to be unlimited and become a source of confusion. For since they are the 'truth', everything else has to give way to them. They take on an absolute priority, or an absolute value, dominating one's thinking, perception, and activity in general. As Bohm writes:

> This kind of trap is very difficult indeed to get out of. For the presupposition of absolute necessity operates before one can think reflectively. By the time one can think in this way that he must get out of the trap, he has been carried very far into it by the operation of the stored up presuppositions. It is generally already too late, because by then, one has begun to relieve his sense of uneasiness about what he is doing by means of various forms of self-deception. For example, one may invent false reasons (or rationalizations) that seem to justify not eliminating contradictions in his overall behaviour, and he does this because the sense of necessity is so absolute that it will yield nothing, while everything else, including truth and observation of fact must give way to it.[2]

Such a 'trap-principle', consisting in attributing an absolute necessity to limited meanings, is quite a common contradiction. It operates not only in individual human beings, but also in social groups, and in society as a whole, becoming in this way a dominant factor in the generative order of society.

> In society, the generative order is deeply affected by what has a very *general* significance. Indeed the generative order may be regarded as the *concrete activity of the general*. This takes the form of general principles, general aims, and generally accepted values, attitudes, and beliefs of all kinds that are associated with the family, work, religion, and country. In going from these general principles to the universal, it is clear that the effect on the generative order will become yet more

powerful. When a given principle is regarded as universally valid, it means that it is taken as absolutely necessary. In other words, things cannot be otherwise, under any circumstances whatsoever. Absolute necessity means 'never to yield' . . . Over a limited period of time, certain values, assumptions, and principles may usefully be regarded as necessary. They are relatively constant, although they should always be open to change when evidence for the necessity of the latter is perceived. The major problem arises, however, when it is assumed, usually tacitly and without awareness and attention, that these values, assumptions, and principles have to be absolutely fixed, because they are taken as necessary for the survival and health of the society and for all that its members hold to be dear. . . General principles, values, and assumptions, which are taken in this way to have absolute necessity, are thus seen as a major source of the destructive misinformation that is polluting the generative order of society.[3]

It is clear that this kind of misinformation[4] is destructive, because it is implicitly conflict. Individuals, social groups, and nations, entrapped in incompatible sets of basic presuppositions, cannot do otherwise than protect themselves against the threat which they represent for each other. This protection takes various forms, including, as was pointed out, self-deception, but also, all kinds of violence, and the recent development of nuclear weapons. In this way, the very means of protection bring about proliferation of further conflict.

The current state of fragmentation can be regarded as a byproduct of this general attempt to defend and maintain different fundamental meanings. In other words, fragmentation of human beings and society can be seen as the somatic result of the self-defensive activity of these meanings.

In my previous paper it was said that the world in which we live is for the most part shaped by meanings that make up the content of human consciousness. Insofar as this man-made world is fragmented, full of conflict and violence, we may suppose that the meanings which make up human consciousness are fundamentally confused. They are picked up by each individual through upbringing, education, tradition, culture, etc. The content of consciousness of the individual human being can be therefore regarded as a particular outcome of these general meanings. What follows is that the pattern of self-entrapping activity which these meanings entail, cannot be said to be something different from the activity of each human being. In this way, confused fundamental meanings seem to constitute the very essence of what we are, and it is only natural to protect the essence by all means, because if the essence is gone we are gone as well.

It is clear that the self-entrapping pattern of the mind's activity with its attendant conflict and disharmony, is nothing new. At least as far as the recorded history of mankind goes, there have always been attempts to bring harmony into human life. This suggests that conflict and disharmony were inseparable from human existence.

Historical examples of dealing with misinformation

Concerning the historical attempts to bring about harmony, it is interesting to note that they were generally directed at somehow making human beings 'see the whole'. Typically, however, this has taken the form of providing an idea of the whole.

One form of these attempts were religious systems. They may be said not only to give an overall scheme of things in terms of their value and origin, but also to provide a set of rules for people to follow in order to fit their whole activity into the overall harmony.

Absolute value was given to God as a source of all that is. Misinformation was acknowledged as taking place on the 'human level', but it was punished as a sin. To avoid sins meant in other words to hold to the correct information, and therefore, to maintain the overall harmony. In order to secure the credibility of the 'original information' concerning the universal scheme of things, this information was regarded as a revealed truth coming out of the very source of all that is. To doubt this was a sin to be punished.

In this way, the whole structure was quite consistent. It could really bring about some limited harmony, insofar as it was generally accepted, and the 'original information' was not confused. In fact, it has been working for several centuries, except that as a way of self-protection, other forms of religious meanings were constantly fought against. The point, however, is that the 'original information' eventually came to be questioned. 'The whole' provided by religion had to be a solid ground which would enable human beings to know not only how to behave in their everyday life, but also how to think about the material universe. This latter question was settled by making Aristotle's philosophy compatible with the religious meanings through replacing his 'unmoved mover' with the Christian form of God. This added quite a substantial content to the overall religious scheme of things.

There was a certain danger in that as well. For in this way Aristotle's view of the universe, or at least its theological interpretation, became a part of the only admitted truth with regard to 'how things are'. In other words, it became a necessary part of fundamental meanings which were to keep order in the life of human beings, if not in the whole universe. Thus, when Aristotle's map of the universe came to be questioned, it was dangerous for the whole religious structure of meanings. It seemed that to question any part of the structure was to question the necessary and universal order arranged by God. In other words, to question was a sinful activity which had to be punished. Indeed, Giordano Bruno was sent to the stake, and Galileo was jailed, and that was part of the way to protect this particular form of the universal order.

Nevertheless, evidence kept accumulating, suggesting that something might be confused concerning the set of meanings provided by religion. To prevent a total chaos, which the collapsing of the religious meanings was believed to imply, attempts were made to provide a corrected version of 'the whole'. Finally, the nature of the material was left to be dealt with by science, whereas what was non-material remained the concern of religion. In this way, the 'original information' got divided into two parts. One part of it was based on revealed truth and belief in it, while the other was based on experiment and logic. The initial idea was that these two parts were not of equal status. The revealed truth was regarded as being of a higher quality than the truth of logic and experiment which was dependent on man.

What is also important to note is that this division in the 'original meanings' went in the first place through man, splitting him into material body and non-material soul, and in the second place, through the whole universe, splitting it into material stuff and ensouled human beings. Since to be of non-material quality was regarded as of a higher value than to be material, it is interesting to see that this may well have originated the process which at present manifests itself as ecological disaster. Of course, it is only one of the numerous consequences of this particular attempt to bring about harmony in human life. The corrected version of 'the whole' made it possible for science to develop, since scientists were left to investigate matter without being sent to the stake when they came out with facts incompatible with religious meanings. However there was also a danger in that, although of a more subtle nature.

Descartes, who set out to elaborate in more detail the corrected version of 'the whole', made it quite clear that there is very little need for non-material elements in the universe. He only needed God for designing the laws of nature, and for providing the universe with a certain amount of movement. All the rest he has shown to be possible for man to figure out by himself. There was also the problem of how to secure that part of the 'original meanings' which was dependent on man. Since one could not any longer use Aristotle's authority, Descartes came out with the notion that clear and distinct ideas are implanted in man by God. Consequently, our knowledge of the universe was regarded as ultimately secured by God who provided *cogito* with clear and distinct, and therefore true, ideas concerning the world.

Although the role of the religious part of the 'original meanings' was not big in Descartes' structure, it was nevertheless crucial. However, it was almost inevitable that with this explicit decreasing of the non-material element, and the increasing content of science, the religious meanings could in time be overlooked altogether. Indeed, the amount of accumulated knowledge appeared at a certain moment large enough to provide man with a new notion of 'the whole', without non-material elements being involved. It was put explicitly in the form of mechanistic philosophy. In this philosophy the 'original information' was based on the belief in the unlimited credibility of the mechanistic approach. This did not explicitly contradict the other belief in the revealed truth. However, since the highest value was given now to the methods of the mechanistic approach, religious 'truths', which could not be subjected to this approach, were disregarded as a kind of illusion.

We can see that this form of 'the whole' did not help very much in bringing about harmony in human life. Insofar as human beings obeyed physical laws, they participated in the kind of harmony which the mechanistic philosophy was concerned with. Furthermore, it was not clear how the 'truth' of the mechanistic idea of the universe was secured. Descartes grounded in God the human ability to perceive the world in the correct way. But if God was an illusion, who or what was to secure the credibility of our ideas of the universe? They might be an illusion as well. On the other hand, the immense success of Newton's physics at that time did not seem to be an outcome of illusion. Consequently, the next generative seed of 'the whole' can be seen in Kant's inquiry into the basis of human knowledge. He did not regard God as an illusion. But by looking more carefully into Descartes' *cogito* he found that the *cogito* is the only author of the structure of the phenomenal world of experience. This obviously solved, or rather dissolved the problem of how human ideas and the external world are related. There were simply no two kinds of things in need of being related. The mind's general forms of understanding, or as he called them the 'categories' of the subject — were entirely responsible for the structure of the phenomenal world.

To put it in modern terms, Kant's claim was that the information content represented by the categories informed the phenomenal structure of the world. In other words, active information, contained in the subject's forms of understanding, organized unformed matter into the unified world of experience. However, Kant's version of 'the whole' was not secured enough. There was no guarantee that the categories were not arbitrary, and even different for each subject. The issue was, what made the categories necessary and universal? Another important point was the rather limited competence of Kant's subject. The categories organized only the phenomenal world of nature. To put the issue simply, Kant's 'whole' did not seem total enough. Accordingly, it was subsequently improved by means of extending the range of the subject's competence. It culminated with Hegel who replaced Kant's subject with the absolute spirit.

It is interesting to note that with Kant, Descartes' God became quite unnecessary with respect to the phenomenal universe which could manage to exist due to the subject's forms of understanding. However, through replacing the subject with the absolute spirit, a new form of God returned to serve as the formative cause of the universe. Thus God, although first taken away, came back, as it were from another side, to secure again the necessity of the universal order.

There was a certain danger in that as well, since the absolute spirit of Hegel was far more concrete than the non-material

God of Descartes. Roughly speaking, the absolute spirit worked on a similar principle to Kant's subject in that it informed the structure of the world. However, the important difference was that it informed not only the world of nature, but the totality of what is, including human beings, society, historical processes, etc. In other words, the absolute spirit unfolded as the whole of manifest existence.

There was a certain purpose in this objectification of the spirit, namely, to rediscover itself in the sense of its coming to self-consciousness in and through man. This teleological activity rendered absolute necessity to all finite forms of existence. In particular, it provided in this way the phenomenal world with a necessity to exist, which was evidently lacking in Kant's 'whole'.

However, necessity concerned here is not only the phenomenal structure of the world, but also all forms of existence extended in space and time. All finite forms were necessary 'moments' of actualization of this immense process which dialectically progressed towards self-realization of the absolute spirit.[5]

There was evidently a danger in this kind of 'the whole'. It was too total, there was no room for sin here. Whatever happened was regarded as a necessary 'moment' of the universal order. Disharmony, conflict, confusion, violence and war, were all necessary aspects of the absolute harmony. Hegel's philosophy was in fact misused by some fascist 'philosophers', and may have played its part in bringing about the historical series of disasters that have followed since.

The other issue was that, concerning Hegel's 'whole', the 'original information' (enfolded in the absolute spirit) was regarded not to be different from the actual world. After the spirit's self-actualization, which Hegel supposed had already been accomplished, knowing became equivalent with being. It may well be so in some subtle sense, but looking superficially at the issue, one might suppose that there was a certain kind of excess concerning this kind of 'the whole'. If a map is not different from the territory, one of these two things might appear rather unnecessary.

To be precise, the very source of the manifest order was the spirit's striving towards self-realization, and in this way the manifest order could be understood as the absolutely necessary order. But it might be easily overlooked, or regarded as not very important. Therefore we should not be surprised that it actually was overlooked, or perhaps ignored, and subsequently Marx came out with the next 'corrected' version of 'the whole'.

In Marx's 'whole' the absolute spirit was taken away, and dialectic was replaced with dialectical materialism. Strangely enough, even without the absolute spirit, dialectical order remained in power over the manifest world. As we know, Marx's 'whole' got eventually actualized in the form of totalitarian social structures, bringing about the next series of divisions between groups of people and nations, with all the attendant conflict and destruction.

The nature of the challenge
The above discussion concerns only a small, though representative fragment of the human activity of dealing with misinformation. The basic pattern of this activity is, as could be seen, that one set of limited meanings which are taken to be unlimited, is replaced with another set of limited meanings with the same necessity attached to them. In consequence, by trying to clear up one kind of misinformation, the very same thing is done again, that is another structure of misinformation is introduced. In this way, misinformation multiplies because new 'necessary' meanings are superimposed on the old ones, making the structure of confusion more and more entangled.

It is not surprising that the present state of the individual and society is the state of thoroughgoing fragmentation, being basically the result of these contradictory attempts *to clear up misinformation by creating more of it*. Insofar as the past meanings have been somatically actualized, they brought about the present form of social structures (including divisions into nations, religions, etc.), and the structure of our material environment. However, what is even more important is that these meanings became inbuilt into the content of our consciousness, being absorbed, as noted earlier, by each of us through education, tradition, culture, etc. In this way, misinformation of the past is active *now*, informing both the outward order of human life and inward order of consciousness. This order of consciousness, with all the conflict and destruction which it implies, seems to be the challenge that faces human beings at present.

As we pointed out, it is not a new situation, but its present display appears to have reached a critical point. It is almost evident that the historical pattern of trying to deal with misinformation cannot be repeated. Furthermore, contemporary approaches do not offer any solution either.

Science cannot help. It seems that in its striving to get more and more results, it has lost the capability of understanding not only its own results, but also, why it is doing what it is doing.

Philosophy cannot help. Modern philosophers work with details of small questions which they manage to accept as having sense within a limited framework. However, they cannot decide whether the framework makes sense. The statement that the world is collapsing is regarded as too general to make sense.

Old religions have lost their meaning (if they ever had any) and fight with each other out of a long tradition. New religions enter the same old pattern with a fresh hope.

Thought cannot help, being basically part of the activity of accumulated meanings, nor can feelings, will, desires, beliefs, intentions, and plans, which are dominated by the same old meanings.

Then, there are contemporary political attempts to bring about harmony. The only thing which distinguishes these attempts from past attempts, is that somehow on the way to protecting some basic meanings, human beings have managed to produce an amount of nuclear weapons capable of annihilating the life of the planet many times. Consequently, the first of these nuclear-based attempts is bound to be the last. This makes it more or less clear that the historical pattern cannot be repeated, unless we do not care about surviving as the human species, or about the life of the planet in general.

To put the whole matter simply, the present challenge cannot be met in terms of the actual order of the mind's activity. The issue is whether this order is the only possible order of the mind's operation. In other words, is this order necessary in the sense of being built into us, so that we cannot do otherwise than to program ourselves in this ultimately destructive way?

Of course, if that is the case, there is no way out. But on the other hand, this would imply a rather strange state of affairs. It would force us to state, taking into account all that has been said thus far about nature, that except for man-made machines, the only mechanical order in nature is the order of consciousness. This would be an exact reversing of the Cartesian view. However, it may well be so, insofar as the present order of consciousness is, as well, man-made, and insofar as we assume that there is no way out.

Another way of looking is not to assume anything about the question. Yet the point is to see that to meet the challenge in a relevant way, means no less than to transform the order of consciousness. Whether there is actually such a possibility is another matter, but the urgency to consider it is evident.

In a sense, Bohm's view is a step in the direction of taking more seriously this possibility. The transformation of consciousness is far more compatible with his view than, for example, with Descartes' view of the universe. Though we should not take Bohm's view as the next set of 'necessary meanings' (nor does he ever propose that it be taken this way), we may consider how his position maps the situation.

What is there to be healed?

Bohm notes that humanity 'has three principal kinds of dimensions — the individual, the social, and the cosmic — and each of these must receive its appropriate attention'.[6] The cosmic dimension, he explains,

> ...is concerned with human relationship to the whole, to the totality of *what is*. From the earliest times it has been considered crucial, for the overall order of the individual and society, that a harmonious relationship be established with this whole. Indeed it was commonly believed that such a relationship would serve to prevent or dissolve the various sorts of difficulties...in connection with destructive 'misinformation' and with the tacit infrastructure of consciousness.[7]

Furthermore, an actual contact with the whole was thought to give the ultimate significance to human life in that it would enable man to see how his life fits into the universal context of all that is.

Human beings have always been trying to establish this contact. It is difficult to say how it got started, but since nothing has fundamentally changed since the beginning, we may well see the basic pattern of these attempts in the historical examples already discussed.

Thus, as we noted, an idea of the whole is introduced and articulated more or less explicitly. What eventually takes place a little later, is a sort of collapse of its credibility. That is, the limitation of the 'original meanings' manifests as a failure of these meanings to produce an expected universal harmony. It is generally felt that 'the whole' is not exactly what it was supposed to be. Consequently, it gives rise to attempts aimed at making 'the whole' better and more credible. The very concept of introducing 'the whole' has not been questioned. What was questioned was its quality. Therefore the subsequent attempts concerned themselves only with improving the quality of 'the whole'.

As could be seen, this has taken various forms, like changing the content of 'the whole' through, for example, adding or taking away the absolute spirit, extending the content by adding to it more knowledge in order to make it more universal, improving the means to make it more certain, etc.[8] Although the content of 'the whole' changed in this way, the basic principle remained the same, namely an absolute necessity attached to whatever would be its content.

To use Bohm's terms, by introducing 'the whole', a certain information content enters the formative level of the mind's order. This content then determines the structure of the signasomatic and soma-significant activity. Absolute necessity attached to the content turns this structure into a kind of self-enclosed trap. That is, one's whole activity consists in carrying out the somatic consequences of the meanings which make up the content, and in assimilating whatever is perceived in terms of these meanings.

What is the way out of the structure which is set up by a not quite viable set of meanings? As traditionally pursued, it is by means of setting up another structure. That is, by means of superimposing a new order on the old order of the mind.

Such an approach is evidently quite a relevant approach in dealing with the material environment, where things can be improved by fitting them into a better kind of designed order. The question is whether this mechanistic approach can be extended into the realm of mind or meaning. We should also ask whether such an extension is not based on the same principle which is behind the failure of the original structure, namely applying meanings beyond the limits of their relevance. This clearly seems to be the case, and thus the traditional way of healing disharmony is in fact the very means of sustaining and perpetuating the confusion which it is supposed to heal.

We may ask what has actually been accomplished in this whole endeavour of trying to heal disharmony, which has continued throughout the ages, or perhaps millennia of human existence? It seems that nothing special has been done, or rather, *nothing at all with regard to the very aim*. There are some byproducts of this activity, like the development of science and technology. But it is clear that the use of these byproducts is ultimately informed by whatever constitutes the basic meanings of mankind.

There is, however, one quite remarkable result of all this endeavour. This is the present somatic set-up of the brain, its basic pattern of activity, engraved into the brain cells through thousands of years of repetitive activity. The challenge to change the mind's order of activity involves, therefore, disentanglement of this somatic set-up of the brain.

The question arises whether this is possible. What seems to be implied by Bohm's view is that this somatic structure, like any other somatic structure, is not an independent form of 'substance', but rather it is a form of 'subsistence'. That is, *its apparent substantial nature is due to a constant activity of more subtle levels of meaning*. A change in these meanings would be therefore a change in the order of this somatic structure.

As has been noted in my previous paper, the overall structure of meaning is capable of unlimited extension. For the mind this implies that it may go beyond any level of meaning. That is, whatever structure of meanings constitutes the content of consciousness, the meaning of these meanings can be perceived. But such a perception is already a change in these meanings in the sense that it makes it possible to see whether they make sense.

Such a capability of going beyond any level of meaning has been called 'intelligence'. We may thus say that intelligence is the activity which is able to change the meanings, and therefore to affect the somatic set-up of the brain that is sustained by these meanings. This would entail a new order of the mind's activity in the sense that if this kind of perception takes place, the mind ceases to be dominated by the meanings in which its activity is entrapped. In other words, *the mind would enter another order which is informed by free, creative perception, or intelligence*.

What has been said here implies something different from replacing destructive meanings with some kind of 'correct' meanings, which obviously would be nothing new. Rather, the concern is a total shift at *the core* of the mind's order of activity, from the existing pattern of programming and reprogramming itself, to the order guided by intelligence. For that to take place, perception has to be very profound indeed, so as to reach the generative source of the pattern. As Krishnamurti used to say, there has to be a *total* insight which can make it possible to see the very essence of the pattern, that is, its basic structure and origin. Such an insight seems to be the necessary step for the mind if it is to enter another order of activity.

To put it differently, what is to be healed is not this or that set of confusions, but *the very way of healing* as it has been pursued from the beginning of mankind up to the present. Taking into account all of what the traditional way of healing entails, we may suppose that the notion of healing the mind by modification of its accumulated content is altogether misdirected. It may be said that by entering this pattern of activity, mankind has taken a 'wrong turn', as Krishnamurti and Bohm call it,[9] which however, as they say, can be diverted through insight into its very origin.

That would imply that the order of the human mind, as it is now, is not necessary, nor is it inevitable for human beings to go on with the 'wrong turn'. In other words, the thought-created order of the human mind does not seem to be its only possible order.

We may suppose that the mind which ceases to be dominated by accumulated meanings would be capable of free, creative perception. If it is not caught again at some stage — that is, if perception is sustained, there seems to be no limit to its activity of going beyond any level of meaning. There is nothing fixed about such a mind, nor is its order limited in any arbitrary way. And that is already different from being bound by the necessity inherent in the accumulated meanings, which is what the present activity of the mind is all about.

As was pointed out in my previous paper, the possibility of going into the meaning of meanings is inseparable from the whole signa-somatic and soma-significant activity. That is to say, it is not limited to any particular context, but rather, it is a key feature of the ordering and forming activity of the whole. That seems to imply that the order of the mind which is capable of sustained and intelligent perception is basically not different from the order of this whole signa-somatic and soma-significant movement. In other words, it is not different from the order of the universe.

All this suggests that it is possible for the human mind to participate in the universal order. One may suppose that if this possibility were actualized, the need to impose any additional, thought-created order on the mind would cease to exist. This means that the present structure of human consciousness would cease to exist, along with all the confusion and conflict that it entails.

A step in a new direction

One has to note that there is a traditional danger here of taking this whole discussed map as a description of 'how things really are', which is again an attempt to order the mind starting, as it were, from the wrong end. This, however, does not deny that the map can be viable up to a point. What we need to emphasize is that a rigid commitment to any map entails the notion of absolute necessity, and that is bound sooner or later to bring about the same kind of confusion which was supposed to be cleared up by the map. This is an important point, since that is what usually seems to take place in human approaches to the issue of healing disharmony.

As we noted earlier, there are religious approaches which try to heal the situation by providing a view of the cosmic order, with all the rewards and punishments involved that are supposed to make human beings conform to this order. There are also philosophical approaches which, even if they do not involve rewards and punishments, nevertheless try to show that it is a logical necessity to accept a given view of the universal order. Both of these approaches are similar in that they aim at a modification of the accumulated meanings in the way which would make the activity flowing out of them more harmonious. The problem, however, is that none of these approaches have produced the expected harmony in human life. On the contrary; absolute commitment to different notions of the universal order has resulted in the proliferation of further fragmentation and conflict.

These approaches do not exhaust human attempts to deal with the situation. There is also another, more radical tradition. What it proposes is that instead of modifying the content of accumulated meanings, we should get rid of them altogether, because it is just these meanings that are regarded as the source of disharmony.

There are two main lines of this tradition. The one associated with Vedanta maintains that there is ultimately something ordered and permanent in human beings, which is not different from the very essence of the universe. If it could only be uncovered, by getting rid of all the unnecessary accumulation of meanings, the human mind would become one with the cosmic order. Another line, namely Buddhism, goes a step further. It claims that even this notion of something ordered and permanent in man, which is supposed to be covered up by misinformation, has to be taken away, because it is still a part of misinformation.

Although these approaches are not explicitly attached to any particular notion of the ultimate order whose nature, they say, cannot be articulated, they are evidently attached to their advocated ways of getting rid of all the superimposed orders. And so, they do not bring about much more harmony than the other approaches. Their commitment to different ways of trying to heal the situation entails the same notion of absolute necessity which entraps groups of people within a host of incompatible concepts, giving rise in this way to the same proliferation of divisions and conflicts.

Perhaps the kind of perception around which the formalized attempts to heal disharmony got built was not always bound by the accumulated meanings. For example, a few individuals whom religious traditions regard as their originators are reputed to have had quite different mode of perception from that of the ordinary mind. If that were an actual fact, we may suppose that in some cases perception might well have been free and creative.

If there were indeed such individuals, their value for the rest of humanity would be considerable if only an actual communication could be established with them. That is, if their perception could be shared, i.e., actualized as common for human beings. The question is, however, whether free, creative perception can be communicated, and what it would mean. Evidently, it is not a matter of conveying an idea or description which then becomes a part of the accumulated meanings.

Suppose that there is a perception that the overall order of consciousness does not make sense. Such a perception is strongly resisted by the self-defensive activity of the accumulated meanings. Usually this resistance takes the form of either ignoring whatever is pointed out as entirely irrelevant, which is the end of communication, or turning it into a belief, that is, into a fixed meaning superimposed on all the other meanings which make up consciousness, which is another form of escaping communication. In this way, communication is not only cut off, but the possibility of learning is denied, since absolute commitment to any belief holds the mind entrapped within a limited pattern.

How then can communication take place? Krishnamurti, for example, says that it is necessary to listen. However, the kind of listening he is referring to is not a case of accepting or rejecting whatever one hears according to whether it fits or does not fit one's idiosyncrasy. What seems to be implied is that the kind of listening which is called for is already a form of free perception in that it is not bound by the necessity inherent in the listener's idiosyncrasy. This means that it is already a change in how the mind works, and that may eventually open the way to a more fundamental transformation of the mind's overall order of activity.

But suppose that there are no such individuals around, which quite generally appears to be the case. Then all that is left seems to be that we have to listen to each other. In fact, the very listening may be more important than the actual presence of an individual who apparently is no longer bound by the accumulated meanings. If there is no listening, whether such an individual is present or absent makes no difference. This presence may have a profound significance in some other sense, but considering the nature of the present challenge, something else seems to have a priority, since not so much time is left. Whatever potential of the mind would be represented by such an individual, there is a very small chance of its general actualization, if the rest of humanity remain as they are.

One may ask how the notion of listening to each other can be at all relevant in the situation when we all seem to be dominated by the same meanings. A significant insight into this question is given by Bohm's proposal to explore and experiment with what he calls 'dialogue'.

The term *dialogue* is derived from a Greek word, with *dia* meaning 'through' and *logos* signifying 'the word'. Here 'the word'

does not refer to mere sounds but to their meaning. So dialogue can be considered as a free flow of meaning between
people in communication, in the sense of a stream that flows
between banks.[10]

As he emphasizes, dialogue is something different from an
ordinary conversation or discussion where people argue from
their fixed positions, and that leads either to confrontation or
to agreement, if whatever may present a threat to any of the
positions is not avoided altogether. In other words, an ordinary discussion does not lead beyond the meanings which constitute the participants' collective idiosyncrasy. It is thus
seriously limited by the form of the 'banks' represented by
the various points of view of the participants.

What Bohm seems to suggest, using the metaphor of the
stream, is that the flow of meaning involves both the stream
and its banks. That is, a free flow is primary, and it is actualized as a constant two-way activity of the stream shaping the
banks and the banks shaping the stream.

> In dialogue it is necessary that people be able to face their dis-
> agreements without confrontations and be willing to explore
> points of view to which they do not personally subscribe. If
> they are able to engage in such a dialogue without evasion
> or anger, they will find that no fixed position is so important
> that it is worth holding at the expense of destroying the dia-
> logue itself.[11]

For that to be possible —

> What is essential is that each participant is, as it were, sus-
> pending his or her point of view, while also holding other
> points of view in a suspended form and giving full attention
> to what they mean ... Such a thoroughgoing suspension of
> tacit individual and cultural infrastructures, in the context of
> full attention to their contents, frees the mind to move in new
> ways... The mind is then able to respond to creative new per-
> ceptions going beyond the particular points of view that have
> been suspended.[12]

It should be emphasized that what needs to be suspended in
this way is the self-defensive activity of each participant's idiosyncrasy which prevents listening. If that takes place, the
mind's activity ceases to be dominated by the accumulated content of meanings, and in this sense we may say that the mind
begins to move in a new way.

Basically this is what is called for in the case of each individual: to be able to give attention to one's accumulated meanings, while suspending the necessity of carrying out their activity. This is what is required, if the mind is ever to be free of its self-created program. The content of dialogue provides, as it were, better conditions for that to take place. In a group of people with various backgrounds, it is easy to see that the commitment of others with all the destructive consequences involved is not different from one's own commitment, and that the absolute necessity inherent in all these commitments is in fact of a relative nature. In this way, the notion of 'being right' loses its importance which in turn opens the way to the possibility of a creative response to the whole dialogue situation.

What is particularly important however is that by giving full attention to one's own and others' content of accumulation, suspending at the same time its activity, one's particular content ceases to be different from the collective content of the group. In other words, one can see that what is going on in the group is a manifest display of the activity of one's own mind. This provides the participants with the possibility of learning about the 'individual mind' as it is reflected in the 'group mind' and vice versa. This movement of learning may lead to creative perception of a new meaning, which in the dialogue-context of no separation between the individual and collective mind would be a common meaning for all the participants.

Thus one aspect of the significance of dialogue is the creation of a new, common meaning shared by the whole group. As Bohm says, this may be called 'microculture', insofar as '...in essence culture *is* meaning as shared in society. And here "meaning" is not only *significance*, but also *intention, purpose*, and *value*.'[13]

However, as was suggested, precondition of this creation of a common meaning is that the rigid socio-cultural commitments of the participants are dissolved. This brings out another significant aspect of such a creative dialogue. As was noted earlier, idiosyncrasy is a particular outcome of the general accumulation of meanings. In other words, the content of one's consciousness, that is, one's misinformation, commitments, ideas, etc., have their ultimate source in the general socio-cultural accumulation. Therefore dissolution of this general accumulation seems to be the necessary step in clearing up

one's individual misinformation. Besides, it is evident that misinformation in the socio-cultural context is most destructive
in its consequences.

Although it is very valuable to create a common meaning,
it does not seem to be the ultimate end of dialogue. When both
socio-cultural and individual misinformation is cleared up, it
is only the beginning of a new order of the mind's activity.
Then the mind participating in dialogue is in fact participating in a creative movement of unfolding ever more subtle and
new meanings, and as was suggested, there are no barriers
to this movement. It might be that participation in this movement *is* the actual contact with the whole that human beings
have always been seeking to establish.

Notes and References
1. See, for example, Bohm, D., *Unfolding Meaning*, ed. D. Factor, Foundation House Publications, Mickleton House, 1985:
p. 82.
2. Bohm, D., 'Insight, Knowledge, Science and Human
Values', *Teacher's College Records 82*, 380-402: p. 54.
3. Bohm, D., & Peat, F.D., *Science Order And Creativity*, Bantam, 1987: p. 238-9.
4. 'It should be clear that by "misinformation" is meant a form
of *generative information* that is inappropriate, rather than simply incorrect statements of fact. In a similar way a small "mistake" in DNA can have disastrous consequences because it
forms part of the generative order of the organism and may
set the whole process in the wrong direction.' (ibid: p. 237).
5. Hegel's extension of Kant's structure is in some respects
similar to the extension of the quantum particle theory to the
quantum field theory (as discussed in my previous paper). That
is, manifest forms and the structure of their activity are
regarded by Hegel as phases (i.e., moments) of the overall
(dialectical) movement whose structure is 'informed' by the
information content of the absolute spirit (i.e., by what he calls
'logos').
6. *ibid*: p. 248.
7. *ibid*: p. 251.
8. It is interesting to note that the concept of trying to make
'the whole' more certain may have to do with what Heidegger points to as a change in the meaning of the notion of 'truth'
which took place over the ages. That is, from the ancient notion

of 'aletheia' as unhiddenness or unconcealment, through the Medieval notion of 'revealedness', to the modern notion of 'certitude'. Evidently, this requirement to guarantee the correctness of the idea of the whole by logical means is quite a modern one. The more ancient method of making the idea of the whole convincing, which we can see, for example, in the Old Testament, is for the most part violence, and occasionally, miracles.

9. See Bohm, D., & Krishnamurti, J., *The Ending of Time*, Victor Gollancz, London, 1985.
10. Bohm & Peat, *op. cit*: p.241.
11. *ibid*: p. 242.
12. *ibid*: p. 243.
13. *ibid*: p. 354.

About the Authors

Srinivas Aravamudan is studying for a PhD in English at Cornell University. His main interests are literary and social theory, colonial discourse, and its relationship with the rise of liberalism and nationalism.

Matti Bergström is Emeritus Professor and was for many years Head of Department of Physiology at the University of Helsinki. He is the author of *The Physiology of the Brain and the Psyche, The Green Theory* and co-author of *The Brain and Evolution* (all in Finnish).

David Bohm is Emeritus Professor of Theoretical Physics at Birkbeck College, University of London. He is the author of *Quantum Theory, Causality and Chance in Modern Physics, The Special Theory of Relativity, Wholeness and the Implicate Order, Unfolding Meaning* and the co-author of *The Ending of Time* and *Science, Order and Creativity.*

John Briggs is Associate Professor of English at Connecticut State University and on the faculty of the New School for Social Research. He is the author of *Fire in the Crucible: The Alchemy of Creative Genius* and co-author of *Looking Glass Universe: The Emerging Science of Wholeness, The Logic of Poetry* and *Turbulent Mirror: The Science of Chaos, Wholeness and Change.*

Larry Dossey, M.D. is Chief of Staff, Medical City Dallas Hospital and an Adjunct Professor in the Department of Psychology, North Texas State University, and he practises internal medicine with the Dallas Diagnostic Association. He is the author of *Space, Time and Medicine, Beyond Illness* and *Mind Beyond Body* (forthcoming).

Arleta Griffor graduated in Mathematics at Wrockaw University in Poland, where she also taught and did research for five years, before becoming a research student in Philosophy of Science at Warsaw University. She moved to Sweden in 1982 and is now studying towards a PhD in Philosophy of Religion at the University of Uppsala, Sweden.

Frank B. McCluskey took his PhD from the New School of Social Research. He has been a postdoctoral fellow at Yale University and is now Associate Professor of Philosophy at Mercy College in Dobbs Ferry, N.Y.

F. David Peat, a physicist, was for many years a fellow with the National Research Council of Canada. He is now a scientific consultant and science writer, and the author of *In Search of Nicola Tesla, Artificial Intelligence* and *Synchronicity: The Bridge between Matter and Mind*, and the co-author of *Looking Glass Universe, Science, Order and Creativity* and *Turbulent Mirror*.

Paavo Pylkkänen obtained an MSc in Logic and Scientific Method at the University of Sussex and is now studying towards a PhD in Theoretical Philosophy at the University of Helsinki. His interests include the philosophy of cognitive science and the implications of quantum theory to our overall world-view.

David Schrum obtained a PhD in Theoretical Chemistry from the Queen's University, Kingston and now teaches at Cambrian College of Applied Arts and Technology in Sudbury, Canada.

David Shainberg, M.D. is a painter in New York. He is also a psychoanalyst, but no longer practises psychiatry. He is the author of *The Transforming Self*.

Rupert Sheldrake was Director of Studies in Biochemistry and Cell Biology at Clare College, University of Cambridge and a Research Fellow of the Royal Society. He is now a Consultant Physiologist at the International Crops Research Institute in Hyderabad, India, and a science writer. He is the author of *New Science of Life: The Hypothesis of Formative Causation* and *The Presence of the Past: Morphic Resonance and the Habits of Nature*.

Francis Frode Steen graduated in History of Ideas at St. John's College, New Mexico, and at the University of Oslo. He is now a free-lance writer.

Karl Georg Wikman graduated in Mathematics and Physics at the University of Gothenburg, Sweden, and is now Director of the Swedish Herbal Institute Ltd in Gothenburg.

Maurice Wilkins is Emeritus Professor of Biophysics at King's College, University of London and won a Nobel prize for his work on the structure of DNA.

THE RIGHT TO BE HUMAN
A Biography of Abraham Maslow

Edward Hoffman

Abraham Maslow (1908-1970), one of the founders of humanistic psychology, stands as a great visionary of modern psychology and related social thought. The range of his contribution is fully revealed in this singular portrait, which includes material from Maslow's published and unpublished works and from private diaries and correspondence with Aldous Huxley, Gregory Bateson, Margaret Mead, Ruth Benedict, and other collaborators. For this biography, Edward Hoffman, Ph.D., obtained over 200 personal reminiscences from Maslow's family, friends, and associates, including Rollo May, B. F. Skinner, and Carl Rogers.

More than any other psychologist in recent years Maslow has powerfully affected the way we think about ourselves. He advanced an entirely original concept of human nature — the hierarchy of inborn needs — that turned psychology on its heels. In contrast to classical approaches that studied human weakness and neurosis, Maslow focused on healthy, exceptional, high-achieving individuals. He systematically explored what he described as 'peak experiences' and originated many concepts related to the 'self-actualized' individual that helped launch the fields of humanistic and transpersonal psychology.

An intuitive, interdisciplinary thinker, Maslow also applied his theories to business and management, theology, politics, criminology, and education, making his forward-looking work vitally important to significant contemporary social issues, and his story is also the story of an important era in psychology.

THE ESSENCE OF SPIRITUAL PHILOSOPHY

Dr Haridas Chaudhuri

This book brings together further selections from the writings and lectures of the distinguished philosopher and spiritual teacher Haridas Chaudhuri. Drawing on both Hindu and Buddhist traditions and referring to the teachings of other great religions and to the thought of Western philosophers such as Kierkegaard, Hegel, and Bergson, the collection presents a unique synthesis of the philosophy of the spiritual life.

Dr Chaudhuri points out the many similarities between Eastern and Western philosophical systems and demonstrates how their various insights can illuminate each other. Using his own special philosophical perspective, perceiving the dialetical process as operating eternally at all levels of consciousness and creating progressively more rich and open-ended syntheses, he shows how an evolution of consciousness is taking place on both the individual and collective level.

Human beings are by nature spiritual, and the fulfilment of our spiritual potential should be the principal work in the life of each person, so that wholeness, balance, harmony, and integration can help us toward the creation of the kingdom of heaven on earth. Dr Chaudhuri's teachings provide valuable guidance as to how this fulfilment may be achieved, ranging over such diverse subjects as the problems of faith, free will and determinism, and the nature and practice of meditation, and includes modern theories of depth psychology as well as ancient mystical traditions. The book culminates in a helpful introductory exposition of the *Bardo Thodol* or *Tibetan Book of the Dead*.